Masculinity and Male Homosexuality
in Britain, 1861–1913

Masculinity and Male Homosexuality in Britain, 1861–1913

Sean Brady

First published in 2005 by
PALGRAVE MACMILLAN
Houndmills, Basingstoke, Hampshire RG21 6XS and
175 Fifth Avenue, New York, N.Y. 10010
Companies and representatives throughout the world.

PALGRAVE MACMILLAN is the global academic imprint of the Palgrave Macmillan division of St. Martin's Press, LLC and of Palgrave Macmillan Ltd. Macmillan® is a registered trademark in the United States, United Kingdom and other countries. Palgrave is a registered trademark in the European Union and other countries.

ISBN-13: 978–1–4039–4713–0 Paperback
ISBN-10: 1–4039–4713–9 Paperback

This book is printed on paper suitable for recycling and made from fully managed and sustained forest sources. Logging, pulping and manufacturing processes are expected to conform to the environmental regulations of the country of origin.

A catalogue record for this book is available from the British Library.

Library of Congress Cataloging-in-Publication Data

Brady, Sean, 1964–
      Masculinity and male homosexuality in Britain, 1861–1913 / Sean Brady.
         p. cm.
      Includes bibliographical references and index.
      ISBN 1–4039–4713–9 (cloth)
         1. Homosexuality, Male – Great Britain – History – 19th century.
      2. Homosexuality, Male – Great Britain – History – 20th century.
      3. Homosexuality, Male – Great Britain – Historiography. 4. Masculinity – Great Britain – History – 19th century. 5. Masculinity – Great Britain – History – 20th century. 6. Gay men – Great Britain – Social conditions – 19th century. 7. Gay men – Great Britain – Social conditions – 20th century. 8. Gay men – Great Britain – Identity. I. Title.
HQ76.2.G7B63 2005
306.76′62′094109034—dc22   2005043180

Printed and bound in Great Britain by
CPI Antony Rowe, Chippenham and Eastbourne

To the memory of James Neale-Kennerley, 1960–99

Contents

Acknowledgements

I owe a debt of gratitude to many people for their support and encouragement in recent years, but the following people require particular mention in regard to this work.

Joanna Bourke and John Tosh, for their supervision, mentorship, rigour, patience and friendship. Thanks also to Joanna Bourke and Julie Peakman for their editorial advice with the final manuscript.

Abiding thanks to the following, without whose guidance and encouragement this book would not have been possible:

Jad Adams, Sally Alexander, the late Alan Bray, Kathryn Castle, Harry Cocks, Matt Cook, Ivan Crozier, David Feldman, Martin Finn, Lesley Hall, Shiela Lecoeur, Anthea Lehmann, Jim MacPhearson, Carmen Mangion, Gary Maughan, Sharon Nassauer, Julie Peakman, Dorothy Porter and Philip Timmins.

The librarians, archivists and staff at Birkbeck College Library: Senate House Library, UL: The British Library: The British Library Newspaper Collections, Colindale: The National Archives, Kew: Sheffield City Archives: The Wellcome Trust Library: The London Library.

The staff and students of the School of History, Classics and Archaeology, Birkbeck College, University of London.

Thanks also to the Arts and Humanities Research Board.

Introduction

> We are, all of us, composite beings, made up, heavens knows
> how, out of the compromises we have effected between
> our impulses and instincts and the social laws which gird us
> around.
>
> John Addington Symonds, *Memoirs*, 1889

In late nineteenth- and early twentieth-century Britain, the existence or
extent of sex between men was, with rare exceptions, denied or ignored
by the legislature, the national newspapers and the medical profession.
This book argues that the culture of resistance in Britain to public discussion of sex and sexuality between men was perpetuated to protect the
precarious status of Victorian and Edwardian masculinity. Masculinity, it
is argued here, meant a man being married. Furthermore, married men
had, increasingly during this period, to demonstrate their masculinity
through their abilities to support their spouses as housewives. This onerous
responsibility did not end there. For men to be seen as fully masculine,
freedom of movement between home, work and the public association
with other men were prerequisites. It is the emphasis and consideration of the linked system of home, the workplace, the all male association
and, in addition, the street, that offers the most potential to examine
the social dynamics of masculinity in this period. The inherent contra-
dictions and instability of the often-stifling domesticity of home, its clash
with the demands of the workplace, the temptations of all male association and the presentation of masculinity in the street, was held in a
precarious balance. This makes it easier to understand why masculine
insecurity had such wide social ramifications in this period.[1] If it were
widely discussed that men also had sex with other men, and that emotional, sexual and domestic alternatives could exist outside the family

1

and chaste homosocial associations, then the structure of society in this period would have been shaken at its foundations.

In its examination of male homosexuality, this book reviews the differing and often conflicting approaches to the 'history of homosexuality'. In doing so, it attempts to place the question of male homosexuality in a broader historical framework, through an exploration of the meaning of masculinity as a social status in this period. Institutions of authority, such as the national newspapers, the legislature and medicine are examined. This revised analysis is used to contextualise the lives and thoughts of two British homosexual men of this period, John Addington Symonds (1840–92) and Edward Carpenter (1844–1929).

The lives of these men highlight, with poignancy, the extent to which masculinity as a social status affected the self-making of British homosexual men between the late 1850s and the eve of the First World War. The evidence includes, letters, diaries and memoirs, as well as critiques of 'Uranianism' by Symonds and Carpenter. The methodological approach of this book also encompasses the wider study of fleeting sexual experiences between men in institutional settings, such as the public school, army barracks and prison, and informal locations, such as the public parks and toilets. Homoeroticism was implicit in many masculine friendships in the period. Late Victorian and Edwardian society tacitly accepted situations that were full of potential for sex between men, as long as these were not alluded to in public discussion. When exposed in sexual scandal, institutions of authority and newspaper journalists presented the 'unnatural crime' as exceptional. The scandals were seen as isolated incidents. Criminal convictions were notoriously difficult to secure. Should a conviction be secured, punishment was severe and those convicted were regarded as extremely rare and aberrant types of men. This cultural context is not emphasised in well-established histories in this field. The institutional and social perceptions of sex between men in Britain do not conform to concepts of a historically specific construction of homosexual 'identity' that have dominated historiography until recently.

This book is part of a new generation of historical research that challenges arguments for the medical and legal construction of homosexual identity in Britain in this period. In addition, there are fundamental advantages over extant methodologies in an approach to the question of male homosexuality that takes account of the influence of masculinity as a social status. Established histories, in the medico-legal tradition, present male homosexual identity formations as if, in the 1870s, or the 1890s, there was in Britain a revolutionary and sudden change that 'produced' them. The examination of masculinity as a social status in Britain offers more potential to examine the homosexual self-making of those men bold enough to embrace and explore their desires for other men, and over a much broader timeframe. The question of male homosexuality then becomes, like other historical questions for this period, more reflective of the gradual, piecemeal and incidental changes in British society.

1
History

The study of male homosexuality in late Victorian and early twentieth-century Britain has received considerable attention in recent decades, though research of historical evidence is far from exhaustive. The problems facing the historian in this field are greater than the addition of new evidence to the historical lexicon. There are significant intellectual disagreements to contend with. In part, these contentious debates are symptomatic of the tensions arising between academic disciplines regarding their own traditions of approach to the 'subject' of the male homosexual. The notion that sexuality and homosexuality in particular were subjects within the remit of the historian has only gained credibility in the last 30 years. Much of the historiography in this field challenges the long-standing claims of disciplines such as sex psychology and the genetic sciences that sexuality belongs exclusively to the realm of scientific enquiry. However, the methodological and ideological approaches adopted by many historians engaging with sexual identity formations in the late nineteenth and early twentieth centuries make many of the studies in this field highly problematic as works of historical writing.

In his most recent work, *Making Sexual History* (2000), Jeffrey Weeks, still one of the most significant historians in the field of male homosexuality, addresses the question 'Who makes sexual history?'[1] Weeks argues that until a generation ago, the question would have been 'absurd'. Weeks states that, prior to the late 1960s,

> it was taken for granted that the truths of sex were timeless. ... the substratum of erotic energy and gendered relationships remained locked into biological of the social life, susceptible to understanding. ... there was a world of social life, susceptible to understanding through learning the laws of society or of historical necessity; and there was

the domain of the essential, graspable only through uncovering the laws of nature.[2]

Weeks argues that 'sexual knowledge' was the domain of psychologists, anthropologists, biologists and sexologists. He acknowledges that when he conducted his first study of the history of sexuality in Britain, *Sex, Politics and Society* (1980), the near absence of sociological and historical study in this field created the sense that he was entering '*terra incognita*'. Weeks' pioneering historiographical work fundamentally questioned the premise that homosexuality belonged to the realms of 'essential nature' and demonstrated the historical processes involved in the construction of these arguments by the discipline of sex psychology in its formative years in the late nineteenth century.

Weeks' innovative approach to the historical interpretation of these processes is indebted to the seminal article: 'The Homosexual Role', by the sociologist Mary McIntosh in 1968.[3] McIntosh demonstrated, through her groundbreaking arguments in 'The Homosexual Role', that male homosexuality in twentieth-century scholarship was considered to be a 'condition' and therefore fell within the remit of sex psychologists and psychiatrists. McIntosh's fundamental argument in 'The Homosexual Role' was that the pathologised 'condition' of homosexuality in late nineteenth- and twentieth-century Western culture was not scientific fact, but an ethnocentric development of the highly pejorative and per- vasive European Christian interpretation of same sex behaviour between males. In addition, the criminality of this pathologised 'species' served to keep men law abiding. This tendency in the developing human sciences to make conclusions that were inherently ethnocentric was identified as early as 1906 by the American sociologist, W. G. Sumner.[4] By the late 1960s, the sociology of deviant behaviour, such as crime, was approached with an awareness of cultural specificity, eschewing the tendency of earlier scholarly enquiry to pathologise certain behaviours. However, McIntosh argued that homosexuality, and male homosexuality in par- ticular, remained the field of enquiry unaffected by the developments in sociological approaches in the late 1960s.[5] At the time of the publication of McIntosh's article, male homosexuality was still regarded as pathology and therefore not a field of sociological enquiry.[6] McIntosh argued that the persistence in construing homosexuality as pathology, rather than social phenomenon, was evidence of the continuation of centuries of vilification of homosexuality in Western culture and bore little relation- ship to accurate scientific analysis. McIntosh concluded that until the social sciences regarded male homosexuality as a social phenomenon, rather than a pathological, and therefore potentially treatable condition, meaningful questions about male homosexual groups and individuals could not be formulated.

McIntosh's approach has provided, in essence, the basis of most contemporary sociological studies of gay men, lesbians, and same sex identities and communities. The medico-legal analysis of homosexual identity formations does not address the 'will-o'-the-wisp of the causes of homosexuality' which, as Weeks states, dominated the 'essentialist' discipline of sex psychology.[7] Instead, the formation of the varieties of sexualised identities based on same sex desire in differing societies, owes more to cultural meaning and values given to this persistent manifestation in the spectrum of human sexual experience. Furthermore, the historically pathologised and criminalised category of the homosexual male was more a reflection of the society that produced it, than anything to do with the nature of same sex desire. The significance of the arguments for the social construction of sexual identities in any given culture, and therefore in any given historical culture, cannot be underestimated.

The socio-constructionist analysis has opened the subject of homosexuality to the sociologist and the historian. If, as the socio-constructionist analysis argues, sexualised identities are not simply the manifestations of nature, but determined by societal context, then developments and changes in identity formations over time may be examined, as with other historical processes. Unfortunately, fundamental aspects of the medico-legal approach to the history of sexualised identities limit its effectiveness as an analytical approach to homosexual identities or as a methodological tool for the historian of Britain. Sociologists who have applied the socio-constructionist model to studies of homosexuality have tended to imply a purposive effort at social control in relation to the construction of 'the homosexual' in Western culture. Although Weeks acknowledges the 'defects of the structionalist–functionalist approach'[8] in this branch of sociology, the historiography influenced by medico-legal approaches in sociology has the same tendency to regard the 'producers' of the 'construct' of homosexuality in monolithic terms. Socio-constructionism identifies the institutions within society that are associated historically and contemporaneously with control of sexuality between men. The attention given to institutions, such as the legislative and medical bodies, in an analysis of the 'production' of a homosexual 'species' is understandable. There is evidence of classification of same sex behaviour between men within these institutions in modern times, which appears to yield readily to the medico-legal analysis. There is, however, the inherent assumption in this approach that the classification of homosexuality in legal and medical discourses implies the explicit will, throughout these institutions, to control sex between men. This assumption is highly problematic for the historian and, for that matter, the sociologist. There is a lack of attention to the agency of individuals involved in the legislative process and in developments in medicine. Also, assumptions are made about the power of these institutions, at a given point in time, to control and shape behaviour throughout society. It is possible to demonstrate the pervasive and purposive role of an institution such as medicine in identifying 'deviant' sexual personalities and taking drastic measures to control them in the context of totalitarian regimes, like the German Third Reich in the late 1930s. But an examination of the Victorian British state and its potential to 'construct' deviant personalities and then control them reveals a very different pattern of power over society. To be sure, the application of the Contagious Diseases Acts of 1864, 1868 and 1869, empowered the state and, by extension, medicine, forcibly to examine any woman considered to be engaging in prostitution, for evidence of venereal disease. However, the instigators of this brutal piece of social legislation intended the Acts to apply only to the civilian population in contact with the army in garrison towns. The Acts became a source of major concern for social reformers and, through their campaigning, they turned it into a national scandal and the legislation was eventually repealed. But the original vision of the Acts, however misplaced, was not intended to control all of society. Indeed, the legislators felt that they could only enforce sexual control in areas where civilian society engaged with the military, and even this exercise proved unmanageable without provoking significant outcry.

Historians have emphasised that notions of the 'specialised' sexual aberrant in medical discourse date from the late nineteenth century. But there is a tendency in historiography to interpret a change in scientific thinking relating to sexual deviance as the point of diffusion of ideas throughout the disciplines of psychiatry and psychology, or even the entire institution of medicine. The fundamental argument in the analysis of identity formation centred on same sex desire since Weeks' work is that identities are 'produced' by the institutions of the dominant culture.

The importance of questioning the place of these institutions in constructing a male homosexual identity in Britain is emphasised by the examination of Michael Foucault's work. It is difficult to overestimate the influence of Foucault in this field. A huge body of critical literature exists in which attempts are made to define, critique and utilise Foucault's analysis. It is rare to find a work of contemporary scholarship in the field of sexuality that does not refer to him. Criticism of Foucault's three-volume work *The History of Sexuality* centres on the lack of historical agency in his arguments and his polemical, totalised and anti-empiricist conclusions. Weeks acknowledges Foucault in his later work, but argues that much of the substance of the medico-legal analysis of homosexuality was well established amongst British academics in the field by the time Foucault published his work.[9] Foucault shared with the seminal socio-constructionists the belief that discursive practices, embodied in institutions, form the 'social objects' which discourse purports to describe. In the formation of homosexual identities, Foucault argued that

> there is no question that the appearance in nineteenth-century psychiatry, jurisprudence, and literature of a whole series of discourses on the species and subspecies of homosexuality, inversion ... made possible a strong advance of social controls into this area of 'perversity'; but it also made possible the formation of a 'reverse' discourse: homosexuality began to speak on its own behalf. To demand that its legitimacy or 'naturality' be acknowledged, often in the same vocabulary, using the same categories by which it was medically disqualified.[10]

Contained in this short paragraph are the most significant theoretical contributions offered by Foucault to historicising male homosexuality. Foucault's claim that a burgeoning discourse on male homosexuality existed in the nineteenth century forms a fundamental part of his arguments against the 'repressive hypothesis' of Victorian sexuality.[11] Also, Foucault's argument that the formation of homosexual identities was centred on the production of a 'reverse discourse' has been of significance in contemporary scholarship. Nonetheless, there is little to distinguish Foucault's analysis of homosexual identity formations from other socio-constructionist arguments. Foucault's originality was to offer a 'wider theoretical context' for homosexual identity formations than had hitherto been the case.[12]

There are fundamental problems with Foucault's analysis of Victorian sexuality and the formation of proscribed sexual identities, beyond the familiar criticisms of his work. Foucault's arguments against the 'repressive hypothesis' of Victorian sexuality have been accepted as 'convincing' by historians since Weeks. Foucault argued that modern 'sexual liberation', far from emanating from 'Victorian repression', is part of a discursive legacy over centuries in the Western world which constituted 'a mechanism of increasing incitement' to talk about sex. Foucault's stated aim in this work was to counter what he perceived as an over simplistic analysis of sexual repression in the historical past being propagated by 'sexual revolutionaries' in the late 1970s. However, an examination of the basis of Foucault's arguments problematises the application of his methodology to the examination of nineteenth-century Britain. The 'veritable discursive explosion' of sex that he describes, was a predominantly continental European phenomenon. To be sure, eighteenth- and nineteenth-century pamphleteers in England, who concentrated on the perils of onanism and other sexual pitfalls, appear to yield readily to Foucault's analysis. But in Foucault's analysis, the 'explosion' of discourse on sex culminated in the constitution of 'a science of sexuality' in the late nineteenth century.[13]

Again, Foucault, or more precisely the historians for whom Foucault's methodology has informed their own works, fail to emphasise that the works of continental sexology were repressed and censored in nineteenth- and early twentieth-century Britain. British science was remarkable for its resistance to enquiry on matters of sexuality and its hostility towards foreign scientific writings in this field. Foucault regards the willingness to be discursive about sex in the West as dating from the seventeenth century and accelerating in the nineteenth century. He identifies the historical root of the phenomenon of 'institutional incitement to speak about sex' in the reforms of the Counter Reformation Roman Catholic Church. The Church 'stepped up the rhythm' of the confessional, insisting upon 'rules of meticulous self examination'. 'All' had to enter into the articulation of 'confession and guidance' and sex, 'its aspects, its correlations, and its effects' had to be 'pursued down to their slenderest ramifications'.[14]

The emphasis upon Roman Catholic tradition in Foucault's arguments may provide some resonance in the examination of developments in sexual discourse and sex psychology in Roman Catholic countries. Indeed, the notable sex psychologists of the late nineteenth and early twentieth centuries emanated from states and regions with strong Roman Catholic traditions, such as France, Austria, Italy and Southern Germany. However, Britain had no tradition of Counter Reformation confessorial practices. Foucault regards nineteenth-century British 'puritanism' as a 'historical accident. ... a tactical diversion in the great process of transforming sex into discourse'.[15] At least Foucault acknowledges that in part of the West, the experience of sex in discourse was contrary to continental developments. It is not entirely surprising that a leading professor of the History of Systems of Thought at the *College de France* might, in philosophical argument, relegate British 'reticences' to the confines of 'historical accident' and cultural aberration. However, his persistent use of the term *'Victorien'*[16] as a generic descriptor for all that is from the nineteenth century contradicts his relegation of British culture to the margins of his main arguments. It could only be from such an academic position that a historian/philosopher might ignore the fact that the 'historical accident' of nineteenth-century Britain had governed much of the globe and had influenced the Protestant outlook of the United States. There has been little recognition of the Gallocentric nature of Foucault's analysis in historiography in this field.[17] When viewed strictly for its utility as a methodology for examining nineteenth-century Britain, Foucault's universal polemic on *The History of Sexuality* in the West appears as little more than a historio-philosophical analysis of the French and, by extension, Roman Catholic European cultural context.

The arguments that institutional discourses and 'reverse discourse' alone 'produced' homosexual-type identities at a given point in the late nineteenth century and that this action was diffused throughout 'Western' culture in this period must be refuted. The particularities of the British paradigm confound the application of existing methodological approaches to the question of male homosexual identities in this country. In addition to this, the theoretical strictures of existing methodologies exclude enquiry into a range of 'aberrant' male (homo)sexualities in the period in question, because they do not fall into the subject specific remit of these approaches. Also, the emphasis of methodologies on institutions, and concomitant 'reverse discourse' excludes historical evidence that does not fit into the methodological framework. With the exception of Foucault's flawed attempt at a wider theoretical framework for questioning sexual identity formations, the established methodologies approach the examination of the period with the narrowest of theoretical frameworks.

David Halperin argues that before 1892, when the taxonomic term 'homosexuality' first appeared in English in a translation of Krafft-Ebing's *Psychopathia Sexualis*, 'there was no homosexuality, only sexual inversion'.[18] Halperin's work presupposes that 'science' in the English-speaking world was engaged in the pursuit of taxonomic classification of sexuality and that *Psychopatia Sexualis* was a freely available text. However, this book demonstrates that in Britain there was a marked resistance in this period among the medical community to regard homosexuality as a subject fit for scientific enquiry. Nearly all developments in early sexology were Continental achievements. The significant exception was, of course, the work of the English sexologist, Havelock Ellis. But Ellis' work was suppressed by the English authorities throughout this period; his ideas did not receive significant attention in Britain until the early 1920s. Even during the first half of the twentieth century, when North American and continental European psychiatry was predominantly influenced by Freud, British psychiatry distinctively eschewed the ideas of Ellis and Freud, dismissing them as 'an unhealthy interest in the workings of the mind'.[19]

Halperin acknowledges that sex between men pre-existed 1892, but argues that before the scientific construction of the word 'homosexuality', there was, in English, 'no conceptual apparatus available for identifying a person's fixed and determinate sexual orientation'. Halperin emphasises the distinctions between homosexuality and its precursor 'sexual inversion' in scientific discourse: ' "Sexual Inversion" referred to a broad range of deviant gender behaviour, of which homosexual desire was only a logical but indistinct aspect, while "homosexuality" focused on the narrower issue of sexual object choice.'[20] The conceptual isolation of sexuality from concepts of masculinity and femininity, constructed concurrently by Havelock Ellis and Freud, made possible a 'new taxonomy of sexual behaviours and psychologies based entirely on the anatomical sex of the persons engaged in a sexual act (same sex vs. different sex)'.[21] Robert Padgug argues that the scientifically constructed category of homosexuality, took a group of closely related sexual acts and converted them into case studies of people, divided into homosexuals or heterosexuals. Padgug argues that this 'conversion of acts into roles/personalities and ultimately into entire subcultures' did not exist before the late nineteenth century.[22]

The medico-legal argument that taxonomic classification and pathologisation of sex between men 'produced' sexual identities and subcultures is highly problematic. Historians in this field have tended to promulgate a highly mechanical notion of the ability of a scientific discipline or a legislative body to 'produce' the sexualised identities of individuals throughout society. Sociological studies surveying the experiences of British elderly gay men in the 1980s highlight that many of the men interviewed had never heard the term 'homosexual' until the 1950s.[23] If this finding is juxtaposed with the reluctance of British psychiatry to engage with sexological theories until the mid-twentieth century, then the irresistible conclusion to be drawn, using the medico-legal analysis, is that there were no 'identities' or communities based on same sex desire between men in Britain before the 1950s. This is clearly a problematic historical claim; historical studies have shown that there were more venues available in eighteenth-century London for men to meet for the purposes of sexual liaison and sexualised association than in London in the 1950s. Also, nineteenth-century British society was remarkable in Europe for its intense hostility towards sexuality between men and demonstrated sophisticated, but tacit knowledge of types and coteries of men who indulged in this passion. It is arguable, using Padgug's analysis of this historical pattern, that coteries and communities predating late nineteenth-century sexological taxonomy were not 'homosexual'.

Recent historians, such as George Chauncey in his study, *Gay New York* (1995), argues that the thriving 'gay' subculture in New York City of the 1920s existed without the taxonomy of sexology. Chauncey places the dominance of 'a world in which men were divided into "homosexuals" and "heterosexuals" ' as late as the 1940s and 1950s.[24]

Recent historical studies, such as Chauncey's, have been, predominantly, influenced by literary criticism in the Lacanian, post-modernist, post-structuralist approach to the question of male homosexuality in history. These works, influenced by critics such as Eve Sedgwick, have highlighted the rigidity and universalising tendencies inherent in the medico-legal account of homosexual identity formation. Queer theorists, such as Sedgwick, promulgate a kaleidoscopic array of theoretical possibilities for 'gay studies'. Homosexuality becomes homosexualities, gay as a nomenclature for all queer men is challenged and masculinity becomes masculinities. Queer Theory promises limitless possibilities for elucidating differences and multivalence in the analysis of queer, and the languages and meaning of queer.[25] Sedgwick, and other critical theorists, sensitive to the disaster of AIDS, perceived a breakdown in sexual identity categories that had served as a politically unifying force since the late 1960s. The 're-naturalising of identity categories' made gay activists and theorists radically rethink about identity. Sex between men did not mean gay and that men could experience a 'sexuality' with other men without ever being identified as gay.

Queer Theory has, undoubtedly, challenged theorists and historians to take account of region, religion, class and race in an account of homosexual identity formation. H. G. Cocks' recent work, *Nameless Offences: Homosexual Desire in the Nineteenth Century* (2003), argues that cultural oppression and secrecy about the phenomenon of sex between men, fostered an 'epistemology of the closet'. From the eighteenth century to the twentieth, homosexual 'self-making' and the languages of the closet were influenced by a variety of cultural pressures, including science, religion, spirituality and class.[26] For Cocks, the secrecy and social negation of sexual desire between men, and its namelessness and ambivalence in law in Britain provided perverse opportunities for its expression, that held an affinity with the language of the law. This created, in practice, a relative space of impunity that existed in private where homosexuality might be expressed.[27] Cocks' work has, through detailed and meticulous assembly of evidence, done much to analyse the existence of homosexual 'self-making' and the extent of awareness of the nameless offence, long before the watershed of the 1880s and 1890s, articulated by historians since Weeks. However, Cocks' work gives the impression that the homosexual 'self-making' of men like John Addington Symonds and Edward Carpenter, offered either a satisfactory expression of their desires or the location for their 'self-making'. Cocks' work identifies that the locations of 'the closet' tended to be large cities, such as London. Men of Symonds' and Carpenter's class undoubtedly did enter these spaces of homosexual impunity and language, but at considerable risk to their status and masculinity, if exposed or even suspected of doing so.

But both Symonds and Carpenter themselves rarely, if ever, used the spaces of the nineteenth-century closet identified by Cocks for either fleeting sexual adventure or their exploration of homosexual self-making. Both men looked beyond Britain for this and both, in their differing ways, rejected the society they were born into in their quests to satisfy their sexual longings and understand their senses of self. Cocks' work has done much to move the question of homosexual identity and self-making away from the emphasis upon law 'producing' a criminal homo-sexual identity in this period. But in many respects, the work leaves the place of medical discourse in this process unchallenged. Cocks' work admits the writings of sex psychologists amongst a *bricolage* of influences, such as spirituality and religious alternatives, in homosexual self-making among this class of men. The work fails to emphasise the context of how men like Symonds first came into contact with the ideas of the sex psychologists – certainly not in Britain, for such works were entirely Continental publications, proscribed and available only in limited num-bers on the black market, or in bowdlerised, pirated editions.

As an alternative, this book seeks to build on Cocks' arguments in rela-tion to the law and formulate an approach to the question of homosex-uality in nineteenth and early twentieth-century Britain that challenges the meaning of homosexual 'identity' for this period, as used by historians since Weeks. The book also questions how the social and cultural context of Britain could 'produce' a relatively sophisticated conception of a vili-fied 'type' of male who would have sex with other males, in the absence of legal and scientific clarifications. Fortunately, recent historiographical developments question the rigour with which historians in this field have examined the context and influence of the sex psychologists in the nineteenth century. One recent historian, Harry Oosterhuis, has also re-evaluated the meaning and application of the term 'homosexual identity' and its relationship to the sex psychologists. In addition, recent developments in questions of gender in the nineteenth century and, in particular, perceptions of masculinity have provided historiography that analyse the importance of masculinity in social structures. This book examines the significance of sex and sexuality between men in this period through a synthesis of these recent, but disconnected methodological developments.

In the following chapters, the works of Weeks and others influenced by Weeks and Foucault are critically re-evaluated and revised. Medico-legal studies, such as Weeks' are dependent upon an analysis of homosexual identity formations that view the legislative framework for punishment of sex between men as working in conjunction, almost in harmony with, concomitant developments in sex psychology. As stated, Weeks argues that the sex psychologists in the late nineteenth century constructed homosexuality as a pathology. In combination with increasing prosecutions after the 1885 Criminal Law Amendment Act, the male homosexual was constructed in Britain to be, according to Weeks, a species of criminal lunatic. However, the British parliament and the Home Office demonstrated a marked reluctance to either clarify legal categories of crimes of sex between males or engage with developments in sex psychology during this period. The central weakness in Weeks' analyses, republished in 2000 and perpetuated through numerous works by other historians, is that purposive criminal control and punishment of sex between men was inimical to the arguments of the early 'sexologists'. Sexologists, such as Ulrichs, Westphal, Krafft-Ebing and Havelock Ellis argued that homosexuality could not be criminal because it was a naturally occurring aberration from or degeneration of the normal sexual instinct.

More recently researched historiographies than Weeks' studies in the field emphasise how, viewed strictly in the context of their times, the late nineteenth-century sexologists were regarded as the prophets of liberation by feminists and many homosexual men. For instance, Chris Nottingham's study, *The Pursuit of Serenity* (1999), revises the common historiographical assessment of Havelock Ellis. Ellis has tended to be presented by historians as an oppressive, patriarchal pathologiser of women and homosexual men. Nottingham reviews Ellis in the context of the politics of late nineteenth-century Britain, releasing him from the totemic status he has been accorded with in the modern lexicon of sex psychological analyses, predominantly in North America, during the twentieth century. The re-evaluation of Ellis' political activities in England in the late nineteenth century more accurately contextualises the radical, almost counter-cultural and maverick figure he was in the period. In many respects, Ellis was at the margins of Victorian society. Nottingham argues, however, that it was Ellis' radicalism, modernism and forward thinking that ensured him his place, along with later sex psychologists such as Kinsey and Masters and Johnson, in any discussion of the discipline.[28]

Similar recent historical revision has been accorded to the reputation of Richard von Krafft-Ebing. Krafft-Ebing was the Viennese psychiatrist who published *Psychopathia Sexualis* in 1886 and dominates in Weeks' analysis of the construction of the modern homosexual in Britain.[29] In *Psychopathia Sexualis*, Krafft-Ebing categorised and 'classified virtually all non-procreative sexualities'.[30] Historians in the Weeks/Foucauldian tradition have condemned Krafft-Ebing and his work for 'endorsing traditional views of sexuality; for opposing sexual liberation; for espousing the heterosexual standard, homophobia, and Roman Catholic faith in the teleology of sexuality ... [and]for urging the state to control as much as possible all forms of "immorality" '.[31] Harry Oosterhuis' recent and highly influential revisionist study of Krafft-Ebing and his work criticises historians for barely doing justice to Krafft-Ebing's reputation and the accurate assessment of his importance in the context of his time. In *Stepchildren of Nature* (2000), Oosterhuis criticises historians such as Weeks, Foucault, Bullough and numerous others, for evaluating Krafft-Ebing from an entirely 'presentist perspective'.[32] Oosterhuis states that one 'cannot escape the impression that many [historians] base their knowledge of [Krafft-Ebing's] work on what others have written about it and only a cursory reading of *Psychopathia Sexualis*'.[33] Throughout his magisterial study of Krafft-Ebing's work, Oosterhuis demonstrates the effects of a highly presentist historiographical assessment of his reputation. Krafft-Ebing barely appears in recent and important cultural historiographies of modernism in fin de siècle Vienna. Also, the condemnation of his place in the history of sexuality and psychiatry has resulted in a serious underestimation of the influence of Krafft-Ebing in the ideas of Ellis and Freud.

Oosterhuis' work has attracted much recent critical acclaim since its publication in 2000 and for good reason. His study does not simply examine Krafft-Ebing's published texts in detail. Oosterhuis was allowed unique access to Krafft-Ebing's personal archive. The archive had been held privately by Krafft-Ebing's family since his death in 1902 and, as well as yielding an invaluable source of correspondence and manuscripts, contains 1386 files of Krafft-Ebing's patients, including letters and autobiographical accounts from patients. Oosterhuis states that before his contact with Krafft-Ebing's descendants, 'his family was hardly aware of their historical significance and nobody showed an interest in them'.[34] Through meticulous examination of this archive, Oosterhuis has demonstrated how Krafft-Ebing was regarded by his patients as a liberator through articulating their sexual propensities in the language of science, rather than in the language of moral or criminal opprobrium usually accorded them in contemporary Austria and Germany. There are, however, fundamental limitations in Oosterhuis' work application to cultural, social and individual interpretations of sex between males in the late nineteenth century. He accurately revises Krafft-Ebing as a radical, modernistic figure in Austrian psychiatry. Krafft-Ebing, like Freud, was central to the modernist concept of sexuality and sexual identity that dominated Western thinking in the mid-twentieth century. This notwithstanding, Oosterhuis historicises the formation of homosexual identities in the late nineteenth century entirely through the prism of Krafft-Ebing's practice as a psychiatrist.

For Oosterhuis, modern sexual identities, such as the male homosexual, could only be formulated in the late nineteenth century through identification with and, more specifically contact with and expression through, the interpretations of the sex psychologist. Even if correspondents did not agree with all of Krafft-Ebing's classifications and pathologisations, Oosterhuis argues that the 'psychological criterion of self-awareness made the crucial difference between modern homosexual identity and the sodomitical role'.[35] Oosterhuis' concept of sexual identity formation is highly specific and narrow. He has reduced the historical application of the term to its slenderest ramifications, much more so than scholars such as Weeks and Foucault. Oosterhuis regards the possession of homosexual identity in this period as attributable only to those directly influenced by Krafft-Ebing. Oosterhuis states that

> sexual categories and identities were not only scientific inventions and imposed from above by the power of organized medical opinion. The medicalization of sexuality has to be viewed as a process in which new meanings were attached to existing behaviors and feelings.[36]

Oosterhuis identifies that in developing city life at the end of the nineteenth century, 'previously isolated individuals, who might have felt their desires to be odd and unique, found others with similar predilections'.[37] Oosterhuis' emphasis on the historical geography of homosexual identity formation in this period is of paramount importance. For 'modern' homosexual identities to be discerned in the late nineteenth century, certain conditions had to be met. Krafft-Ebing was working at a time when in Vienna, Berlin and Paris, the habitation of the vast majority of his homosexual correspondents, scientific enquiry of sexuality between men and other perversions was tolerated. To be sure, the publications of sex psychologists such as Krafft-Ebing received serious concerns and consternation from much of the continental journalistic commentary on the subject. However, *Psychopathia Sexualis* was, in Krafft-Ebing's life time, freely published in numerous editions and copies amounting to tens of thousands and was widely available to a general readership in the German-speaking lands and France. Also, Vienna, Berlin and Paris of the fin de siècle contained 'networks and specialized meeting places .... private circles, certain cafes, restaurants ... bathhouses ... theaters' where homosexual men could meet, all of which 'could foster a sense of community'. Some homosexual gatherings were even widely publicised and regarded as big social events, such as the 'fancy balls of urnings in Berlin'.[38] In other words, homosexuals and their community activities were more or less tolerated in these cities.

Oosterhuis differentiates his analysis of male homosexual identity, much as Krafft-Ebing did, from other categories of sexuality between men evident in the nineteenth century. Sodomites, effeminate cross-dressers, male prostitutes, married men who occasionally or even frequently indulged in same sex activity and the 'situational' same sex activity associated with prisons or the army barracks, fell outside of the modern, medicalised homosexual identity developed by Krafft-Ebing, his patients and the consciously homosexual readership of *Psychopathia Sexualis*. Oosterhuis regards the new homosexuals as 'the best represented and also the most articulate' of Krafft-Ebing's correspondents and case histories. Oosterhuis acknowledges that, during the past two centuries

> several, older and newer, variants [of homosexuality] could exist alongside one another, whereby differences in class, gender and status as well as geographical variation played an important role.[39]

This argument is an important departure in the historical analysis of modern homosexual identity formations. Oosterhuis argues that 'the homosexual' identity at the fin de siècle was limited to men who eschewed marriage in order to form sexual and emotional relationships with members of their own sex. In Krafft-Ebing's case studies, the 'homosexual' found that the 'new ... identity was hard to reconcile ... with ... marriage and family life'.[40] The process of formation of identity came about through engagement and correspondence with Krafft-Ebing.[41] Oosterhuis' concept of homosexual identity formation is precise and pedantic. If this conception of homosexual identity is applied to late nineteenth-century Britain, it is arguable that male homosexual identities did not exist in this culture. Even modern male 'homosexual' identities that dominate the historiography of Britain in the period, such as those formed by John Addington Symonds and Oscar Wilde, fall outside an Oosterhuisian concept of historical homosexual identity formation.

Neither of these individuals had much difficulty, for most of their adult lives, in reconciling marriage and family life with their sexual and emotional relationships with men. Even Symonds, whose unpublished scholarly works critiqued and deconstructed the formulations of the Continental sex psychologists, including Krafft-Ebing's, fashioned an understanding of his own desires that was, albeit anxiously, compatible with his married and family life.[42] The works of Continental sex psychologists, such as Krafft-Ebing's, were simply not available in Britain in the numbers required for modern homosexual identity formations to flourish on the scale found on the Continent. Even Krafft-Ebing's work, which was translated into English in intermittent and expensive 'pirated and unauthorised editions' in the period, attained a 'scabrous British reputation as little more than a work of scientific pornography'.[43]

There was no socially tolerated home-grown science of inversion theories in Britain in the period; the works of Continental specialists were condemned by the medical authorities and their availability was severely curtailed in this country. Also, attempts to publish an English discipline of inversion theory in 1898 were severely proscribed by the authorities. And yet the period contained numerous examples of homosexual-type lives, 'identities' and subcultures, as well as broader manifestations of sexuality between men in Britain, at least in its urban spaces.[44] If Oosterhuis' meticulous analysis of homosexual identity formation is accepted and applied, then the use of 'identity' as is prevalent in the works of Weeks and others needs to be abandoned for the historical analysis of sexuality between men in Britain. Simply labelling individuals such as Symonds, Carpenter, Horatio Brown, Algernon Swinburne, Wilde and others in the period as 'sodomites' insufficiently describes the complexities of their lives and certainly contradicts their own perceptions of their sexual desires for other men. Cocks' work has done much to articulate the existence of homosexual self-making, rather than homosexual identity, in the period. This development has moved the question of homosexuality away from the purposiveness of legislative discourse in constructing male homosexual identity. However, this work and others that use a Queer Theoretical framework, leave the basic tenets of Weeks' analysis of homosexual identity construction intact. This book, instead, attempts to deconstruct the basic analysis of modern homosexual identity formation propounded by Weeks and others and argue that other, more significant social pressures were central to the homosexual self-making of British men such as Symonds and Carpenter. The namelessness of the propensity in law, argued by Cocks and built upon here, was matched by the namelessness of the propensity in the scientific community in Britain.[45]

This peculiarly British attitude towards sex and sexuality between men, that could not even tolerate scientific discussion of the phenomenon, is best understood through an examination of gender structures in the period and, in particular, masculinity. Recent historiographical developments that adopt a gendered approach to history have produced historiographies for a wide range of historical questions for the period. Historians who have developed a gendered approach to historical questions have predominantly done so in response to the 'cordoned off' approach adopted by feminist historians since the 1970s. Feminist historians, who have produced a vast body of influential women's histories, displayed strong separatist tendencies to treat the study of women in isolation. This approach to historical enquiry is resonant with the subject specificity of medico-legal 'histories of homosexuality' and the approach persists in the form of Women's Studies courses in university departments. However, the criticism of the 'cordoned off' approach has been almost exclusively levelled at feminist history and historians and there is no gendered critique that addresses the 'cordoned off' approaches of histories of homosexuality. The reasons for this lack of critical attention may be due to the presence of ethnic-like lesbian and gay identities and subcultures in British society; the category of 'women' as an isolated subject for enquiry is far less defensible, considering that this category constitutes just over half the population. The call for a more 'gendered' approach to history was made as early as 1975 by the feminist historian, Natalie Davis. Davis argued that historians 'should be interested in the history of both men and women [and] that [feminist historians] should not be working only on the subjugated sex any more than an historian of class can focus entirely on peasants'.[46]

Feminist historians have gradually begun to realise that the adoption of a gendered approach, which encourages the gaze of the historian upon men and masculinity as well as the historical subjugation of women, is full of 'subversive potential'.[47] Taking their lead from developments in sociological theory, historians have adapted contemporary sociological theories of gender formation to historical enquiry.[48] The sociologist Bob Connell and others in his wake have, since the 1980s, developed the conceptual apparatus of gender as a series of historically constructed social structures. Developed in reaction to the insufficiencies of essentialism in the gender categories of masculine and feminine in early sociology, sociologists such as Connell promote the understanding of a relational account of gender. This development has moved sociological enquiry away from determinist 'role theories' to an understanding of the 'different dimensions or structures of gender, the relation between bodies and society, and the patterning or configuration of gender'.[49]

Masculinity is best understood as a fluid and mutable configuration of socially constructed gender norms.

Gendered considerations have barely affected the historiography of male homosexual identity formations in Britain in the late nineteenth and early twentieth centuries. Cocks' recent work is a notable exception. Cocks recognises the historiographical potential in engaging in an examination of dominant masculine culture in Britain in the nineteenth century when addressing questions of the place of sexuality between men in this period. He argues that 'any history of same sex desire has to be a history of masculinity' and attempts in his work to break with the legislative focus on the construction of homosexual identities.[50] His work concentrates instead on the prevalence of the sodomy trial in late eighteenth- and nineteenth-century England and Wales. Cocks establishes, through painstaking examination of newspaper reportage, crown court and magistrates court records, that trials for sodomy and related sexual misdemeanours between men were increasingly frequent and widespread throughout the nineteenth century. His research is important in this field. His work refutes the dominant argument in historiography since Weeks', that perceptions of sexuality between men were poorly formed, or even non-existent in Britain before the 'Stella and Fanny' trial of 1871. Cocks' study also demonstrates that historians, such as Weeks, have based their influential arguments about this lack of societal awareness on the reactions to no more than three prominent scandal trials between 1871 and 1895. Cocks' work amply demonstrates that throughout the country, individuals were willing to report cases of sex between men to the magistrates. Cocks argues that the developments in punishing sex between men in the nineteenth century owed little to the ambivalent developments in statute law, policing and the reforming zeal of the state. Contrary to the medico-legal analyses in this field, the British State in the nineteenth century displayed a marked reluctance either to clarify or to control sexuality between men in any explicit sense. Instead, the change that occurred during the nineteenth century in this area was the willingness among individuals to enforce the laws that did exist. Cocks' careful statistical analyses also demonstrate 'an absolute increase in the numbers of committals for sodomy and assault with intent to commit sodomy in England and Wales' during the nineteenth century.[51]

Unfortunately, Cocks' approach to potential historical connections between perceptions of masculinity and the problems posed by sex and sexuality between men is limited and problematic. Cocks recognises the potential provided by an examination of masculinity to discuss the existence of, and cultural meanings attached to, sexuality between men before the medico-legal watershed of the 1870s. However, Cocks limits his analysis to the deleterious effects of the sodomy trial on the 'character' and 'manliness' of the bourgeois male and the importance of 'character' and 'manliness' in trials concerning men of this class. This book demonstrates that the possession of a respectable 'character' in trials of this nature between 1861 and 1885 was essential to defendants, irrespective of class. Also, the possession of a respectable 'character' was of paramount importance in prosecution witnesses, irrespective of the class or sex of the witness.

Cocks' work falls short of the full potential to formulate an analysis of the role of masculinity as a social status in male homosexual self-making in Britain in the late nineteenth century. For Cocks, masculinity in this period consists of little more than 'manliness' and 'character', which was arguably little more than the presentation of masculinity by males of the middle classes. Problematically, the self-making of homosexual men in the period is presented as an, albeit liminal, form of masculinity, in a spectrum of possibilities in the period.[52] Recent works that take account of masculinity in historical questions have tended to emphasise, in a post-modernist approach to the question, the multivalence of masculinity. Similarly, Queer Theory, in its application to contemporary notions of 'gay', underpins political theory and social action that emphasises the multivalence of 'Queer'. Undoubtedly, these developments encourage interesting and potentially limitless possibilities for analysing (and forming) multiple Queer and 'straight' masculinities in modern North American and European societies.[53] However, it is highly debatable that men in late nineteenth- and early twentieth-century Britain perceived that anything other that one form of masculinity offered them the social status of fully masculine adult men.

This book adopts a concept of masculinity that takes account of masculinity as a social status. Masculinity as an area of historical enquiry has undergone significant development as a workable historical question by John Tosh. Historians have begun to recognise in recent years the 'invisibility' of men and masculinity in history and historical writing – men were the norm against which women and children were measured. Many historians in the past decade have taken 'masculinity' as their focus of enquiry and the titles in print in historical and literary studies which boast 'masculinity' as the topic exceeds 200, the majority published since 1997. However, the bulk of these works that address nineteenth-century Britain, tend to concentrate on Victorian codes of manliness as inscribed in novels, such as *Tom Brown's Schooldays* or *John Halifax, Gentleman*, in the attempt to historicise masculinity. The problem with most of these studies, as highlighted by Tosh, is that the cultural representation of British masculinity in the nineteenth century appears as 'an entirely elite affair'. Tosh argues that studies which emphasise masculinity as multiform in differing classes risk construing masculinity as a second-order feature, contingent on other social identities, such as class. Tosh's analysis of masculinity looks beyond its (mis)conception as merely a set of cultural attributes and he develops his methodology, along the lines of Connell, of masculinity as a social status, placing it as central to historical enquiry.

Tosh argues that masculinity as a social status was not reducible to class status. Instead, masculinity in nineteenth-century Britain had its 'own pecking order which [was] ultimately to do with the upholding of patriarchal power rather than a particular class order'. This concept of 'hegemonic masculinity' emphasises patriarchy in its literal sense as 'father-rule'. Hegemonic masculinity not only emphasised the authority of paterfamilias over his wife and family, but also stigmatised masculine traits that undermined this position, such as the inability to maintain domestic masculine authority through alcoholism, or dependence upon a wife's earnings. The emphasis of early trades unions and Chartist organisations on the effects of unemployment on masculine domestic authority has been evaluated by some gender historians as the development of a concept of masculinity amongst the working classes that 'was middle-class'.[54] But a close examination of trades union and Chartist material emphasises a model of domesticity that was distinctly different from its middle-class counterparts. In the middle-class domestic model of the early nineteenth century, a wife was kept in ignorance of her enfranchised husband's political affairs, whereas the Chartist model promoted the political involvement of wives. However, the political activism of wives in Chartist concepts was the promotion of their husbands' right to the vote as the head of the household.[55] But the emphasis of the authority of paterfamilias in both middle-class and Chartist domestic models is an example of 'hegemonic masculinity' cutting across 'more familiar social hierarchies'. The extent to which masculinity as a social status could be described as 'hegemonic' in the nineteenth century is problematic. Significant sections of the working classes remained disenfranchised and unable to support housewifery. More recent work by Tosh recognises the role of politics in creating 'exclusionary practices' in formations of masculinity.[56] As the benchmark of social inclusion and as a social status, masculinity became dominant by the end of the century.[57]

Tosh argues that masculinity as a social status required public demonstration in three distinct areas: the home, the workplace and all male associations. Public demonstration of the authority of men over women, whether women were present or not, in these distinct areas was a vital element in acquiring full masculine status, irrespective of social class. This inherently unstable system was prone to attack through male unemployment, feminist assertions and, most significantly for the methodology of this book, masculine traits considered subversive to patriarchy. Tosh identifies, in brief, the increasingly problematic status of bachelors in the nineteenth century in an exclusively uxorious concept of masculinity as social status. He also identifies how sexuality between men 'struck at the roots of the family, flouted the work ethic, and subverted the camaraderie of all male association ... the crime [was that homosexuality] undermined patriarchy from within or discredited it in the eyes of women'. Tosh argues that masculinity targeted the persona of the exclusive homosexual 'when medical theory identified a congenitally defective "third sex" '.[58] It is not the brief of Tosh's methodological article to deal with the 'emergence' of male homosexual identities. Nonetheless, Tosh recognises the difficulties in the scholarship in this field, as to exactly how homosexual 'identities' did emerge.

It is the contention of this book that the interests of upholding and perpetuating a concept of masculinity as a social status, centred on uxorious sexuality (meaning the expression of male sexuality exclusively and entirely with a wife), fostered a pervasive social perception of the vilified, effeminate, unmanly sodomite in Britain that was not dependent on the classifications of sex psychology. In 'The Homosexual Role', McIntosh traces the development of a vilified social concept of the exclusive sodomite from the seventeenth century in England and argued that this conception developed as a 'social role' to keep men law abiding. As this book demonstrates, the legal definitions in this respect, even after amendments in 1885, remained ambivalent. However, the promulgation of perceptions of masculine social status, which transcended class definitions and were arguably central to class formations in the modern era, provides a much more powerful and pervasive cultural dynamic in the stigmatisation of sex between men in the late nineteenth and twentieth centuries. Historians have demonstrated a haphazard pattern of social control of sex between men in the early modern period in Britain. However, after the 1750s, formalised marriage, and therefore the uxorious focus of masculinity as a social status, became more widely encouraged. Also, by 1840, the age at marriage had become lower for both sexes and its incidence much more widespread, particularly in the wake of rapid urbanisation. This had been fostered by the extension of premises licensed to perform marriages, such as Non-Conformist chapels, and the registration of marriages by the state.

Another dimension of masculinity as a trans-class social status in Britain in this period, not emphasised by Tosh's methodological article but central to Connell's most recent work is the imperative of nationality and perception of position of nation in the world order in cultural concepts of masculinity.[59] The degree to which the social status of masculinity was central to nineteenth-century British perceptions of its pre-eminence in the world order is demonstrated by 'subaltern' histori-ographies that adopt a gendered approach. For example, Mrinalini Sinah traces the development of sexually oppressive colonial policy in late nineteenth-century India and the construct of the sexually dissolute 'effeminate Bengali', which was concomitant with developments in English domestic perceptions of 'manliness', masculinity and strictly uxorious sexuality.[60] It is this context of British perceptions of its moral and political pre-eminence in the world in the late nineteenth and early twentieth centuries that offers the best potential to examine British con-cepts of sex between men in this period. In the British perception of masculinity, any social toleration of sex between men not only undermined masculinity as a social status in the metropolitan space of mainland Britain, but also threatened the cultural self-perception of pre-eminence in the wider world. It is this analysis that also potentially explains the resistance in Britain to Continental developments in sex psychology until well into the twentieth century. The following chapters demonstrate that there was a pervasive and tacit awareness of sex between men and the concept of the effeminate, exclusive sodomite served to socially control men to contain their sexuality to the uxorious ideal. But to have allowed British science to classify the phenomenon would have constituted an admission to the world that this kind of sexuality existed amidst British masculinity. Official, journalistic and medical denial of the existence or extent of sex between men were for reasons of maintaining the precarious balance of masculinity as a social status.

2
Masculinity

In recent years, historians of masculinity have demonstrated the increasing importance of the family and domesticity in national life in nineteenth- and early twentieth-century Britain. Central to these studies is the examination of fatherhood. Emphasis was placed in public discourse on an ideal of the uxorious husband and the authoritative father as the basis for the stability of society. In addition, men had to be able to demonstrate their masculinity in the workplace and the all male association. Maintenance of masculinity as a social status affected and influenced cultural and social perceptions of the phenomena of sex and sexuality between men. Historians of masculinity, notably John Tosh and Megan Doolittle, stress the inherent instability of masculinity structures that required men to uphold authority in the home, and preserve parity with male peers in the workplace and all male associations.[1] In addition, masculine authority over women and children, as well as over men who were not considered to be fully masculine, had to be maintained in the street and in public places, in order for masculinity to be seen to be preserved and bolstered.

The existence of sex and sexuality between men created a dilemma in a society that placed so much emphasis on the family and the responsibilities and expectations of individual male heads of the household. In this context, masculinity is described here as a singular, dominant construction. In contrast, some historians in this field emphasise the plurality of masculinities in this period. John Hammerton argues that cross-dressers, 'homosexuals', 'the domesticated Chartist' and so on, demonstrated a range of masculinities in nineteenth-century Britain.[2] However, the important point in historicising masculinity, is that aberrant men, such as cross-dressers and homosexuals, were not considered fully masculine. Domesticated Chartists, on the other hand, did demonstrate full masculinity. 'Moral force' Chartist men promulgated a concept of domesticity that placed husbands firmly at the head of the household.[3] Chartist women were, undoubtedly, politically active, which distinguished them from their middle-class counterparts, but their campaigns centred on achieving the vote for their husbands.[4] The ideal of the male head of household was valorised to such an extent in Britain that it 'cuts across more familiar social hierarchies', such as class.[5] This does not mean that 'masculinity' is presented here as an essentialist male identity. Rather, men who did not fulfil social and cultural expectations of masculinity in the period, such as young bachelors, risked being marginalised and considered not fully masculine.[6]

Institutions of British authority, such as national newspapers, government, the legislature and the profession of medicine, placed so much emphasis on this expectation of masculinity and masculine behaviour, that it had a direct effect on how British people regarded sex between men. As the following chapters demonstrate, sex and sexuality between men were tacitly well-understood phenomena. Nonetheless, it is striking, in comparison to Continental states, how little public discourse of this matter was conducted or tolerated.[7] Discourse of this nature was ignored or suppressed in order to preserve and present masculinity in this country as free from unnatural practices between men. In 1871, the Lord Chief Justice concluded that '[sodomy] has not yet tainted the habits of the men of this country – for that thank heaven'. The occasion for his comments was the landmark 'Stella and Fanny' trial, examined in detail in this book. In this sodomy trial, which involved cross-dressed defendants and the posthumous reputation of Lord Arthur Clinton, MP, British medical experts were unable to provide conclusive evidence of physical signs of sodomy. This was in sharp contrast to their French counterparts, who had published treatises on the phenomenon and had used French men suspected of the vice in their studies. The lack of expertise within British medical circles was taken to indicate that the unnatural vice existed amongst Frenchmen, but not amongst British men. The trial also forbade, in English case law, the possibility of physical studies of the Continental type being conducted here.[8] Studies of sex between men proliferated in states such as France, the German Empire, the Austrian Empire and Italy. By preventing scientific enquiry into the physical aspects of sex between men, the Lord Chief Justice, in effect, preserved the reputation of masculinity in this country from the taint of unnatural vice.

The comments and actions of the Lord Chief Justice are indicative of authoritative attitudes towards sex between men throughout the period in question. When British society was forced to face the existence of the phenomenon, such as in a prominent sodomy trial, the men involved were ostracised, vilified and cast as highly unusual aberrations, beyond the pale of acceptable masculinity.[9] At other times, British society preferred to ignore this phenomenon. Public silence on this matter was exercised to such an extent that national newspapers barely reported cases of unnatural crime between 1872 and 1885, at a time when prosecutions actually increased.[10] In 1896, after the furore of the trials of Oscar Wilde, the Lord Chancellor, Lord Halsbury, presented the Publication of Indecent Evidence Bill to the House of Lords. Halsbury's Bill was intended to make publication of details of trials for 'unnatural crime', meaning crimes of sex acts between men, a criminal offence. This Bill will be examined in detail in this chapter. The Publication of Indecent Evidence Bill reflected, in its conception, a significant tendency towards silence on the matter of sex between men for much of the second half of the nineteenth century.

British legislation, on close examination, was archaic and highly ambivalent in respect to any kind of homosexual category. The Buggery Act of 1533 remained the basis for legislation until 1967. Also, the infamous Criminal Law Amendment Act of 1885 simply made all sex acts between all males criminal, rather than indicating any kind of special legal classification.[11] In comparison, Continental states appeared to tolerate a burgeoning scientific discourse on the matter.[12] Legislation in these states either allowed consensual sex between adult males, or had legislative arrangements that were more tolerant than Britain. For instance, France had decriminalised sex between consenting adult males with the implementation of the *Codes Napoleon* 1805.[13] Also, the *Codes Napoleon* were adopted by Italy in 1889.[14]

Continental states affected by the *Codes Napoleon* were able to tolerate the legality of sex between men on the grounds of right of contract between male citizens.[15] Because British society experienced no revolutions or invasions, rights of citizenship for British men were achieved through piecemeal concession, expansion and reform of the traditional parliamentary franchise after 1832, rather than constitutional and revolutionary changes.[16] Importantly, rights of citizenship, as expressed through the vote, still excluded significant numbers of men as late as 1914 in Britain. It is remarkable also, in the context of its European neighbours, how little the legislative arrangements for punishing sex between men changed in Britain in the nineteenth and twentieth centuries.[17] However, British society did experience profound structural transformations during the century. After 1850, Britain became the first predominantly urban society. Britain was also the first industrial nation.

Much controversy exists amongst historians about the developments and structures of class and society in Britain.[18] Part of the problem for historians is the relatively gradual, uneven and complex transformations in class structures and political representation in the period. This is why the examination of masculinity is important for historians in an analysis of British society. As Tosh states, gender relations and masculinity as a social status 'enlarges the range of factors relevant to the historian of social identity or social change'.[19] In order to evaluate the significance of masculinity in cultural and social abhorrence of sex and sexuality between men, the implications of masculinity as a social status in class formations need to be assessed.

Tosh's work in this field examines the demonstration of masculinity amongst middle-class men.[20] This emphasis is understandable in the context of the nineteenth century, as middle-class values increasingly dominated significant arenas of public life, such as parliamentary and municipal politics. Tosh acknowledges that dominant groups, such as the middle classes, valorised particular features of their ideals of manliness that might have conflicted with manly codes amongst aristocratic or working-class groups. However, ideals of manliness were not the same as masculinity as a social status. Masculinity had its 'own pecking order' which was ultimately concerned with upholding the power of 'father rule', rather than particular class solidarity or orders.[21] Men had to maintain their masculinity in the workplace, home and all male association. Tosh argues that it was the clash and tensions between these aspects of a man's life that formed the dynamics of masculinity. In particular, the 'clash between work and home' was the source of much tension in the attempt to maintain masculine ascendancy over women. Tosh argues that, for the upper middle classes, stifling domesticity, promulgated in the mid-nineteenth century, became increasingly associated with 'ennui, routine and feminine constraint' by the turn of the century. The rise in club membership and a vogue for adventure amongst this class of men, were indicative of the 'respective pulls of home and the homosocial world'.[22] This system of linked elements, which were often contradictory and unstable, was central to masculinity as a social status. Masculine 'independence' was the key indicator of achieving full masculinity. Contemporaries dignified work, sole maintenance of the family and free association with one's peers.[23] Nineteenth-century middle-class life yields readily to this analysis. The resonance of this analysis is also demonstrated by examination of British working-class life and structures.

At the end of the nineteenth century, Britain was a working-class nation, in the broadest sense of the term. Seventy five per cent of the working population were urban manual workers. However, as Ross McKibbin demonstrates in *Ideologies of Class: Social Relations in Britain 1880–1950* (1990), this did not translate into collective Socialist or Marxist politics, unlike in their European counterparts. Only 15 per cent of the employed workforce were members of a trade union. McKibbin argues that on close analysis, the 'huge British proletariat disperses itself and its "collective" element becomes remarkably thin'.[24] The small-scale organisation of the British industrial economy meant that collective activities of male employees were either fractured or non-existent. A collective sense of class between working men in this sector was undermined by close connections between employer, or the employer's middlemen, and employees.[25] McKibbin distinguishes between the working-class men employed by thousands of small industrial firms and the 'lower working-class' man, challenged by insecurity of employment and concomitant poverty. He argues that the conditions of both the small firm employee and the lower working-class man, excluded collectivist politics.[26]

At the lowest end of the social scale, 'simple poverty' excluded the conditions for collective, class-based politics. As McKibbin states, 'the sheer struggle for survival demanded so much time and physical energy that there was little left of either for any kind of active politics'. In addition, the peripatetic nature of residence amongst the poorest classes 'implied votelessness'.[27] Reforms of the franchise in 1867 and 1884 extended the vote, in principal, to the working-class man who was head of his household.[28] Being head of household had not necessarily been contingent on maleness. But by the end of the century, the head of household 'was constructed as the only individual in the household ... who could fully engage with civil society and the public world'.[29] Participation in the franchise was undoubtedly an exclusive male preserve in the nineteenth century. Women who were heads of their household were severely limited in their scope to 'command ... authority relationships available to men'. Nonetheless, employment and domestic insecurity meant that, before 1918, half of adult working-class men could not participate in the elementary act of voting in parliamentary elections.[30] Unemployment, illness and domestic mobility affected not only a working man's citizenship, but also his masculine status. Tosh argues that even for the majority of men who wielded little social and economic power, 'loss of masculine self-respect was as much an occupational hazard as loss of income'. Work and a viable household were highly vulnerable 'to the vicissitudes of the economic cycle'.[31]

The ability of men at the lowest end of the social scale to support their families was the subject of middle-class concern and commentary. Helen Tandy, a social worker in East London and member of the Charity

Organisation Society, commented in 1895 on the circumstances for marriage amongst the poor with whom she worked. Tandy described the brief courtship and marriage of many couples she encountered: 'the causes which lead to [marriage] are often almost inconceivably slight – a fit of pique, a taunt from some companion, the desire for a lark, or a bet'.[32] Clearly, Tandy appraised the working-class people she encountered entirely from her own socially elevated perspective. However, her comments are indicative of how socially altruistic associations, such as the Charity Organisation Society, created influential benchmarks by which the working classes were judged.[33] Tandy railed against the 'recklessness' of many working-class marriages in East London. 'Capital they have none', she argued, 'beyond what they may possess of strength and skill'. Tandy regarded the role of earning income as the husband's responsibility. So, it appeared, did husbands, even in 'reckless' marriages. Many of the couples she encountered had small children, the care of whom was regarded as the domain of wives. Tandy cited the case of 'A. B.', who was 'aged twenty-one, and has a wife and three children to support; he does it by turning a piano-organ to the accompaniment of a tin whistle'. She lamented this man's circumstances, as imprudent marriage and fatherhood had

> obliged him to do whatever he could to keep her. He is a well-made, active, rather intelligent young fellow, capable of doing better things by nature, but hopelessly dragged down by the responsibilities he has so recklessly assumed.[34]

The organ grinder had married at sixteen. Tandy was promulgating ideas of 'Social Utopia' in her article.[35] For Tandy, social utopia meant 'no one will enter upon the responsibilities of marriage without a fair prospect of being able to bring up a family in decency and comfort'.[36]

Many of the poor she encountered regarded marriage as the only acceptable way for couples to set up homes independent of their overcrowded families. Tandy claimed that the 'troops of ragged, dirty, stunted little urchins, neglected, and crippled in mind and body ... are the offspring of these reckless marriages'. Her particular concern was for the 'ruined lives of the parents' of these tatterdemalions:

> The fathers, with all self-respect crushed out of them, are reduced to picking up odd jobs at the street corner. ... This question of imprudent marriage shows itself as one of the most serious of modern social life.[37]

Tandy had strongly entrenched views about masculine responsibilities in the matter of work and family. She did, however, acknowledge that not all the marriages she encountered were reckless. Tandy acknowledged that if the couple were of the 'better sort' of the poorer classes, they would have as 'good a chance of happiness as any'. For couples who were

> the more thoughtful, and more carefully brought up.... acquaintance ... is fostered by treatings to the theatre and music hall, and culminates when Jack gets a rise in wages and Jane has saved up enough for a wedding dress and her share of the furniture.[38]

In other words, the eponymous 'Jack' was able to attain full adult masculinity and support his wife. Tandy recognised that most wives in this class were employed in the first year of marriage, until children came along. The double income was used to procure items of luxury for the home. This was an insurance against future hardships, as luxury items such as 'elaborate tea-services' could be pawned if the family fell on hard times.[39]

It is clear from Tandy's statements that adequately paid work was considered essential to maintenance of masculine social status. However, even the British working-class male who earned enough to be the breadwinner for his family was unlikely to incline towards class-based community solidarity. McKibbin argues that a collective sense of class amongst the better-off working-class men was 'aetiolated almost to non-existence' by British employment patterns. Proletarian service sector workers, such as shop assistants, attendants, warehousemen and storemen, remained 'almost immune from working-class politics'. An 'enforced individualism', fostered by 'over-disciplined', status-conscious, deferential and isolated working practices, characterised this expanding sector of working-class employment. Developments in class solidarity were detectable in government employment, such as the Post Office, and co-operative societies showed 'some advance in organisation'. But for the majority, employment patterns encouraged either 'an insurance agent Liberalism ... or a rather craven Toryism or no politics at all'.[40] Even in the industrial sectors, the predominance of small firms discouraged class solidarity and fostered individualism from neighbours of the same class.

McKibbin argues that the loyalty of the employee of the small or middling industrial firm to his workplace overrode solidarity with other workers outside his firm and living in his neighbourhood. For communitarian solidarity to thrive, a man's prime loyalties needed to be his family and neighbourhood. However, McKibbin argues that for British working-class men, it is doubtful that the class basis of their neighbourhood was the locus of their political loyalties. Men took pleasure in their families, but 'home was where they lived, work was where they had their social being'.[41] The prime interests of their wives were care of children and household. Even if men disliked their work, they frequently enjoyed the social relations with other men created by the workplace. Occupational loyalty and peer esteem amongst workmates often transcended neighbourhood loyalty. In a culture where 'the prime determinant of political allegiance was work', it was unlikely that neighbours in differing kinds of employment would necessarily share a political outlook based on class interests. McKibbin also emphasises the 'divorce' between the interests of working-class husbands and wives in the arena of politics. Disenfranchisement of women undoubtedly reinforced the notion that 'politics was a male preoccupation'. Moreover, the housewifery of this class also detached married women from the social and political arenas where their husbands might engage. McKibbin cites Lady Bell, commenting in 1908 on the apolitical character of most working-class housewives in Middlesborough:

> Many of the most respectable women among the poor regard it as a credit to themselves that their lives are bounded up by their household cares. How often one hears them say in a tone of pride that they never go anywhere ... and that they never speak to anyone![42]

The intense domesticity this described was only possible if the husband continued to earn a breadwinner's wage. As Joanna Bourke states in *Working-Class Cultures in Britain 1890–1960* (1994), from the late nineteenth century, 'many working-class women thought that housewifery was something worth striving towards'.[43] Bourke's study demonstrates the economic viability of housewifery for many working-class families. Housewifery could also invest working-class wives with significant control of the domestic space. Bourke does not underestimate the risks of economic dependence on the male breadwinner. She states that 'the family is a confrontational unit: husbands may be tyrannical [and] wages may be skimmed'. Attempts by wives to control the domestic space were efforts at 'reducing their own powerlessness'.[44]

Bourke's study may emphasise the pivotal nature of the housewife within the working-class household. However, the working-class wife's own desires for this domestic role was utterly dependent on the wage her husband brought home and the proportion given to her. In a politically fragmented and uncommunitarian working class, maintenance of masculinity as a social status was essential to the viability and aspirations of the working-class family unit. Tosh emphasises the cultural weight attached by trades unions and middle-class commentators to the male breadwinner wage from the mid-nineteenth century. Increasing emphasis was placed 'on the man's unaided labours', ignoring the prevalence of women's paid employment amongst the poorest sections of the community. Working-class housewifery may have conferred some domestic power, aspiration and control for women. But the dignity of the male breadwinner and his place at the head of his family commanded more cultural attention. As Tosh argues

> home might be the 'woman's sphere', but the husband who abdicated from his rights in the cause of a quiet life was in common opinion less than a man, and he was the common butt of music hall humour.[45]

In the late nineteenth and early twentieth centuries, the masculinity of the working-class breadwinner and his middle-class 'betters' shared rudimentary factors. If his residency was settled for more than one year, then the working-class male head of household could vote. If he did vote, he was most likely to vote for either the Liberal or Conservative parties. Lady Bell, who remarked on the gender divisions in working-class marriages in Middlesborough, commented that

> at the most acute moment of the Free Trade discussion ... in which most of the workmen ... took one side or the other, the women ... seemed quite indifferent. When they were asked what their husbands' views were, the majority had not an idea ... and had no views of their own upon it.[46]

The 'workmen' cited by Lady Bell were, in all probability, breadwinners. The involvement of these 'workmen' in political debate demonstrated their independent masculine social status. These working-class husbands could enjoy the comforts and benefits of housewifery, without the necessity of discussing their work or politics with their wives. These men had the freedom to move from the domestic space to the public arenas of work and political decisions. Indeed, the upholding of housewifery was contingent upon a working man's ability to do this. The subject of this particular debate, free trade, demonstrates the importance of working men in mainstream political arguments. Politics based on working-class solidarity on the Continent were firmly allied to Marxist or quasi-Marxist ideologies, which rejected the capitalist system. The question of free trade, an undoubtedly capitalist concern, had a greater ideological value for British working-class men 'beyond any conceivable socialist doctrine'. Even the Labour Party, founded in 1900 and ostensibly a movement representing the working classes, did not promulgate rejectionist ideologies. McKibbin argues that Labour MPs and the Labour movement worked entirely within the existing capitalist and parliamentary system. In the 1905 general election, the majority of working-class male voters were not persuaded by the Conservative policy, 'tariff reform means jobs for all'.[47] This policy was deliberately promoted by the Conservative Party to appeal to working-class men who could vote. However, the Liberal Party policy of free trade succeeded with working-class men because of its 'analogy to unfettered collective bargaining'. Free trade permitted a relative autonomy and propriety for working-class men and had become the technique by which market capitalism was justified to this class of voters.[48] Also, free trade offered guarantees of cheaper food, a prerequisite in the successful maintenance of working-class housewifery.[49]

Bourke argues that increasing numbers of working men were able to support housewives by 1900.[50] This created an elite within the mass of manual workers – those men who were able to support their wives and families and maintain their political and social loyalties outside the home and neighbourhood. These families stood in sharp contrast to men who were unemployed and dependent on intermittent, casual work and the earnings of women. Of course, vicissitudes in the economic cycle and peripatetic living arrangements could cast the elite working-class man out of the franchise and the ability to support his wife. But it is clear that, by the end of the nineteenth century, half of Britain's male manual workers were able to participate in the franchise and support their families.

Inability to head a settled household left half of male manual workers outside of this basic demonstration of masculinity as a social status. Tosh labels masculine social status as 'hegemonic masculinity'. He has adapted this sociological concept for historical analysis. As a sociological concept, hegemonic masculinity describes the 'solidarity' of men in all classes in developed countries in upholding patriarchal power. An example of this is the persistence in assumptions that paid work is a male birthright. The upholding of masculinity involves marshalling men with very different class interests into a hegemony of dominant power over women. Tosh acknowledges that historical application of the theory of hegemonic masculinity is limited, but he argues that 'it becomes increasingly relevant from the 1880s, when the role of the stage and the printed word in shaping gender identification was already in evidence'.[51] This argument is problematised by divisions in the British working class. As Tandy's observations highlighted, theatre and music hall attendance were the preserve of the 'better sort' of working-class couple.[52] Married couples at the lowest end of the social scale with 'reckless' courtships would have been unlikely to experience exposure to the gender norms presented by these forms of entertainment.[53]

Given that half of manual workers were, at one time or another in their lives, unable to maintain the rudiments of masculine social status, because of the vicissitudes of employment, hegemonic masculinity does not gain its analytical resonance until well into the twentieth century. Bourke's study demonstrates that masculinity as a social status became a realistic aspiration for most working-class men after the First World War. However, masculinity as a social status undoubtedly became dominant in society in the second half of the nineteenth century. Social commentators, such as Tandy, constructed the working-class man who could not support his wife as separate from society, emphasising the physical degeneracy of the offspring from such marriages. Sunday newspapers aimed at a working-class readership, such as *Reynolds' Newspaper* and *Lloyd's Weekly Newspaper*, valorised and dignified the working-class man who could support his family.[54] Trades unions emphasised the importance of the male breadwinner in this class. Although British trades unions commanded only a minority of working-class membership, Eric Hobsbawm argues that British trades unions enjoyed, after 1875, a legal status and privilege unparalleled in Europe. However, trades unions in Britain remained disorganised and decentralised along certain craft and occupational lines.[55] This notwithstanding, working-class men who were members of a trades union had distinct ideals of the conditions necessary for respectable, self-respecting masculine social status. Increasingly, political party policies attempted to appeal to the respectable sections of working-class men who were eligible to vote.

By the end of the nineteenth century, masculinity as a social status dominated and was increasingly viewed as the normal and desirable structure in families of all classes. Men who were unable to maintain their wives and families and operate in the realm of work and politics were regarded as outside society. The status of fatherhood in all classes became central to notions of social stability. Megan Doolittle's study, *Missing Fathers: Assembling a History of Fatherhood in Mid-Nineteenth Century England* (1996), emphasises the construction of fatherhood in legal and social concepts in the nineteenth century. Doolittle examines family disputes in the courts and fatherhood in working-class autobiographies.

Only a tiny minority of families used the courts for disputes. However, the impact of disputes, usually from the divorce courts, was wide. Doolittle states that cases involving custody of children were sensational because 'they touched upon those points in the workings of families which were most vulnerable to controversy'.[56] The privileged rights of fathers were challenged throughout the second half of the nineteenth century. The development of the divorce court, legislation protecting married women's property and 'organised protest by first wave feminists' were distinctive characteristics in developing public perceptions of the status of the family. But these attempts at reform were undermined by the decisions of the judiciary, 'concerned to defend a construction of fatherhood which they personally also occupied'.[57] Doolittle argues that the status of fatherhood was undoubtedly questioned, but that criticism and reform did little except to sharpen definitions of fatherhood and its power. This construction of fatherhood remained dominant and not seriously threatened until well into the twentieth century. Although mothers had more legal rights than their forebears at the end of the nineteenth century, state and medical intervention in the family resulted in targeting mothers as the 'inadequate parent' in matters of childcare and family cohesion. Mothers of all classes were expected to be house-wives. Those who were not were increasingly viewed as problematic and on the margins of society. Doolittle argues that society's expectations of mothers, in all classes, increased.[58]

Men of all classes became 'dependent upon their dependents' in this period. In other words, the male breadwinner expected provision of 'hot meals, clean clothes, and a comfortable chair by the fireside' from their wives. Husbands, in turn, were expected to provide for their families. As Doolittle states, for many working-class men, their

> sense of adult masculinity was usually linked very closely to marriage and parenthood and the heavy responsibilities this implied. While few explicitly expressed a desire for children, almost all had children to care for. ... None saw parenthood as a choice, more as an inevitable consequence of marriage and full adulthood.[59]

Factory legislation and the introduction of compulsory education after 1870 meant that working-class men had to provide for their children until they were adolescent. At the end of the century, working-class fathers had a much more sharply defined and onerous sense of respon-sibilities to live up to than their forebears.[60] Doolittle also argues that fatherhood was almost entirely contained within marriage after 1834.

The bastardy clauses of the Poor Law had great significance for fatherhood, in that

> illegitimate children lost any tenuous rights of care and protection from their fathers, and fathers had much wider discretion in choosing whether or not to accept responsibility for their children.[61]

Men had the unprecedented power to ruin an unmarried woman's reputation through fathering illegitimate children. Women in this circumstance had no recourse to law. Marriage became the only socially acceptable expression of sex. Bourke states that between the 1870s and the First World War, illegitimacy rates steadily declined. Also, rates of premarital sex, though notoriously difficult to assess, were low amongst women born before 1904 and lowest amongst working-class women. The greatest sexual offence among women was not necessarily premarital sex, but 'the carelessness of being "caught out" by pregnancy'.[62] Given the legal status of bastardy after 1834, women were imperilled by premarital pregnancy and could only be rescued by recognition of the pregnancy by the father, through marriage.

Men may have had rights over women in the late nineteenth century, but this predominance did not remain unchallenged. The social purity movements of the 1870s and 1880s specifically attacked male lust and power over women's lives and bodies. In *City of Dreadful Delight: Narratives of Sexual Danger in Late-Victorian London* (1992), Judith Walkowitz examines the development of social purity doctrines that enjoined men to exercise 'sexual self-control'.[63] In the 1870s and 1880s, campaigns were mounted to repeal the notorious Contagious Diseases Acts. The Acts had empowered the state to force women suspected of prostitution in garrison towns, to undergo medical examination for venereal disease. Repeal campaigns were particularly popular amongst workingmen. Walkowitz demonstrates the incongruous coalition of 'middle-class moral reformers, feminists, and radical workingmen' around the single issue of repeal of the Contagious Diseases Acts. The repeal campaigns and propaganda were widely reported in newspapers that catered to the working-class reader, throughout the country. The repealers warned workingmen that the Acts could 'impose disgusting examination' on their 'virtuous wives and daughters'.[64] Walkowitz argues that this propaganda was readily integrated into 'traditional political categories of popular radicalism'. Working-class newspapers, such as *Reynolds' Newspaper*, presented the working man's wife and daughters as his property, and in need of protection from the sexual attentions of disreputable men. Josephine Butler, the social activist who spearheaded the repeal campaigns, did give radical new meaning to the portrayal of women in her propaganda. She dignified 'the figure of the suffering fallen woman', inverting the prevailing view of 'fallen women' as pollutants of men. Butler 'defended them as victims of male pollution, as women who had been invaded by men's bodies, men's laws, and by that steel penis, the speculum'. However, in most other respects, Butler and the Repeal campaigns 'adhered faithfully to the gender and class expectations of traditional stage melodrama'.[65] The campaigns portrayed women as passive victims and 'involuntary actors in their own history, without sexual passion'.[66] The Acts were successfully repealed in 1886. In 1885, a much more widespread and populist campaign was mounted to raise the age of consent for girls. The 'Maiden Tribute' campaign was stimulated by scurrilous reporting in the *Pall Mall Gazette* of an apparent prevalence of child prostitution. Again, the campaign enjoined working men to protect the virtues of their daughters from the debauched attentions of dissolute aristocratic men.

The 'Maiden Tribute' campaign resulted in mass demonstrations and a successful lobbying of parliament. The Criminal Law Amendment Act of 1885, introduced to parliament as a result of the 'Maiden Tribute' campaign, raised the age of consent for girls to sixteen. Organisations emanated from the various social purity campaigns that specifically targeted male sexuality as a social problem to be contained. For example, the White Cross League and the Alliance of Honour were highly popular movements that mainly attracted the attentions of the respectable working class. Radical working men, trades unionists and socialists supported the movements, which appeared to attack 'upper-class profligates'.[67] These social purity movements published numerous pamphlets aimed at insisting upon sexual purity in men. Lesley Hall, in her study *Forbidden by God, Despised by Men* (1992), examines literature published by the social purity organisations in the 1880s and 1890s. Hall argues that this literature encouraged 'a high and single standard of chastity' among men.[68] This literature was widely disseminated. One publication, *True Manliness* (1889), had sold over a million copies by 1909. This was in addition to its dissemination in *The Blanco Book* (1903), a compilation of White Cross League publications produced for issue to soldiers.

Hall argues that *True Manliness* and others in its genre, enjoined men to preserve their sexual expression exclusively for marriage. As well as condemning unmarried fornication, the pamphlet provided 'dramatic metaphors' for the perils of masturbation. This literature argued that

> a 'real man' had sexual urges [but] a true man was able to control these. He was in charge of what his body did, not its victim.

If this dynamic were reversed it boded ill, reflecting upon his very manhood.[69]

Of course, anti-masturbation literature had been in evidence since the eighteenth century. But Hall argues that the late nineteenth and early twentieth centuries was the era of greatest anxieties about the perils of masturbation for British masculinity. The literature in this era gave 'enormous weight to the deleteriousness of the habit', and used medical authority to substantiate its claims. Particular concerns were expressed about the 'evil habit' being learned from other boys in adolescence. Hall states that 'rather surprisingly the fears were not of creating a permanent homosexual or "inverted" tendency through adolescent homoerotic experimentation'.[70] The absence of this possibility, in a genre that relied upon fears of a variety of medical conditions emanating from masturbation, is of historical significance. British doctors avoided discussion and examination of sexuality between men. British medical treatises that concentrated on the perils of masturbation made no connection between 'self abuse' and 'inversion'.[71] However, Continental medical literature on the subject of inversion specifically targeted habits of self-abuse as one of its causes. Experts in this field in the 1870s and 1880s, such as Richard von Krafft-Ebing and Alois Geigel, theorised that homosexuality was caused by early habits of masturbation in an otherwise healthy male.[72]

The absence of connection between masturbation and inversion in British medical and social purity literature is significant to the historiography of homosexuality in Britain. Historians who examine the Criminal Law Amendment Act of 1885, such as Walkowitz and Hall, have tended to concentrate on the broader implications of the campaign and its concomitant legislation. Clause 11 of the Act also criminalised all sexual act between men. Both Hall and Walkowitz cite Jeffrey Weeks' work in this area. Without providing evidence, Weeks connects the ideologies of the social purity campaigns with the passing of Clause into law.[73] However, as F. B. Smith demonstrates, the social purity movements did not articulate, at any point, the need to control sex between men. They did not even mention that this propensity existed among British men at all. Clause 11 was introduced at the very end of the passage of the Bill through parliament, without debate. In all probability, the clause was introduced by Henry Labouchere, MP, as a wrecking amendment.[74] The passage of Clause 11 into law is examined in Chapter 4. But this aspect of the legislation was neither recognised in the campaign, nor by the campaigners in the aftermath of the Act.

In the wave of male social purity literature after the Criminal Law Amendment Act, Hall detects tensions between the 'perception of an urgent need to warn of impending dangers and fear of putting undesirable ideas into formerly untouched minds'.[75] Clearly, in the minds of the social purity campaigners, the danger of masturbation creating a gener-ation of sexually dissolute husbands and fathers, outweighed fears of acknowledging the existence of masturbation. But to suggest that masturbation might cause the propensity for 'inversion' was anathema. There was little available medical literature in Britain that discussed the aetiology of this propensity.[76] Men of this kind existed, but when society was forced to face their existence, such as in a sodomy trial, the men involved were cast as highly unusual aberrations. As trials of these kinds were rarely reported in the national newspapers, Victorian society was, by and large, spared even this intrusion.[77] Any suggestion that sexual desire for other men might be caused by masturbation habits amongst the bulk of the male population increased the possibility of its existence.

Clause 11 passed into law quietly and without comment. However, within a few years of the legislation, Oscar Wilde was spectacularly pun-ished with a conviction of gross indecency. The Wilde trials of 1895 are presented by historians as the events that crystallised the notion of 'the homosexual' in British society. But too much emphasis on the Wilde tri-als alone in historiography, distorts patterns of opprobrium for sexuality between men in Britain. As stated, historians in the Weeks/Foucault tradition argue that 'homosexual identity' was constructed by medical and legal classification of this 'species' of abnormal male in the late nineteenth century. However, the legal authorities that incarcerated Wilde did not recognise any special criminal or pathological category of male who would have sex with other men.[78] This is demonstrated by the fate of a petition made by Wilde for clemency, on the grounds of madness. On 2nd July 1896, Wilde petitioned the Home Office for early release from Reading Gaol. Wilde argued that his offences were forms of

> sexual madness and are recognised as such not merely by modern pathological science, but by much modern legislation, notably in France, Austria and Italy where the laws affecting these misdemeanours have been repressed, on the grounds that they are diseases to be cared for by a physician.[79]

Wilde cited arguments from scientific works in his plea, all of them Continental. Wilde blamed his 'erotomania' for bringing him from 'noble distinction to the convict's cell'. He also blamed the 'horrible iso-lation' of prison life as deleterious to his sanity and expressed the wish to 'pass directly from the common gaol to the common lunatic asylum'.

Wilde expressed the hope that 'medical science as humane treatment' would restore 'a nature that once knew purity'.[80]

The Home Office arranged for a medical enquiry in late July 1896, to assess Wilde's sanity. The Home Office officials recorded that the medical panel did

> not consider that there is danger of the prisoner becoming insane and they are supported by the medical officer [for Reading gaol], who says that Wilde's health has improved and he has gained flesh.[81]

Absolutely no acknowledgement was made by these medical men of the grounds for Wilde's appeal. Wilde's claims of 'sexual madness' were not recognised by the medical enquiry's investigation. To the men at the Home Office, Wilde was simply a common criminal who, by his sexual actions, had cast himself outside society. At the beginning of the trials, Wilde had a wife, family and successful literary career. Through his foolhardy libel suit against the Marquis of Queensbury, Wilde had 'forced' the authorities to act against him. Wilde was not considered to be suffering 'sexual madness'. But he had undoubtedly forfeited his masculine social status. Wilde was ostracised, vilified, incarcerated and never again allowed to have contact with his children. After his release, he was forced to live in exile from Britain.

Much concern was expressed after the Wilde trials about the impact of such a case on the reputation of masculinity in Britain. In March 1896, the Lord Chancellor, Lord Halsbury, motioned a Bill in the House of Lords in reaction to the widespread newspaper reporting of the Wilde trials. Halsbury's Publication of Indecent Evidence Bill proposed to make it a criminal offence to publish details of court cases involving sex between men. Halsbury and the Lords who debated the Bill found it impossible to name the particular crime to which the proposed legislation referred. Halsbury argued that 'the great evil with which the Bill seemed to deal was very great and urgently required a remedy'.[82] In response to procedural demands for evidence of his claims, Halsbury stated that 'he could not and would not reproduce a mass of indecent and obscene matter in their Lordship's House taken from newspapers'. Halsbury appealed to the Lords' common sense in the matter, stating that

> no noble Lord would be able to contradict him when he said that … cases had been published in the newspapers containing details of the most grossly indecent character.[83]

Halsbury's reference to 'grossly indecent' crimes left the House in no doubt as to what they were debating. The crime of gross indecency referred to Clause 11 of the Criminal Law Amendment Act of 1885, which criminalised sexual acts between men other than sodomy. The Prime Minister, Lord Salisbury, agreed that the subject of the Bill was nearly impossible to debate: 'in discussing the evil to which the Bill relates we are rather hampered by the disagreeable character of the subject'.[84]

Halsbury's Bill was the first occasion that the subject had been debated in parliament in the modern era. Halsbury proposed to make it a criminal offence to report details of 'grossly indecent' cases in the newspapers. He even proposed that such cases might be heard *in camera*. Halsbury gave his reasons for insisting on press silence in this matter, believing that

> many fathers of families, who had to apply an *index expurgatorius* at the breakfast table, would be grateful to their Lordships if they passed this bill and mitigated the indecency to which publication was given in some newspapers.

Halsbury questioned whether it was to 'the public advantage that such publications should be sown broadcast all over the country amongst persons of both sexes and of all ages'.[85] He feared that recognition of the existence of the 'evil' and 'grossly indecent' crime undermined paternal authority in the home. The Prime Minister supported Halsbury's aims for the bill. Salisbury argued that

> it is precisely the class of cases ... which produces to my mind the most flagrant evil that we have to deal with. The reason why the publication of that class of cases is so much to be deprecated is not merely because it offends our taste and makes the reading of newspapers disgusting, but because it is a well-ascertained fact that the publication of details in cases of that kind has a horrible, though undoubtedly direct, action in producing an imitation of the crime by other people.[86]

Salisbury evidently feared that publication of cases of sex between men advertised the existence of the vice. If sex between men was recognised to exist, then Salisbury feared that other British men might also indulge in the vice. Censorship of the newspapers would have kept the general public, and family dependants in particular, in ignorance of this vice.

The Publication of Indecent Evidence Bill never passed into law. Although 'all were in entire sympathy with the object of the Bill', some of the Lords were wary about the infringement of the liberty of the press.

But Lord Rosebery, the Liberal leader, argued that the Bill was an overreaction to the matter of debate. Rosebery asked the House whether the 'evil [is] as great as it has been asserted to be'. He argued that 'the amount of indecent evidence that is published in newspapers of large circulation is extremely small and a diminishing quantity'.[87] Rosebery highlighted that the Bill proposed to censor details of cases from the high courts, but offered no control over arraignments at magistrates courts. He argued that 'no conceivable Ministry, no Lord Chancellor would dream of giving powers to a Bench of Magistrates to order what evidence should or should not be published'. Rosebery added that he did not think that the 'evil' was, in fact, much in evidence in Britain: 'you are going to legislate with respect to a corner, a fragment of an evil which is not itself great and which has a tendency to become less and less every day'.[88] Rosebery suggested, to cheers in the House, that the 'evil' was so rare amongst British men, that special legislation in the matter was unnecessary. He also made the popular suggestion that the 'evil' was disappearing from society. Rosebery conceded that 'there is in the papers, on very rare occasions, a certain amount of evidence which is not altogether agreeable reading for ourselves and our families'. But Rosebery asked the House, 'Would it not be better to leave the matter alone?'[89] He argued that the press already exercised 'wisdom and common sense' in reporting such cases.[90]

Rosebery appears to be correct in his assessment of the reticence of the press in this matter. Only a tiny fraction of cases of sodomy and gross indecency were reported in the newspapers in the 1890s.[91] Rosebery suggested that the evil was so rare among British men that Halsbury's 'unconstitutional innovation' was unwarranted. Had the government proceeded with the Bill, a huge constitutional debate would have been sparked about press freedoms. The Liberal Lord Glensk stated that 'it was most regrettable that such a Bill should ever have been introduced'. Like Rosebery, Glensk 'entirely denied that the publication of objectionable matter was on the increase. On the contrary, the tendency was altogether in the other direction'. Glensk urged the House to ignore this matter, rather than subjecting 'the Press to a new tribunal by extending an arbitrary power to a judge'.[92]

This unique debate articulated, for the first time in a public arena, the deep fear of suggesting that sex between men was a prevalent phenomenon in Britain. All the participants in the debate were concerned with preserving masculine social status from the threat posed by phenomenon. The Conservative government was clearly willing to contemplate press censorship in the matter in order to assist 'fathers of families' to maintain discipline and authority over the morals of their families. Advertising the existence of the 'evil' threatened to undermine masculinity by provoking a spread of the vice. The objections of the opposition are even more revealing of prevailing attitudes. The vice was so reprehensible and so rare amongst British men, argued the Liberals, that no action needed to be taken to curb its reporting in the newspapers. Rosebery lauded the 'wisdom and common sense of the public at large', and indicated that the press would respect and uphold these sensibilities when rare cases of 'gross indecency' occurred.[93] It was better to ignore the matter completely, rather than risk extensive constitutional reform. This course of action guaranteed that the issue of freedom of the press, and the 'evil' that prompted this debate, would be kept firmly out of the newspapers.

Rosebery's instincts on the matter were well founded. Newspapers shied away from reporting such cases, indicating that most of the public preferred not to be confronted with the issue. Also, the authorities could and did use the obscene libel laws to prosecute a publication that contravened prevailing standards of taste. Havelock Ellis' study, *Sexual Inversion*, was a scientific treatise on the subject of sex between men similar to Continental publications in this field. But when Ellis attempted to publish and sell *Sexual Inversion* in 1898, the book was banned as a work of obscene libel.[94] The first work to be successfully published in Britain on this subject was Edward Carpenter's apologia, *The Intermediate Sex*.[95] Its existence was ignored by the mainstream press. The *British Medical Journal* did not review it until 1909, and excoriated the piece. However, *The Intermediate Sex* attracted the attention of M. D. O'Brien. O'Brien was a member of the England Patriotic and Anti-Socialist Association, an organisation based in Salford that campaigned for 'individualism and freedom' for men in Britain. He was the author of articles arguing for 'Free Libraries' for the poor, 'The Natural Right to Freedom' and 'Socialism tested by Facts'.[96] O'Brien was, like Carpenter, a resident of Sheffield and vehemently opposed to Carpenter's socialist politics. O'Brien conducted a campaign against Carpenter in the *Yorkshire Post*, and privately printed a pamphlet, *Socialism and Infamy*, lambasting Carpenter's ideas on 'homogenic love', or sexuality between men.

In his letters to the *Yorkshire Post*, O'Brien claimed that Carpenter's ideas on 'homogenic' comradeship were deleterious to the birth rate:

> It is not unlikely that the decline in the birth rate will greatly increase. This movement, partly open and partly carried on under the surface, has for its object the establishment of what is called 'comradeship' as

a social institution ... those who go in for it are not naturally inclined to marry or beget children.[97]

O'Brien was much more explicit in his pamphlet about what he objected to in Carpenter's work. O'Brien attacked

the disgusting, loathsome and socially destructive vice which you [Carpenter] have the boldness to hold up for approval, if not for adoption.[98]

O'Brien found the subject material for Carpenter's book reprehensible, and argued that 'homogenic love' should be called 'homogenic lust'. He claimed that the publication

brings you within the reach of the criminal law ... Desire for carnal intercourse with one's own sex [is] a morbid appetite, the product probably of cultivation, which sinks those who possess it to the lowest depths of depravity ... that it is possible for a human creature to fall.[99]

O'Brien's tirade against 'homogenic love' centred on the effects this vice would have on the masculinity of the citizens of Sheffield:

Do you think that the practice of homogenic love is likely to promote either the moral, the mental or the physical welfare of Sheffield? Do you think it is calculated to make Sheffield's citizens better husbands, better fathers or better sons? Is this vice good for Sheffield, or is it bad for Sheffield? ... Is it a sound investment for the steel city's sons to invest in? Is it fitted to make mechanics more skillful, intelligent and inventive? Will it increase the industry and efficiency of merchants, organisers, managers and directors of labour, or of commercial travellers who have to compete for orders in all parts of the civilised world?[100]

O'Brien was concerned that, if Carpenter's work were associated with the City of Sheffield, trade in the city would be irrevocably damaged:

Is the infamy which is said to have brought destruction upon Sodom and Gomorrah likely to bring in one form or another anything less than destruction on the trade of Sheffield?[101]

O'Brien's tirade was confined to a privately printed pamphlet and *Socialism and Infamy* was never published. However, O'Brien's opinions on the deleteriousness of 'homogenic love' are revealing. He regarded the vice, which he felt excluded women, as detrimental to the family and the birth rate. Also, the vice flouted the work ethic and sense of citizenship upon which the commercial success of Sheffield was based. It is interesting that O'Brien regarded all classes of male citizens as being fundamentally threatened by the existence of the vice in the city. O'Brien argued that Carpenter and his friends had evaded prosecution, because 'these charges are not pressed home ... those who make them do not like their names to be mixed up in anything so vile and loathsome'. O'Brien argued that the 'vile' practices advocated by Carpenter 'quite unfits its slaves for the duties of the married state, and causes them to turn from their wives to the male "comrades" who are more capable of satisfying their unnatural appetites'. In other words, toleration of 'homogenic love' threatened marriage, one of the fundamental prerequisites for masculine social status. O'Brien suggested that 'homogenic love' might turn some men from the onerous duties and responsibilities of full masculinity and procreative, uxorious sex. Men would, somehow, be enslaved by irresponsible, exclusively pleasure-orientated sex with other men and abandon their wives. O'Brien accused Carpenter and his comrades of threatening to overthrow 'private property, private homes and private families' through advocacy of 'homogenic love'. O'Brien blamed Carpenter's socialism for the tenor of comradeship in his work:

> The socialist and anti-private property principle of unexclusiveness ... strikes inevitably at the monogamic union, without which the separate private family, composed of children who have ... the same father and mother, cannot in the very nature of the case exist.[102]

'Homogenic love' threatened, according to O'Brien, 'separate and private family life'. He argued that, if Carpenter's ideas were to be adopted, 'what vicious, effeminate and unnatural creatures all men would become'.[103] For O'Brien, the success of the City of Sheffield was contingent upon a robust sense of individualist masculinity. O'Brien was in no doubt that masculinity required men to be uxorious and that association of male citizens be free from any taint of sexuality.

Of course, O'Brien's criticism of *The Intermediate Sex* was never published and his defamation of Carpenter was confined to the pages of the local newspaper. But O'Brien's thoughts on this matter reflected the tenor of the House of Lords debate in 1896. Sex between men threatened the fabric and stability of society. Between the late 1860s and the first decade of the twentieth century, masculinity as a social status became the dominant indicator of social inclusion. For men to be considered fully masculine, they had to be married. Angus McLaren's study, *The Trials of Masculinity* (1997), argues that bachelorhood became an increasingly ambivalent and problematic status for adult men. McLaren states that the male world became split between 'the married and the unmarried'. Although the 'loss of freedoms attendant upon marriage [were] ritually lamented' in popular male culture, men who remained celibate were regarded by their peers as 'not having attained full adult status'. Also, doctors cited the overrepresentation of single males in asylums as evidence of 'the social dangers posed by bachelors'.[104] In addition to being married, men had to demonstrate their masculinity through their abilities to support their wives and families. Attainment of full adult masculinity was contingent upon the ability of men to move freely from the home to the workplace and all male associations. In this period, masculine social status became the benchmark of middle-class independence and citizenship.

Masculine social status also became the benchmark of working-class respectability and citizenship in this period. Trades unions and working-class newspapers valorised the skills and independent character of the working man and his ability to support his wife and family. Indeed, a working man's masculinity became contingent upon this and trades unions promoted the male breadwinner wage as essential to working-class dignity. The atomised structure of the British working class meant that a working man was much more likely to find political solidarity with work mates and his employer than communitarian solidarity with his working-class neighbours. The Franchise Acts of 1867 and 1884 extended the vote to working-class men who were head of their households. Both the Liberal and Conservative parties became dependent upon the voting intentions of this class of men, and election policies were developed and designed to appeal to their interests. However, economic vicissitudes meant that only half of working men had the domestic stability to qualify for the vote. Masculinity as a social status dominated, but had not developed what Connell regards as its 'hegemonic' qualities, apparent in the mid-twentieth century.[105] Nonetheless, at the end of the nineteenth century, married working-class men who could not support their families became the subject of social concern and were constructed by social commentators as separate from society. By 1900, working-class housewifery and full masculine social status became realistically achievable for increasing numbers of working-class families.

From the 1870s, men's sexual power over women was being vigorously questioned by popular mass campaigns. Men were required to exercise stringent self-control in their expression of sex. These campaigns were particularly popular with the respectable working classes. Working-class men were enjoined to protect their wives and daughters from sexual predators and violators. The campaigns encouraged working-class men to regard their wives and daughters as property, in need of defence and protection. These campaigns resulted in changes to legislation. Campaigns for male social purity remained very popular. Pamphlets warning about the perils of masturbation by men reached at least a million homes. However, this literature did not claim that masturbation would cause inversion, or the sexual desire for other men. Medical theories of inversion on the Continent specifically targeted masturbation in the aetiology of male homosexuality. In Britain, these theories were ignored in social purity campaigns.

Masculinity as a social status required men to undertake onerous and often conflicting responsibilities. Recognition of an alternative to acceptable masculinity threatened to undermine the basis of British society. Sex and sexuality between men complicated the free association of independent male citizens. Admitting that this kind of vice existed among men challenged the ability of 'fathers of families' to maintain authority in their homes. In the House of Lords debate in 1896, attempts were made to ban completely publication of details of court cases involving 'unnatural crime'. The government of the day was prepared to infringe the constitutional liberties of the press in order to remove the existence of this 'evil' from the public consciousness. In the event, arguments that the 'evil' was almost absent and in decline in Britain, prevailed. It was better to ignore the phenomenon, than advertise its existence by controversial constitutional change. To the British, sexuality between men threatened the structure of the family and flouted the work ethic. If recognised and tolerated, the phenomenon had the potential to tempt some men away from their procreative duties to their wives. Sexuality between men and its communitarian overtones also threatened the ability of independent men to maintain work, trade, commerce and politics.

The debate surrounding Halsbury's Publication of Indecent Evidence Bill and O'Brien's tirade in *Socialism and Infamy* give clear and explicit reasons why British society had great difficulty in discussing the existence of the phenomenon. But these outbursts were rare responses to moments of crisis in British masculinity. Halsbury had been moved to curb press freedoms in reaction to the embarrassing and international spectacle of the Wilde trials. O'Brien was also responding to what he perceived as a crisis for masculinity – the successful publication of *The Intermediate Sex*. Both the House of Lords debate and O'Brien's critique were unusual and explicit responses to the phenomenon. However, the sensibilities and defence of masculinity expressed by the Lords and by O'Brien, are detectable in other evidence of the phenomenon in the period.

3
National Newspapers

Highly prominent, scandalous and infrequent trials for the 'unnatural' and 'nameless' crime of sodomy in the late nineteenth century have attracted a great deal of historiographical attention. Until very recently, significant historical analyses have been based on the proceedings and reportage of no more than three trials of this kind, occurring between 1871 and 1895. Historians of British homosexuality have tended to concentrate upon the 'Stella and Fanny' trial of 1871, the Cleveland Street scandal in 1889, and the trials of Oscar Wilde in 1895. These trials, involving men of the highest social visibility and status in late Victorian society, have formed the bases of arguments relating to formations of homosexual identities and perceptions of homosexuality in British society. The 'Stella and Fanny' trials of 1870 and 1871 were conducted following the arrest of two cross-dressed actors, Ernest Boulton and William Park. As the case against Boulton and Park emerged, it transpired that Boulton, or 'Stella', was probably having a sodomitical relationship with Lord Arthur Clinton, MP. The case attracted widespread newspaper coverage. The publicity surrounding the 'Stella and Fanny' trial of 1871 and the collapse of the trial on the grounds of lack of evidence is used by Weeks and many others to argue that perceptions of sexuality between men were barely formulated in British society at this time. The Cleveland Street scandal and the trials of Oscar Wilde are presented as a new and unprecedented trope in newspaper reporting and public knowledge. In contrast, Cocks' work on the sodomy trial in English society demonstrates that trials for sodomy in England were not only extensive in this period, but also proliferated after 1800. Through the meticulous analysis of judicial returns in the parliamentary records, Cocks argues that in the 1860s alone there was an average of 60 indictments a year for sodomy. It is, however, impossible to ascertain from these statistics, the proportion of indictments that referred to sexual offences between men. After all, the Buggery Act of 1533, which still remained the basis of legislation, included sexual acts performed by men with animals and other men and included anal penetration of women within its legislative scope.

Weeks, Cohen and others regard changes in British legislation, particularly the 1885 Labouchere Amendment to the Criminal Law Amendment Act, as the classification and categorisation of a homosexual 'species' in legal arrangements.[1] Nevertheless, as Montgomery-Hyde's work highlights, the sixteenth-century Buggery Act remained the basis for legislation in proscribing sex between men until its repeal in 1967.[2] Alterations to this legislation in the nineteenth century certainly widened its scope to establish in law that all sexual acts between men were criminal. But the legislation that criminalised sex between men in the period in question never, in essence, distinguished between bestiality, heterosexual sodomy or homosexual sex. This ambivalence in the legal definitions up to 1967 defies the medico-legal analysis of a purposive, legislative categorisation of the homosexual.

Cocks acknowledges that indictments for sodomy in the nineteenth century cannot be read simply as indictments for sex between men. His careful statistical analysis of, hitherto neglected, magistrate and assize court records establishes a distinct pattern in nineteenth-century England for indictments using the Buggery Act. In rural areas, indictments for bestiality were proportionately higher than for sexual acts between men, though indictments for the latter were by no means non-existent. In urban areas, which were the loci for the majority of sodomy indictments, the indictments were, almost exclusively, for sexual acts between men. Cocks' research has led him to urban court records beyond London and has demonstrated evidence of indictments for sexuality between men in cities such as Manchester.[3]

Cocks' work is significant to the arguments in this book because he demonstrates that sodomy indictments in urban areas referred almost exclusively to sexual acts between men. Also, Cocks establishes that there was an absolute increase in sodomy indictments during the nineteenth century. Reproach towards sex between men after 1861 was ambivalent and often contradictory. There was an increasing willingness, particularly in urban spaces, to report sexual acts between men to the authorities. Urban dwelling had become, after 1850, the mode of living for the majority of the population. In the second half of the nineteenth century, the moral rectitude of urban dwellers, in particular the enfranchised middle and working classes became impossible for the authorities to ignore. Notwithstanding this changing pattern of power, the authorities, which in this circumstance meant the courts, the police, the Home Office and, ultimately, parliament, demonstrated a marked reticence in clarifying definitions, sentencing policies, or the classification of sexuality between men.

The statistical and legal evidence demonstrates that to the urban dweller, motivated to report sex between men to the authorities, sodomy was understood almost exclusively to mean sex between men. It is not necessarily the case that rural interpretations of sodomy and buggery were vague simply because the availability of animals in the countryside made the incidence of bestiality more likely. It must not be forgotten that a town or city of the mid-to-late nineteenth century had an enormous population of domestic animals.[4] Horses, cows and poultry were kept in the towns and cities in abundance and these were the animals that almost invariably featured in buggery trials that involved animals, throughout the nineteenth century and for much of the twentieth.[5] The nineteenth-century urban dweller would undoubtedly have understood the modern meaning of bestiality. Instead, the urban dweller differentiated this crime from sex between men, not through alienation from animals, but for specific social purposes. Tacit awareness of the existence of sexuality between men was widespread in society, particularly amongst urban dwellers, and an established notion before the 'Stella and Fanny' trial in 1871. In a predominantly urbanised society that, increasingly, expected its men to marry, irrespective of class, there was little room for toleration of sexual aberrance. The uxorious focus of masculinity as a social status excluded and characterised masculine traits that threatened its stability. The man, who engaged in sex with other men, was arguably the most destabilising of all.[6]

Newspaper reports and legal indictments frequently described sex between men as 'filthy', amongst other terms.[7] Mary Douglas argues that in cultural terms, dirt and filth exist, not absolutely, but 'in the eye of the beholder'. Toleration of agreed cultural conceptions of dirt 'offends against order'.[8] If late nineteenth-century urban society regarded sex between men as dirt, then this form of sex and its perpetrators posed a threat to order. Controlling and eliminating perceived dirt would act as 'a positive effort to control the environment'.[9] However, as sex between men fundamentally threatened the balances of power within gender relations and therefore society as a whole, recognition of the existence and extent of this form of 'dirt' would have been almost too destabilising to contemplate. Powerful cultural mores prevailed to keep it well hidden, both by society as a whole and by its perpetrators.

When it was not confronted with this form of 'dirt', late nineteenth-century British society could and would forget its existence. Those with vested interests in maintaining the balance of gender relations would not readily admit to the extent of this form of 'dirt'; only when confronted with irrefutable evidence of it, could this group consent to recognise its existence. Thus confronted, the 'filthy' men involved in sexual acts with each other had to be regarded as aberrant and rare; to do otherwise would threaten order. This helps to illustrate why the characterisation and exclusion of the type of man who would engage in sex with other men is often elusive and shadowy in the historical records for this period. This chapter demonstrates the reasons for the relative elusiveness of this form of sexuality in public narratives in the period in question. There is an opaqueness in the 'public' historical record; between 1872 and the mid-1880s, there was a decline in references to cases of sex between men in *The Times*. This does not mean that cultural awareness of sex and sexuality between men became non-existent: quite the reverse. From the sparse evidence that does exist, a pattern of complicit secrecy and silence on the subject emerges. At a time when British masculinity was deliberately projected as the pre-eminent and moral exemplar throughout the expanding Empire and in relation to its European neighbours, even *The Times* fell silent on the subject of trials for sex between men. It is a further paradox that this period of opaqueness, 1872 to 1885, are also the earliest years for which we have significant evidence of self-making centred on desire between men in Britain.[10]

It appears that the national press refused to acknowledge the extent of such occurrences, in the hope that the phenomenon of sex between British men might simply disappear.[11] Metropolitan sodomy indictments did not abate in this period and the earliest evidence of modern homosexual self-making emanates from these years, so sex and sexuality between men clearly did not disappear.[12] It is significant that the single case of unnatural crime reported between 1872 and 1885 in *The Times* involved a member of the German embassy. In 1881, Count Guido zu Lynar, secretary to the German ambassador, was discovered committing an unnatural act with a corporal from the Scots Guards. Following the arrests, the German ambassador claimed diplomatic immunity for zu Lynar. The representative of the German embassy told the magistrate's court that 'the German government regarded this matter with the utmost regret ... [and] would, of course, institute the fullest enquiries into the case of the Count'.[13] *The Times* clearly reported this case because of the diplomatic impasse created by the Count's sexual impropriety. Also, the nationality of the Count meant that the case did not threaten

British notions of masculinity. Indeed, the exceptionality of the case served to reinforce these perceptions. Even the corporal from the Scots Guards, John Cameron, was presented in the report as not fully British, or at least on the margins of acceptable Britishness. On his arrest, Cameron told Inspector Chisholm that 'had he known what the [Count] had brought him to the house for he would have knocked his brains out'. This discussion was conducted 'in Gaelic, both [Inspector Chisholm] and the prisoner conversing in that dialect'. It is impossible to ascertain whether the conversation, between an Inspector of the Metropolitan Police and a corporal in the Scots Guards, did take place in Gaelic. Cameron made a 'long statement in which he tried to show that the evidence for the prosecution was altogether untrue'.[14] This statement was made, presumably, in English. Undoubtedly, Gaelic was spoken in Irish migrant quarters of the city, but less so by the 1880s.[15] The speaking of Scots Gaelic would have been an even rarer phenomenon. A conversation in Gaelic, either Irish or Scots, would have been a highly unusual occurrence between such men in London. However, the report gave prominence to this piece of evidence, and no other, for the defendant. This had the effect of rendering both defendants as foreign, or at least peripheral, to British society, and the case itself as highly unusual and aberrant.

Evidence of an adjuration for press refrain and silence on the subject of sex between men is difficult, but not impossible, to discern. Recommendations of silence on this subject did arise intermittently in the early to mid-nineteenth century. In 1825, *The Times* editorial explicitly recommended silence on the subject as a remedy for 'this horrible and increasing crime' following a spate of sodomy trials involving audacious 'unnatural gangs'.[16] This notwithstanding, *The Times* continued to report unnatural crime with some consistency until the early 1870s. However, *The Times* commentary in 1825 reflected a broader tendency in early nineteenth-century publishing to shrink from publicising sodomy trials. For instance, the publication of sodomy trial proceedings in pamphlet form for general circulation, which had been widely available in the eighteenth century, virtually ceased after 1800.[17] But the newspapers and in particular *The Times*, continued to report sodomy trials, albeit in sketchy and veiled detail. *The Times* occasionally justified this reportage on the grounds that the cases were tried before juries and therefore, in the interests of justice, at least the minimum of details needed to be circulated in the public domain. But other voices argued that the publication of sodomy trials in the press simply advertised the extent to which sexuality between men existed. In the 1830s,

T. E. Baker urged Robert Peel, then Home Secretary, to decriminalise or at least reduce the sentencing for the capital crime of sodomy. Although Baker, a reform-minded campaigner, was writing in the 1830s, his sentiments were echoed in practice throughout the century. Baker urged Peel to decriminalise sodomy on the grounds that

> if no notice were taken of this crime in our civil courts and newspapers, it would in my opinion become less frequent, for thousands would never know the present existence of this unnatural offence, nor should we be shocked and disgusted by the frequent public allusion to it. For purposes of justice, very offensive evidence must often be heard in trials, the publication of which afterwards for general circulation, can produce little but unmixed evil.[18]

An examination of this document from the decades before the records fall virtually silent on the subject of sex between men is important, not least because its premises were constructed to create a general silence in the matter. However, throughout the 1850s and 1860s, *The Times*, almost exceptionally among mainstream newspapers, continued to report and comment upon unnatural crimes between men that came to attention through the police and criminal courts.[19] *The Times* did not, by any means, report every case that came to the attention of the courts. Reports of unnatural crime in its pages numbered no more than three incidents in any given year. Cocks' work demonstrates that the incidence of metropolitan sodomy indictments alone was much greater than the number of unnatural crimes reported in *The Times* would indicate. The style of reportage of unnatural crime was more succinct and gave less detail than in earlier decades. The pattern of reporting was, however, not consistent. As Cocks' work demonstrates, the cases that made it to the pages of *The Times* in the 1860s represented only a fraction of sodomy trials conducted. An examination of the unnatural crimes that did make it to the papers reveals little to suggest why these trials, over others during the decade, were reported. The only consistency in reporting was that unnatural crime meant, to the metropolitan journalists and readership of *The Times*, sex between men. The cases reported involved men from highly diverse backgrounds: labourers, soldiers, cigar-makers, cab drivers and coffee-shop proprietors, as well as solicitors and men of the cloth. The paradigm of cross-class same sexuality, much examined by historians of the 1890s, does not feature as the major source of alarm in the articles.

The pattern of sexual contact between the men in the 1860s' reportage was, in the main, connection between men of similar class status and the cash nexus rarely featured. Discrepancy in age between defendants did feature and it is evident that the courts regarded the elder participant as the more culpable, even in cases where the younger man could in no way be regarded as a minor. In the case of *Regina v. Ketch and Slade*, both defendants were found guilty of the 'unnatural offence'. Ketch, a printer who was aged 22, was sentenced to 12 years penal servitude and Slade, a dealer aged 60, was sentenced to 15 years penal servitude as 'the elder'.[20] There is no inference in this article or the Central Criminal Court entry for the trial whether the older defendant with the greater sentence was penalised more heavily because of a particular act, such as being the penetrator in anal sex. Both parties were equally guilty and it seems as though Slade received the heavier sentence because his seniority in years and marginally higher social status conferred the greater responsibility for the crime. The courts of the 1860s were clear that sex between men was a crime for both participants, even though the legislation governing the crime remained highly ambivalent as to who was the criminal in crimes of buggery. At a trial in 1871, reported in *The Times*, George Brett was accused of numerous 'abominable offences' over a period of years from 1867 with William Morrell, a deserter from the Dragoon Guards. Morrell reported the crime and was the prosecution's only witness. Although the details are sketchy, Morrell was portrayed by the prosecution as the victim and recipient of the 'abominable offences'.[21] However, the case was thrown out of the Central Criminal Court because, according to the record, 'there was no corroboration of the prosecutor's evidence, which, even if true, showed consent on his part'.[22]

The language used by *Times'* journalists in the 1860s to describe cases of unnatural crime merits examination – to assess the understanding of sexuality between men amongst journalists. With some caution, inferences can also be made from articles covering unnatural crime as to the level of understanding of sexuality between men amongst the readership of *The Times*. All the cases reported in the newspaper in the 1860s would have had to satisfy the conditions of Lord Campbell's 1857 Obscene Publications Act. The articles from the 1860s give less detail than equivalent articles covering unnatural crime from the 1820s and 1830s. However, the reader of the articles in the 1860s was left in no doubt as to the nature of the 'unnatural crime' being described. This indicates a level of understanding of the existence and implications of sex between men in the 1860s, at least amongst the upper middle-class readership of *The Times*. Notwithstanding the constraints on publication in the 1860s, the articles remain highly illustrative of the sexual incidents they were reporting. An example of this is contained in the reporting of a sodomy trial from 1863. *The Times* reported a trial from the Central Criminal Court, which it regarded as a 'disgusting case' and that for the sake of decency and, no doubt, avoidance of prosecution under the 1857 Obscene Publications Act, stated that 'many of the particulars ... cannot be reported'. The trial involved two men; Charles Rees, aged 32, whose given occupation was a servant and John Tyson, aged 26, who was a soldier in the Scots Fusilier Guards. The prisoner Rees was a lodger in a boarding house in Paris Street, Westminster, which was the scene of the crime. The principal witness of the crime was 'a very respectably dressed woman named Mary-Ann Powell' who was a fellow lodger in the house. Mrs Powell had been asked by the landlady of the house to sit up late to ensure that another lodger, named Nicholls, 'did not walk off with his luggage, leaving the rent unpaid'. To accomplish this request, Mrs Powell had stationed herself behind the door of the front parlour; but Nicholls did not appear from his room with his luggage. Instead, Mr Rees and the guardsman 'came down the stairs from Nicholls' room'. Mrs Powell stated that they were 'behaving towards each other in a very indecent manner' as they proceeded towards the back kitchen of the house. The intrepid witness followed the two, who had shut the kitchen door. She could hear their lewd conversation and, by looking through the two keyholes in the door, had 'a full view of what took place between the prisoners'. Mrs Powell fled upstairs to inform the mistress of the house and managed to return to the scene of the crime in time to hear 'the sound of copper money handed by Rees to the soldier'.[23]

Short of describing the sexual acts that took place, the writer of this and other reports of unnatural crime leaves the reader in little doubt as to the nature of the crime committed. In spite of the evidence of the witness, *The Times* reported that Rees and Tyson were found not guilty by the jury. Unfortunately, the Central Criminal Court record of the trial gives only meagre details of the case, simply recording a verdict of 'not guilty' for 'unnatural crime'.[24] However, the *Times* article alluded to why the case collapsed against Rees and Tyson. The prosecution's only witness, Mrs Powell, transpired to be not as 'respectable' as her first appearance in court indicated. She was separated from her husband, a sergeant in the Dragoon Guards. Although she had made a living as a milliner after her separation, 'she had abandoned that means of obtaining a livelihood since she had picked up with a gentleman in the neighbourhood of Pimlico'. Mrs Powell was, in the considerations of the time, a 'kept woman' at best and, more than likely, a prostitute. Also, her gentleman caller could not corroborate her evidence: 'the gentleman was in bed in her room on the night of this occurrence, but she had not told him until afterwards of the scene she had witnessed through the keyhole because at the time he was asleep'. Mrs Powell's arrangements for accommodation implied dishonesty or the potential for dishonesty. Crowded lodgings, with other men who were not her relatives present in the house and without a spouse to protect her, meant that she was living in a space that was potentially disreputable for her character. Mrs Powell's lack of protection from her spouse and her living circumstances posed a threat of encountering an 'unnatural' incident.

During the 'Stella and Fanny' trials, the *Pall Mall Gazette* expressed intense concern that newspaper coverage of the trial would be read by women. The act of reading about sexuality between men, even when the incidents occurred in situations unlikely to be visited by the 'respectable' female reader, could endanger the character of 'any one having the faintest pretension to be considered an honest woman'.[25] By the act of witnessing sex between men, Mrs Powell's character was at serious risk. Under scrutiny, the value of Mrs Powell's testimony as a prosecution witness evaporated.[26]

The Paris Street incident raises questions about the importance of the character of witnesses and the accused in sodomy trials. Cocks' work concentrates on the significance of the character of the gentleman accused in nineteenth-century sodomy trials. Cocks argues that the sodomy trial of the high social status offender attracted more attention than offenders from lower down the social scale. Middle- and upper-class criminals generally attracted most newspaper comment; although only 4 per cent of criminal trials involved offenders from these classes, they received an overwhelming majority of attention in the press.[27] However, Cocks' work on character and self-possession and its relationship to 'masculinity' gives the impression that possession of character and moral continence was considered to be exclusively an elite, or even gender-specific preserve. Cocks' work does not emphasise the relevance of character in sodomy trials involving participants from the working classes and from both sexes. The courts and the journalists were evidently concerned with the 'respectability' of trial participants, which included attributes such as occupation, quality of apparel and reputation and it is arguable that these were middle-class benchmarks against which the working-class participant was judged. For *The Times* at least, the wearing of demure apparel, engagement in an 'honest' occupation and secure marital status qualified the working-class participant as 'respectable' and in possession of good character. It is clear from the Paris Street incident that Mrs Powell started the trial as a witness in possession of good character. She was 'very respectably dressed' and was married. However, as the trial progressed, her character started to unravel under scrutiny. By the end of the trial, Mrs Powell appeared as an adulteress, who shared overcrowded lodgings with men that were strangers to her and who possibly held a prejudice against guardsmen, given the occupation of her estranged husband. The guardsman, on the other hand, had his character exonerated by his sergeant major. The sergeant major gave evidence of Tyson's excellent conduct as a long-serving guardsman and added that he regarded Tyson as 'about the last man in the regiment who ... would be connected with such a case as the present'.[28] Historians of homosexuality in nineteenth-century Britain, such as Weeks and, more recently, Matt Cook, make references to the reputation of guardsmen in Victorian London for prostitution. Indeed, guardsmen featured regularly not only in trials, but also in the rare examples of homosexual pornography from the period.[29] Although one must not read too much into the sergeant major's statement, it appears that Tyson's excellent service was insufficient to fulfil the requirements of good character in the context of the sodomy trial. Tyson needed to be 'the last man in the regiment' to engage in sodomy, possibly recognising the propensity of others in the regiment to do so.

It is evident from all *The Times'* articles on unnatural crime in this period that the possession of good character transcended class status and gender. It was important in these cases not to attribute propensity to sodomy to any particular class of men. *The Times* received regular scrutiny from the working-class Sunday newspapers for evidence of class bias.[30] More than this, it would not be in the interests of *The Times* to alienate working-class and lower middle-class men, the bulk of the male population, as potential sodomites in the eyes of its elite readership in an era of extensive franchise reform. Of course, when men of high social status were accused of sodomy, this attracted far more attention than trials involving lower-class men because of the wider social ramifications of their disgrace. The trial of Edward Whitehurst, a prominent solicitor in Westminster, received almost daily attention throughout November 1862 and the trial was covered until its conclusion. Other trials, involving men of no social importance, were often not covered for the duration of the trial. However, what is clear from all the articles in this period, is the reluctance of the courts to put any man on trial for unnatural crime. The character of defendants and witnesses, irrespective of class, appears to feature more prominently than in trials for theft or other crimes.

The reports of unnatural crime nearly all register a tone of disbelief that any honestly occupied man would engage in a crime of this nature. In a magistrate court trial in 1862 involving a cab driver and a gentleman caught together in 'an indecent position' in a public house lavatory by numerous witnesses, the character of the gentleman, Augustus Cordner, was the more reprehensible because this defendant was a drunkard and was 'described as a poet'.[31] In the trial of James Rowton, a school teacher, in 1865, who was accused of unnatural crime involving a 14-year-old boy, the case rested on the jury's assessment of the defendant's character and whether he had the propensity for such a reprehensible act. The defence supplied a succession of character witnesses, who attested Rowton to be a paragon of virtue. However, an adult witness who was taught by Rowton as a boy gave evidence that 'his character is that of a man capable of the grossest indecency and most flagrant immorality'. This evidence was, after some deliberation in the court, deemed inadmissible because the witness 'knew nothing of the neighbourhood's opinion' of Rowton. Rowton's excellent reputation in his local community was clearly enough to influence the jurors to regard the evidence of a former pupil as slanderous.[32]

The emphasis on character in sodomy trials in this period highlights a fundamental ambivalence in the requirements of evidence to secure convictions for unnatural crime. The archaic Buggery Act required proof of anal penetration and emission of semen before convictions could be secured. But a conviction for sodomy was, ostensibly, a more likely outcome in the 1860s than at any point in the history of the Buggery Act to that date. Between 1828 and 1861, changes in the rules of evidence and the punishment for sodomy diminished public controversy over sodomy convictions. A spate of sodomy trials in the 1820s, which, in spite of reliable witnesses, resulted in acquittal for the defendants on the grounds that no evidence of seminal emission could be found, prompted *The Times* to highlight the near impossibility to secure convictions for unnatural crime.[33] *The Times* also highlighted that the capital charge for sodomy made juries very reluctant to convict.[34] In Sir Robert Peel's Offences Against the Person Act of 1828, the requirement of proof was diminished to evidence of penetration only, which resulted in an increase in convictions.[35] Nonetheless, the retention of the capital charge meant that juries were still reluctant to convict for unnatural offences, as men continued to be hanged until 1836 for sodomy and the charge remained a capital indictment until 1861.[36] The diminution of proof in 1828 and removal of the capital charge in 1861 might, as Cohen argues, be regarded as governmental clarification in the punishment and suppression of sexuality between men.[37] Nevertheless, what is striking about the treatment of the Buggery Act during the nineteenth century is how little it was altered and how reluctant the authorities were to interfere with its archaic basis. The Offences Against the Person Act of 1861, finally removed the capital charge for sodomy. It is significant that in 1861, sodomy remained one of only 'seven offences with the capital charge' from the legacy of England's notorious eighteenth-century bloody code.[38] The capital charge for sodomy was quietly dropped in 1861, attracting no comment in *The Times* or other newspapers. The retention of the nominally capital charge for sodomy until 1861, when hundreds of other felonies had gradually lost their capital charges by the early 1830s, was indicative of the legislature's persistent reluctance to regard or address sex between men as a priority for legal clarification. Also, it is evident from *The Times'* articles and the scant references in the court records to the trials reported, that the majority of cases of unnatural crime between 1861 and 1872 did not, in spite of legal developments, result in convictions. *The Times*, unlike its editions from the 1820s and 1830s, did not indulge in arguments for changes in the law to secure easier convictions in respect to unnatural crime. The article writers appear content simply to report the bare facts of a case and publish the verdict.

A significant part of the problem for the courts in securing convictions rested on the meaning of penetration in such trials. Unfortunately, no sodomy trial transcripts survive from the 1860s, but a sodomy indictment from 1841, surviving in the Treasury Solicitors' archive, indicates that prosecution counsels were prepared to stretch the definition of penetration to include oral sex and mutual masturbation under existing legislation.[39] It appears from the newspaper record that the courts occasionally got around the problem of proof of penetration *in ano* by convicting men of the much lesser offence of indecent exposure. In the trial of Thomas Smith and Edward Tanbridge in 1871, it is clear from *The Times'* description of the 'indecent and abominable conduct in a public place ... the facts [of which] were unfit for publication' that a sexual encounter had taken place between the two men.[40] In another case of indecent exposure without sexual assault involving one man and a female witness, the details of the encounter are no less coy. But the reader is allowed to infer from witness statements like 'she swore she saw it, by the side of a high road, in broad daylight' that the woman witnessed genital exposure or, at most, an act of masturbation.[41] On convicting Smith and Tanbridge for indecent exposure, the court sentenced the prisoners to six months imprisonment, adding that 'the heavier punishment would be the contempt and scorn they would be held in by every right minded person'. This possibly conveyed the court's frustration at its inability to secure a conviction for full sodomy, though a conviction would have meant recognition by the state that sodomy existed.

The punishment of 'contempt and scorn' encouraged by the court raises the question of the wider social disgrace of appearing in a law court accused of sodomy. It was not in the interests of masculinity as a social status to have high rates of sodomy convictions and the rules of evidence reflected this. However, when defendants were found not guilty due to lack of reliable or 'respectable' witnesses, or for lack of witness evidence of actual sexual connection, their names appeared in *The Times* for readers to form their own judgements of the individuals involved. In the trial of the cab driver, Robert Godbold and the drunken poet, Augustus Cordner in 1862, the cab driver's name and his badge number were published. This revelation in *The Times*, published before conviction, would have singled out Godbold for opprobrium in the likely event of a not guilty verdict. It would have been highly probable that *The Times'* readers were potential customers of the London cab driver. Although the case was referred for trial before a jury, there is, unfortunately, no record, using either the cab driver's or the poet's names, of the case making it to court and the incident is not referred to again in *The Times*. It is likely that lack of witnesses to sexual penetration meant that there was insufficient evidence for a trial by jury. This notwithstanding, the reader of this incident was allowed to assume that a sexual encounter had taken place between Godbold and Cordner. The principal witness, a globe maker named Mr Penny, attested to seeing Godbold and 'the gentleman' going into the yard of the public house. Suspicions were aroused when

> about a quarter of an hour afterwards someone knocked at the street door and asked for [Godbold] ... [Penny] then went to the yard, and found the watercloset fastened on the inside. He knocked at the door and a voice said 'all right'. He went again, with two or three others, and broke the door open, and found [Godbold] and the other man inside. The other man rushed out and escaped.[42]

Cordner, the gentleman poet, was, by magistrate request, identified and apprehended by the police. Like the cab driver, Cordner denied all charges, claiming he 'knew nothing of the matter, as he was very drunk' at the time.[43] Although sodomy was not proven and therefore did not officially exist in this case, the individuals could be singled out for opprobrium for their dubious behaviour, which forced the authorities to conduct an arraignment for sodomy.

The Times' reporting of cases of unnatural crime throughout the 1860s provides valuable insights into the level of understanding of sex between men, at least amongst its journalists and readership. Also, the participants in the reported trials tended to be from lower or middling social ranks, indicating understanding of sex between men lower down the social scale and a willingness to report incidents to the authorities. *The Times* demonstrated no discernible pattern in the reporting of unnatural crime in the 1860s other than that the abhorred 'unnatural crime' referred exclusively to sex between men. Although *The Times* displayed a strong metropolitan bias in reporting unnatural crime and most of the cases published occurred in the London area, cases of unnatural crime from provincial assizes, such as Durham and Leicester, made it to its pages in these years.

However, it is important to note that *The Times* can be distinguished from other newspapers of the 1860s in that it reported unnatural crime at all. *The Times'* idiosyncrasy in reporting unnatural crime becomes apparent when the publication is compared to the *Manchester Guardian* and the *Daily Telegraph*. In the 1860s, these publications were considered to be the nearest equivalent of *The Times* in the arena of dispassionate journalism. The examination of these newspapers as source material for this or other historical problems is much neglected. Part of the problem is that *The Times* is the only newspaper with a modern index. This notwithstanding, in the nineteenth century the *Manchester Guardian* indexed every article it published in yearbooks. These yearbooks have been examined for the years 1860 to 1872 and 1885 to 1890. There are no references to cases of 'unnatural', 'abominable', 'infamous' or 'nameless' crime in the indices for these years. The yearbooks did not shrink from indicating the nature of other articles, including sexual assault of girls, wife beating, bigamy, infanticide and so on.[44] Cocks highlights that newspapers in this period, if they covered trials for unnatural crime at all, 'tried to cover all traces of its existence with circumlocution and evasion'.[45] To ensure that the newspaper's clerical staff were not being reticent in indicating unnatural crime, the entries for unnatural crime in *The Times* between 1860 and 1871 have been cross-referenced with the relevant editions of the *Manchester Guardian* and in each case, the report was not replicated. Part of the reasons for not reporting cases of this nature was economy of space. In the 1860s, the *Manchester Guardian*, which proudly claimed the status of a national daily and opened London offices in 1867, only ran to four pages daily.[46] The news items were certainly of the character of a national newspaper, with an emphasis on issues affecting the north-west of England, but articles were much more condensed and summarised than *The Times*, which at this date ran to 16 pages daily. All historians in this field recognise the widespread and extensive reporting of the 'Stella and Fanny' Westminster Hall trial of 1871 in the London-based newspapers.[47] The *Manchester Guardian*, exceptionally in this category, made no reference to these trials at any point in the proceedings. This may have been due to the emphasis on issues in the north-west, though the publication's London office was well established by 1871, the *Manchester Guardian* boasted national newspaper status by this date and, according to the *Pall Mall Gazette*, the trial was a scandal of national proportions and an international disgrace.[48] A police raid of a cross-dressers' ball in Manchester in September 1880, examined by Cocks, made it to the pages of the local paper, the *Manchester Evening News*,[49] but again, not to the pages of the *Manchester Guardian*, indicating that incidents of this nature were ignored by the publication. Undoubtedly, further investigations of the newspaper, involving reading of editions, page by page over years, might reveal more cases published. If these cases do exist in the *Manchester Guardian* for this period, then the staff responsible for the index made sure that they would be most difficult to find.

A similar pattern is detectable in the *Daily Telegraph* for this period. The newspaper published ten pages daily and its articles were more expansive than the *Manchester Guardian*'s. The *Daily Telegraph* has no index facility, but the articles from *The Times* have been cross-referenced with the publication. Again, the *Daily Telegraph* did not report the cases of unnatural crime that appeared in *The Times* in the 1860s. The exception to this was the trial of Edward Whitehurst, the Westminster solicitor, in November 1862. The *Daily Telegraph* reported this case as 'an exceptional charge'.[50] It is interesting that out of all the cases of unnatural crime reported in *The Times* in these years, only the incident involving a man of the highest social prominence was reported in the *Daily Telegraph*. The *Daily Telegraph* did not report on unnatural crime again in these years until the 'Stella and Fanny' trials. It is clear from this study of the London-based *Daily Telegraph* that the cases of unnatural crime, as reported in *The Times*, were deliberately ignored by *Daily Telegraph*' journalists. The *Daily Telegraph* reported other crimes from the same court session in which cases of unnatural crime, as reported in *The Times*, were heard. In the 1860s and early 1870s, *The Times* pursued and persisted in a policy of intermittent reporting of cases of unnatural crime, whereas its rival daily publications, the *Manchester Guardian* and the *Daily Telegraph* rarely, if ever, reported these incidents in their pages.

Each reference to unnatural crime in *The Times* has also been cross-referenced with prominent Sunday newspapers, *Reynolds's Weekly Newspaper* and *Lloyd's Weekly Newspaper*. These publications have attracted, in recent years, the attention of historians, mainly because of their style of journalism, which was designed to attract the working-class and lower middle-class reader. These publications competed with each other for these classes of readers and, in combination, had a circulation vastly exceeding that of *The Times*.[51] Of course, the readership of *The Times* differed greatly in class status and educational standards from the readership of these Sunday newspapers. However, by the 1860s, the journalists for all these publications, in spite of their divergent politics, tended to be from equivalent educational and class backgrounds.[52] The bulk of articles of domestic news were informed, for all publications, by the proceedings of the police and crown courts. In many instances, the prominent articles based on law court proceedings in *The Times* for any given week between 1860 and 1885 can be found replicated, in essence, in the Sunday edition of *Reynolds'* and *Lloyd's*.

Reynolds' Weekly and *Lloyd's Weekly* did not, however, follow the lead of *The Times* in reporting unnatural crime. References to cases of unnatural crime in *The Times* cannot be found replicated in these publications between 1860 and 1885. The only exception in the 1860s was an article in *Lloyd's Weekly* in January 1865. In an article headlined 'A Man Dressed in Woman's Clothes', *Lloyd's Weekly* outlined a case that appeared before the Clerkenwell police court. Interestingly, this case was not reported in *The Times*. The defendant, Herman Skaper, was arrested 'dressed in woman's clothes, supposed for some unlawful purpose'.[53] The journalist for this article made the supposition that the transvestite defendant must have been engaging in prostitution. This was not proven in the case and Skaper was discharged with a caution. But it is significant that the supposed connection between male cross-dressing and male prostitution was made, in a lower class journal, some years before the 'revelation' of the sexuality inherent in the 'Stella and Fanny' trial. However, this article in *Lloyd's Weekly* was exceptional. Between 1861 and the mid-1880s, none of these Sunday newspapers, nor for that matter the metropolis-based *London Illustrated News*,[54] reported incidents of unnatural crime. These publications did not flinch from reporting other genres of scandal in intimate detail. A sample of the kind of headlining in *Reynolds'* and *Lloyd's*, taken from a single week in January 1865, demonstrates the interest expressed by these publications in incidents of lurid interest, often with sexualised overtones: 'Charge of Indecent Assault Against an Officer by a Sixteen year-old Maid': 'Wiggins, An Alleged Seducer': 'Sale of a Wife and Two Children': 'Extraordinary Case of the Flogging of a Woman'. Other articles during this particular week concentrated on the suicides declared by the coroner's courts throughout the Kingdom and, most notably, the divorce scandals from the lately instituted Divorce Court.[55]

The reporting of Divorce Court proceedings in the nineteenth-century newspapers is revealing of the different publishing policies of *The Times* and the Sunday newspapers. Although studies of Divorce Court journalism makes no mention of how unnatural crime was reported, the difference in publishing policies demonstrated in the historiography offers some indication for *The Times'* almost solitary persistence in reporting incidents of unnatural crime. Also, the obsession of the Sunday newspapers with Divorce Court scandal journalism offers the potential to historicise the relative silence of these publications on incidents of unnatural crime. Controversy raged in the early 1860s over the reporting of Divorce Court proceedings in the newspapers. An examination of this controversy and the historiography that concentrates on this issue are revealing of the view *The Times* editorial held of its own reportage in comparison to other publications. All the popular newspapers filled its columns with the details from the proceedings of the new Divorce Court, established in 1857. The reportage of predominantly upper- and upper middle-class sexual scandal and matrimonial betrayal, provoked intense disapproval. However, much of the outcry came from the upper echelons of society and included the Queen herself.[56] In the late 1850s, this outcry developed into proposals for a bill to curb press reportage of Divorce Court proceedings. Fortunately, in the interests of press freedom, the Lord Chancellor, Lord Campbell, ruled against such a bill being introduced in Parliament. Nonetheless, the furore over Divorce Court reportage did not abate.[57] In response, *The Times* argued that reporting from the 'Divorce Court is useful and necessary; the evil lies in looking to it for a succession of exciting narratives'.[58] *The Times* regarded itself as the objective and high-minded reporter of 'fact'. *The Times* clearly left it to other publications to produce the 'exciting narrative'. Anne Humpherys, in her study of 'The Newspaper Press and the Divorce Court' (2000), regards the claims of *The Times* for objective reporting as disingenuous. Humpherys may be correct in her analysis of the ability of the press, then or now, to provide genuinely dispassionate reporting.[59] However, *The Times'* persistence in reporting the 'facts' of unnatural crime, at a time when all other publications were almost silent on the subject, reinvests the editorial of *The Times* in the 1860s with some credence to its 'dispassionate' claims for its reportage. Judith Walkowitz, in her study *City of Dreadful Delight*, argues that the popular Sunday newspapers of the 1860s were engaged in the creation of a narrative style of reporting. This reporting was 'organised around themes of sex and crime', which 'reshaped the staid format of news reporting of respectable dailies by incorporating narrative codes of popular literature'.[60]

The Divorce Court proceedings provided the journalists of the Sunday newspapers with factual examples of the kind of fictional material that pervaded the popular melodrama, in the form of the novel or the play. In other words, the scandal stories in the Sunday newspapers were, in spite of their lurid and sexualised content, narratives of family interest. Reportage of divorce scandals would not have been particularly destabilising for the family readership of a Sunday newspaper. The participants in the Divorce Court were, almost invariably in the nineteenth century, members of the moneyed elite. Very few, if any, of the readership of a Sunday newspaper would have found themselves in the Divorce Court in this period. Also, the spectacle of sexual scandal amongst their social superiors would have reinforced political suppositions amongst this class of readership, of the perfidious and dissolute mores of members of the gentry.

The reporting of unnatural crime, however, had, in mid- and late nineteenth-century Britain, no popular narrative template to emulate. The anti-establishment qualities of pornographic productions of the 1820s and the 1830s, spawned by the ultra radical pressmen of the underground press in these years, had disappeared by the mid-century.[61] Even in the 1820s and 1830s, this genre of subversive pornography hardly ever indulged in a homosexual theme. Also, the political and social ambitions of the editorial and journalists of the Sunday newspapers in the 1860s would have gained little or nothing from the melodramatic reporting of crimes of sex between men. Most of the trials for sodomy in the 1860s reported in *The Times*, involved men of a lower or middling social status. Even the trial of Edward Whitehurst did not attract the attention of the Sunday newspapers. The narrative in articles in the Sunday newspapers tended to cast the working-class man as an inherently dignified character, who took pride in and drew his social status from his skills. In this potentially unstable concept of masculine social status, there could be no countenance of aberrant male behaviour, such as sex between men, which might destabilise a working-class man's fragile authority over women and children and his standing with men of his own class. Women and female children in these narratives, on the other hand, displayed the significant tendencies of requiring male protection, particularly from penury and sexual dangers. This genre affected all newspaper reporting with the advent of 'new journalism' in the late 1880s, in the wake of W. T. Stead's sensational *exposé* of sexual exploitation of adolescent girls in The *Pall Mall Gazette*. However, Judith Walkowitz detects this genre of reporting as relatively well developed in the Sunday newspapers by the 1840s.[62]

The political and social preoccupations of the Sunday newspapers and their imperatives of ever-increasing circulation numbers, might explain the near-absence of reporting on sodomy trials in their publications. These arguments do not, however, explain the persistence of *The Times*, almost exclusively, in reporting crimes of this nature in the 1860s. Nor do these arguments explain why *The Times'* reporting of cases of unnatural crime stopped between 1872 and 1885, except for a single incident involving a member of the German diplomatic corps. Although there was no abatement in indictments for sodomy in this period, none of these incidents were reported in *The Times*. Also, there were socially important sodomy trials in these years. For instance, Simeon Solomon, the Pre-Raphaelite artist and Royal Academician, was quietly cast into disgrace and ostracised in 1872 after being caught having sex with another man in a public lavatory. Solomon's public reputation had been seriously diminished by the publication in 1871 of his *Vision of Love Revealed in Sleep*, a poem with distinct homoerotic overtones. Ostensibly a pillar of the Victorian Establishment, his involvement in a sexual scandal, given the preoccupations of the day with respectability, should have been a point of intense abhorrence and concern. However, the newspapers, including *The Times*, were silent about the scandal. Nonetheless, Solomon's disgrace was well known in elevated metropolitan social circles and he was never able to work prominently again.

The idiosyncratic reporting policy of *The Times* in relation to unnatural crime in the 1860s is best understood through examination of the circumstances affecting the near-disappearance of unnatural crime from its pages between 1872 and 1885. One of the most significant factors in this gap in reports of unnatural crime in the pages of *The Times* was the furore created by the widespread publication in the newspapers of the 'Stella and Fanny' trials in 1870 and 1871. With the exception of the *Manchester Guardian*, London-based newspapers such as the *Daily Telegraph*, the *Standard* and the *Pall Mall Gazette*, as well as *The Times*, all gave significant publicity to the trials. Even the Sunday newspapers, *Lloyd's Weekly* and *Reynolds' Newspaper*, published abbreviated accounts of the trials. The 'Stella and Fanny' trial has preoccupied the attentions of all historians of British homosexuality. However, most historians have, almost invariably, tended to concentrate on the last of the trials of *Regina v. Boulton and Others* in Westminster Hall in April and May 1871. The ambivalence in definitions of sodomy and apparent confusion amongst the authorities about the existence of sexuality between men in the Westminster Hall trial has led most historians since Weeks to conclude that there was little understanding of sex and sexuality between men in British society at this time. This argument fits neatly, in chronological terms, into the arguments for the medico-legal construction of the homosexual towards the end of the century.

However, the most recent study of the 'Stella and Fanny' trials, by Charles Upchurch, strongly criticises the emphasis of studies by Neil Bartlett, Weeks, Sinfield and 'innumerable other works ... [which] rarely move beyond the sensationalism of the 1871 newspaper reporting'.[63] No attention is given by historians to the newspaper coverage of the Bow Street proceedings between April and June 1870; as Upchurch states, 'the discrepancies between the arraignment and the trial are not discussed in any of these works. ... what the state and the press chose to omit from the 1871 trial coverage is in fact the key to understanding the cultural significance of the case'.[64] Upchurch detects distinct differences between the reporting of the arraignment in 1870 and the Westminster Hall trial of 1871. In the Bow Street proceedings of 1870, the public was confronted with the 'knowledge' of the sodomitical world of the 'Mary-Anne', or male prostitute. Upchurch argues that the proceedings became 'a month long forum where cross dressing men were able to put forward their own self-representations to a national audience'. These statements became dangerous when connections 'between cross-dressing and same sex desire that were common and often assumed within the community of Mary-Annes' were revealed during the course of the proceedings. Nonetheless, in the 1871 trial, the public 'knowledge' gained during the arraignment had disappeared; 'the newspaper coverage no longer indicated that significant numbers of male cross dressers were regularly seen in the West End [and] evidence indicating that male cross dressers had frequently engaged in acts of anal intercourse was also omitted from the 1871 news coverage'.[65] Upchurch argues that the 'middle-class' men who controlled the newspapers and the state needed 'cross dressers and Mary-Annes to be different to themselves'. In Upchurch's analysis, 'Stella and Fanny's' world and its sexual connection to a member of the House of Commons, demolished 'the public façade of social and moral distance between [this class] and the sodomite'. In order to justify their own privileged position in society, the men responsible for maintaining the 'institutions and ideologies of middle-class power ... manufacture[d] the silences that surrounded the [1871] trial. Their refusal to know or to admit to knowing allowed Boulton and Park to retain their freedom'.[66]

Upchurch's work undoubtedly represents a new departure in the analysis of the cultural relevance of the 'Stella and Fanny' trials. However, Upchurch's work pays little detailed attention to the extent of 'knowing' demonstrated in the newspapers during the Bow Street proceedings. He argues that the 'trial that Boulton and Park eventually faced in 1871 was not an effort to punish their transgressions, but to contain and reshape the challenge they presented in the arraignment of the year before'.[67] Although Upchurch's analysis differs significantly in emphasis to others, his work still presents the Bow Street revelations as being thrust upon an unsuspecting public.

The 'Stella and Fanny' incident came to court because of the discovery of correspondence between Boulton and Lord Arthur Clinton, MP, which strongly suggested a sexual relationship between them. The letters were obtained during a police raid of Boulton's lodgings. The police had been observing Boulton and Park's cross-dressed activities for some time before the raid and the letters were deemed sufficient evidence to bring a felony charge. Undoubtedly, Upchurch is correct in his analysis that the unfolding evidence in the Bow Street proceedings confronted a national readership, albeit the elite readership of *The Times* and the *Daily Telegraph*, with the existence of a cross-dressing, sodomitical community of Mary-Annes in the West End of London. However, close reading of the reports of the Bow Street proceedings in the first few days of the trial reveals another pattern – of tacit 'knowing' amongst substantial sections of the public, at least in the Metropolitan space of London, which is different from that described by Upchurch. On the third day of the trial, 7th May 1870, *The Times* commented on the crowds vying to gain entrance to the courtroom:

> The case excited unusual interest, probably owing to the notoriety acquired by certain young men who, for years past, have been in the habit of visiting places of public resort in feminine attire, and who have been occasionally turned out or compelled to retire to avoid the consequences of the public indignation excited by their presence when detected.[68]

The article added that 'the prisoners appeared in male apparel on this occasion, much to the disappointment apparently of the crowds assembled to see them'.

It is clear from this article that the public in central London were relatively accustomed to the existence of habitual cross-dressers in their midst. Even more remarkable is the familiarity of *The Times* journalists with the phenomenon; in its consistent and singular reporting of unnatural crime during the 1860s, *The Times* failed to report the one incident of suspected unnatural crime involving a cross-dressed defendant, which, uniquely, made it to the pages of *Lloyd's Weekly* in 1865. It is also apparent from *The Times'* article that the public would act with hostility when the cross-dresser was habitual and discerned to be one of the 'certain young men'. The first articles in the 'Stella and Fanny' incident indicate significant public amusement created by the proceedings, possibly because of the unusual spectacle of cross-dressers actually being put in the dock. The Bow Street proceedings certainly attracted the interests of all ranks in society. On 14th May 1870, *The Times* reported that the day's proceedings had attracted

the usual rabble outside, but ample provision had been made. ... to prevent the inconvenient crowding of the court. Nevertheless, the small area of the building was quite full, the audience including many persons of rank, besides many theatrical celebrities, who were probably admitted by special application to the authorities.[69]

Stella and Fanny were established and popular revue actors, so the case undoubtedly aroused the interest of the theatre world. But more than this, *The Times* indicated in these articles that the phenomenon of cross-dressed men was a not unfamiliar sight to the general public in London. The articles also reveal that *The Times* refrained from comment on this tacitly understood metropolitan phenomenon and ignored a trial involving a cross-dressed defendant in the 1860s, whereas the publication would report other incidents of suspected unnatural crime in this period. However, the exposure of public awareness of a cross-dressing culture in London in these articles does not amount to the public necessarily equating cross-dressing with sexuality between men. Cross-dressing had long been associated with theatricality and by the 1860s, pantomime, replete with 'dames', had developed as a Christmas entertainment for middle-class children.[70] More generally, it was acceptable for men to occasionally dress in women's clothes 'for a lark'. This was Skaper's defence in the 1865 trial reported in *Lloyd's Weekly* and accepted by the bench.[71] In the first days of the Bow Street proceedings, Boulton and Park also claimed they were cross-dressed for 'a lark', but *The Times* commented that

> it must be said that the lark was one of a very long duration, extending over years, and carried on with a degree of systematic arrangement unusual, to say the least of it, when harmless diversion was alone in contemplation.[72]

The Times' reference to a more sinister purpose in their habitual cross-dressing, with overtones of unnatural crime, reflects the concern raised in its reporting of the tacitly understood phenomenon of 'certain young men' who habitually cross-dressed in public for immoral purposes. It is clear that the public could discern between mere theatricality and 'larks' and a more habitual form of cross-dressed male who, when discovered, elicited hostility. *The Times* did not explicitly state, but did infer that the habitual cross dressers in London were, in its and the public's assessment, male prostitutes.

In comparison, the *Daily Telegraph* conducted an editorial on the degree to which the theatre going public had been deceived by Boulton and Park's theatrical cross-dressing over the years. As the case developed, the defendants used their theatrical status as a defence for being caught cross-dressed. The *Daily Telegraph* conducted a survey of Boulton and Park's theatrical reviews for performances during the late 1860s. It found that in a series of theatrical performances where Boulton had appeared as a cross-dressed character that the 'prisoner Park does not appear to have taken part in enterprises of this kind'. The article cited reviews from newspapers around the country attesting to the popularity of Boulton's female impersonations. In Essex, an unnamed local paper acclaimed

> the Alice of Mr Boulton, [which] took the audience by surprise; in 'make up', action, gesture and conception, it was a finished picture. ... He drew down thundering plaudits by his talented acting, and especially by his singing, in an imitation mezzo-soprano voice ... which was three times re-demanded.[73]

Another review of Boulton's rendition of 'Alice' was quick to defend the character of this clearly popular performer. In spite of his convincing performance as a woman – 'it is really difficult to believe that he is not really a charming girl' – the review ventured to reassure its readership that Boulton was not a sodomite: 'let it by no means be understood that there is anything of the "social monster" business connected with him'.

The *Daily Telegraph* regarded this assessment as 'ludicrous' in the light of the revelations of the Bow Street proceedings and, given the nature of the proceedings, regarded the publication of the misplaced assessment of Boulton's true character as 'somewhat appropriate'.[74]

Ernest Boulton posed a challenge and caused confusion to nineteenth-century perceptions of appropriate gender behaviour on many levels. His habitual transvestism, revealed in correspondence used as evidence in 1870, transgressed the acceptable contexts for men to dress as women, in the form of 'larks' and on the stage. Much of the correspondence read out in court gave evidence that Boulton, in particular, spent long periods of time attempting to live as a woman and insist on being addressed as a woman; the evidence of witnesses attested that he managed this with considerable success. 'Stella' had calling cards printed, styling 'herself' as 'Lady Arthur Clinton', thereby posing as the spouse of the unmarried Clinton.[75] A cross-dressing friend of Boulton's, named 'Louis', expressed disappointment that Boulton was spending so much of his time in 'role'; 'I am sorry to hear of you going about in "drag" so much'. Louis wanted his 'darling Erne' to adopt a more manly appearance so he could meet his mother as 'Ernest': 'I thought it well to tell her that you are very effeminate, but I hope you will do your best to appear as manly as you can, at least in face'.[76] The correspondence from Louis was the only series to address Boulton by his masculine name. One of the letters from Louis was not read out publicly in court, due to its 'abominable and filthy' contents, indicating that Louis confessed sodomitical practices to 'Erne'.[77] However, even Louis expressed exasperation at the extent to which Boulton lived in 'drag'.

It is arguable that Boulton's sexuality confuses and confounds the modern historian as well as the nineteenth-century public and his 'drag' sodomite friends. As stated, Boulton appears in all histories of homosexuality in Britain, but there are many aspects of Boulton's life that suggest intermittent but concerted attempts at transgendered/transsexual self-making by this individual. This possibility is not recognised in the historiography and may attest to the difficulties in historicising Boulton. The picture is confused further by Boulton's connection with 'twenty other men with painted faces'.[78] It is clear from the correspondence from Louis that 'going about in drag' formed an important part of this particular sodomite's persona. But Louis could and often did appear 'manly' and willingly so. Boulton appears as much more serious in his attempt to live as a woman for most of the time. His 'female personations' on stage allowed him a source of living, but using his male name was essential if this form of burlesque were to be successful. However, the *Daily Telegraph* records an incident where Boulton was cast as a woman playing a female role in a play, which went undetected by the newspapers.[79] Also, as 'Lady Stella Clinton', Boulton could live as a woman and it was this connection with Clinton that attracted the greatest public curiosity in the case. Much evidence attests to Clinton passing Boulton off as a woman at social functions and, significantly, there is no evidence of probable sexual connection with any man other than Clinton. Boulton might have genuinely regarded himself as a woman; but the *demi-monde* of London's 'drag' sodomites of the 1860s was the nearest 'Stella' could find for like-minded companions.[80]

Boulton's particular style of self-making was apparent to the journalists of the day. In its compilation of Boulton's theatre reviews, the *Daily Telegraph* published an extraordinary assessment of Boulton made by an unnamed local newspaper: 'A *Lusus Naturae* – certainly if one of nature's journeymen had not been at work, "Mister" Boulton – we hesitate almost to write this prefix – would have incontestably been a woman.'[81] In an equally extraordinary article, *Reynolds's Weekly Newspaper* chose to remind its Sunday readers that Boulton had a precedent in the popular imagination:

> Thirty seven years ago the town was full of the story of a man in woman's clothes, just as the town is now full of the Boulton and Park business. Early in 1833 there died. ... a person ... known as Lavinia Edwards. Nobody claimed the corpse, and it was finally sold to Guy's hospital, for the purposes of dissection. While the dissection was going on it was suddenly discovered that the supposed woman was a man.

An inquiry revealed that Edwards had successfully passed for years as a woman:

> Upon the provincial stage the man had achieved a certain amount of success, acting as a woman in female parts. ... It seems however that for some years before his death, [he] had left the stage and earned his livelihood on the streets of London. ... The medical testimony was of such a nature as to leave no room for doubt as to the character of the pursuits by which this wretched creature had gained his living.

This barely veiled comment indicated that Edwards had venereal disease in his rectum. *Reynolds'* gave its reasons for reminding the public of this incident:

> Scandals of this kind are short lived; but there are times that it is well old stories should be retold and just at present the story of Lavinia Edwards is not without a moral.[82]

The transgendered/transsexual analysis of Boulton carries with it all the pitfalls of anachronism. However, the contemporary circumstantial evidence of Boulton's possible transgenderism/transsexualism, as distinct from other 'drag' sodomites in this period, further problematises the focus of historians on this particular 'trial' in the analysis of historical understanding of male homosexuality in society. Nonetheless, it is remarkable that *Reynolds'*, which had rarely carried articles on unnatural crime during its existence, should publish this article, which explicitly encouraged discussion of the existence of sexuality between men and aberrant sexual types amongst its working-class readership.[83] The coverage of the 1870 arraignment in *Lloyd's Weekly* and *Reynolds'* did differ in emphasis from the coverage in the elite daily newspapers. As Upchurch argues, the dailies appeared much more concerned, in editorial statements, with the effect of the case on national honour.[84] However, *Lloyd's Weekly* gave unique emphasis to the extent and luxury of Boulton's female wardrobe and made strong suggestions that he could not possibly have afforded such apparel by working as a performer, hinting that prostitution should not be ruled out in the case.[85]

All the newspapers that covered the arraignment of 1870 were dependent upon and reflected tacit knowledge of the existence of sex and sexuality between men. In extension, the public in London were revealed to have knowledge of the existence of 'drag' sodomites in their midst. The term 'drag' passed into usage in these articles without much need to explain its meaning. The character cast by Ernest Boulton, who appeared to embody sodomy and drag, created further confusion and intense concern and interest through his often convincing mock marriage with Lord Arthur Clinton. By the time *Lloyd's Weekly* published its last article on the arraignment proceedings on 29 May 1870, the headlines had developed from 'Men in Women's Clothing' to 'The "Men–Women" at Bow Street'. *Reynolds'* and *Lloyd's Weekly* ceased coverage of the arraignment from this date, though the arraignment proceedings continued until 12 July 1870. The decision was possibly prompted by a demand, made publicly in court on 28 May, from an agent for the Society for the Suppression of Vice, for newspaper coverage of the case to cease. Both publications ignored the demand and received a scathing review of their coverage in the *Pall Mall Gazette* on the 30 May. In explicit support of the Society's actions in court, the *Pall Mall Gazette* lambasted all the papers, but singled out *Reynolds'* for its irresponsibility and 'revolting details' the previous day, no doubt referring also to its article on Lavinia Edwards.

The tone of the *Pall Mall Gazette* article is interesting in its revelations of the cultural knowledge of sexuality between men. The article acknowledged the existence of sexuality between men in classical literature, but warned its elite readership that heroes of classical literature were but 'dust and ashes' in the modern era.[86] The habits of the men of classical literature were, according to the *Pall Mall Gazette*, as ancient and decayed as the civilisations to which they belonged. The classical literature that had survived to the nineteenth century had done so because

> the filth that has come down to us is but a drop of that great sea of impurity in which the pre-Christian mind was wont to revel. ... the worst and most corrupt effusions of the ancient writers were, happily, burned at Constantinople by Christian enthusiasts.

The article writer conducted a review of sexuality between men in various Greek and Roman works of literature, secure in the knowledge that the classically educated readership would be familiar with the idiom.[87] But the article argued most emphatically that this form of sexual connection had no place amongst modern, Christian British men:

> Lais and Antinous have no business anywhere but the Classical dictionary. As long as they remain there, they will ... be mere phantoms with very little power for evil or good. Antinous in 'drag' in the Burlington Arcade, in the police court, and in the columns of the *Daily Telegraph* (supposing him to be a really existing creature) is infinitely more formidable than his half-forgotten prototypes. It is not merely that he is a thing abominable. ... he does not know his epoch, and commits at best a lamentable anachronism, but that he is an example of unspeakable turpitude.[88]

The readers of the *Pall Mall Gazette* and, by extension, *The Times* and the *Daily Telegraph* were gifted, through public school curricula, with insights into sexuality between men in the Classics. The *Pall Mall Gazette* called for an immediate cessation of the publication of the arraignment in the newspapers. It wished to protect 'honest' women and the young from the possibility of this sexuality existing amongst modern British men.

The article also served as an appeal to the sense of duty and responsibility amongst its classically educated male readership to recognise and instruct upon the interminable distance of time and values between the Ancient and the Modern. 'Filth' in the Classics could be grudgingly tolerated because this form of 'filth' existed in cultures long dead and gone. However, this form of 'filth' was inimical to the social structures of the predominant, modern and Christian civilisation of Imperial Britain. The article writer was evidently appealing to the sensibility amongst its readership that Imperial British civilisation would prevail, whereas the classical civilisations had fallen. Since Gibbon, this class of men had understood that the Ancient civilisations had collapsed through the sexual and moral turpitude of its men. In contrast, only the strictest sexual and moral rectitude amongst the men of Modern Imperial Britain would ensure that Imperial British civilisation would survive and continue to surpass the great civilisations of antiquity.

The newspaper reports of the arraignment of 'Stella and Fanny' signifies widespread, but tacit knowledge of forms of sexuality between men. Upchurch's study of the 'Stella and Fanny' trials is correct in its analysis that the knowledge that is evident in the newspaper coverage of the arraignment is distinctly different from the coverage of the trial of 1871. However, evidence of consensus amongst the newspapers and the courts to 'withdraw' from 'knowledge' of the sexuality in the case is not explicit. No correspondence in News International Archive exists that would indicate a specific change in policy in *The Times* at this date. Upchurch highlights that 'there was no mechanism by which the government could have compelled the majority of the major London newspapers to follow its lead in relation to the Boulton and Park case'. The government, through the offices of the Attorney General, had 'recast' the events in the case for the Westminster Hall trial. Many of the witnesses called to the arraignment were absent from the trial and evidence in the arraignment that could have convicted Boulton was not used.[89]

A not guilty verdict was essential for Gladstone's administration. Clinton had been elected as the Liberal candidate for Newark in the 1868 general election, the first to be conducted under the rigours of a much-extended franchise. Clinton was therefore associated with Gladstone's highly contentious reform policies in the first modern Liberal ministry.[90] Clinton had died on 17 June 1870, ostensibly from scarlet fever, before he was due to be called to the arraignment to give evidence. Theo Aronson, in *Prince Eddy and the Homosexual Underworld* (1994), suggests that Clinton's death was too convenient for the authorities and that he had probably committed suicide.[91] Nonetheless, a verdict of guilty of sodomy by association for Clinton, albeit posthumously, would have created enormous difficulties for the Liberal party, facing the rigours of re-election by the extended franchise, voting by the secret ballot that the Liberal government would create in 1872. Upchurch highlights that Gladstone and John Delane, the editor of *The Times* had a series of meetings in mid-July 1870. One of the meetings coincided with the 'shift in *The Times* coverage from favouring the prosecution to strongly supporting the defence, to the point of misrepresentation'.[92] The connection cannot be proved by evidence and Upchurch suggests that, in all probability, 'both institutions desired the suppression of information concerning ... the case ... but each tailored their omissions to meet distinct institutional goals'.

Upchurch portrays *The Times* as providing leadership amongst the daily newspapers, such as the *Daily Telegraph*, which continued to report on the details of the prosecution's case in the arraignment during July 1870. Upchurch highlights that the *Daily Telegraph* was the only newspaper in 1871 to mention discrepancies between the 1870 and 1871 processes. Even then, the publication did not attempt to discern a motive for the discrepancies. Of all the daily newspapers that covered the arraignment in 1870, *The Times'* coverage was, in Upchurch's assessment, the most discreet. Through recognition of the 'symbolic breach in British masculine identity' created by the reporting of the arraignment, *The Times* endeavoured to repair the breach by 'suppression of evidence' in its pages, possibly encouraged by political intervention. However, Upchurch's analysis of the processes involved in suppression of knowledge of unnatural crime in the variety of publications which covered the 'Stella and Fanny' trial is problematised by the evidence of patterns of reporting unnatural crime in the newspapers in the period. Upchurch's assessment of the reporting of the case is an undoubted improvement, both in terms of research and analysis, on other studies. Nonetheless, Upchurch's work replicates a problem that is fundamental to other studies. He also examines the 'Stella and Fanny' trials in isolation from other sodomy trials in the 1860s and 1870s and pays no attention to differing journalistic approaches to unnatural crime in these years.

This lack of attention to the broader context, distorts the pattern of suppression of knowledge apparent in the variety of publications that covered the case. As demonstrated here, *The Times* had, throughout

the 1860s, persisted in a policy of occasionally but consistently reporting unnatural crime in its pages. This policy had, with some modifica-
tions in style, continued without break since the 1820s. During 1870
and 1871, *The Times* reported on incidents of unnatural crime other
than the 'Stella and Fanny' trials. *The Times*, therefore, had considerable
institutional experience in reporting crimes of this nature. In its coverage of the first few days of the arraignment in 1870, *The Times* coverage
indiscreetly indicated the 'knowledge' of the existence of a cross-dressing,
sodomitical culture in London. During the 1860s, *Times'* journalists
had ignored incidents which involved cross-dressed defendants and
therefore was not experienced in reporting this dimension of unnatural
crime in a manner that would not threaten British conceptions of masculine social status. The 'Stella and Fanny' case, with all its damaging
connections to high politics and the governing classes, created such a
sensation of interest that *The Times* could not ignore it. The eventual
shift in emphasis in the reporting of the arraignment in favour of the
defence was entirely consistent with the approach of *The Times* to other
cases of unnatural crime. Securing a verdict of 'not guilty' for sodomy
meant that the crime did not exist. Exposure of the defendants in its
pages would punish the perpetrators with infamy and ostracism for forcing the state to conduct sodomy proceedings. *The Times*, alone amongst
national newspapers, continued to report cases of unnatural crime until
1872, when this pattern of reporting all but disappeared for 13 years.
Even the *Daily Telegraph* was being consistent in its approach to reporting
the 'Stella and Fanny' case. Like other newspapers, it had ignored cases
of unnatural crime, except the case in 1862, when the defendant was a
man of social prominence. No incidents of unnatural crime had involved
men of social prominence again until the 'Stella and Fanny' case.

The other national newspapers, including the *Daily Telegraph*, had, in
comparison with *The Times*, little experience of reporting unnatural
crimes and cases were ignored by nearly all publications in the period.
None of these publications had the experience in styles of reporting this
crime that would not threaten masculinity, preferring to ignore this
deeply threatening phenomenon in its pages. The hysterical sensation
of the 'Stella and Fanny' case resulted, in 1870, in garrulous revelations
in these papers of a sophisticated knowledge of sexuality between men
and 'drag' sodomites, tacitly understood amongst significant sections of
the urban population of Britain. The abandonment of reporting the
arraignment by the Sunday newspapers in May 1870 and the suppression of knowledge during the 1871 by all the newspapers was entirely
consistent with the policies of ignoring unnatural crime by these

publications in the period. *The Times*, the *Pall Mall Gazette* and the Society for the Suppression of Vice were undoubtedly influential in the change of tone adopted by the newspapers, but these publications were reverting to entrenched patterns of ignoring unnatural crime when the 'Stella and Fanny' case abated in July 1870 and disappeared entirely with the collapse of the Westminster Hall trial in 1871.

An explanation of *The Times'* persistent and idiosyncratic pattern of reporting unnatural crime in the 1860s and 1870s resides in the editorial policies exercised by the publication in these years. *The Times'* diminution in reporting unnatural crime after 1872 coincided with fundamental changes in the organisation and outlook of the publication. John Delane had been editor of *The Times* since 1841 and, by the 1860s, had become an 'institution' of national importance in his own right. Describing one individual as an 'institution' is deliberate in this context. Historians in the Weeks/ Foucault tradition historicise institutions, such as newspaper houses and government departments, as faceless, monolithic engines of purposive intent and power. However, an examination of newspapers such as *The Times* and government departments like the Home Office in the nineteenth century, reveals that the senior staff in these 'institutions' numbered but a few and were selected from the most elevated and narrowest of social backgrounds. In the medico-legal approach to the history of homosexuality, one gains no sense of the agency, proportion or intimacy of decision making in British institutions of authority and power, particularly before the mid-1880s.[93] In government departments, at least, the ministers came and went with the changes of government. But in a newspaper like *The Times*, the editor wielded a formidable personal authority of publishing and journalistic policy over a small and permanent staff of journalists. In the case of Delane, his aegis spanned nearly four decades.

Delane's term in office established the reputation of *The Times* and, after the repeal of stamp duty and censorship in 1855, British journalism in general, for critical and politically independent journalism. *The Times*, of course, had long been the organ of the Tory party, a relationship Delane overtly cultivated and extended.[94] But *The Times* regarded it increasingly as a duty, to be forensically critical of whatever party formed the government. Its perception of itself as a national institution in the era of 'free journalism' after 1855 was as unequivocal as it was lofty:

Whenever a newspaper is the established organ of a party, its circulation is limited and its existence precarious and costly. Journalism, therefore, is not the instrument by which the various divisions of the ruling class express themselves: it is rather the instrument by means of which the aggregate intelligence of the nation criticises and controls them all. It is indeed the 'Fourth Estate' of the Realm: not merely the written counterpart and voice of the speaking 'Third'.[95]

The Times recognised that the abolition of the revenue stamp and the disentanglement of the newspapers from the Lord Chancellor's Office would produce ferocious competition amongst an independent and cheap press. *The Times*, leviathan among newspapers, survived this transition as a business organisation. Heavy investments were made in the late 1850s in the mechanisation of printing presses and the distribution of the publication. However, the style of content remained, under Delane, aloof and unchanged.[96] Most other newspapers were, by the late 1860s, beginning to respond to the changes in popular journalism. Although there are no specific references to it in the historiography, Delane's unchanging policy during the 1860s may explain the persistence in reporting unnatural crime. By the 1870s, Delane was regarded as a figure from a previous era on many levels. Although he did not retire officially until 1877, Delane's grip on *The Times* was little more than nominal after his decline in health in 1872. New men of *The Times*, conscious of the wider interests of the contemporary reader and the mortality of *The Times'* traditional constituency, made moves to make *The Times'* journalism more reflective of popular styles.[97]

It is probable that the reporting of unnatural crime in *The Times* of the 1860s was an anachronistic survival of journalistic policy from the 1830s. Delane served his journalist apprenticeship at a time when discussion of the crime of sex between men in the newspapers was more widespread and detailed.[98] It is highly probable that Delane had less difficulty in allowing this crime to be reported than his successors, who were much more sensitive to the reactions of the readership in an era of free journalism and, after 1867, much extended franchise. The new generation of men who took over from Delane in 1872 clearly decided that, in the interests of preserving social and gender stability in Britain, *The Times* should conform to the policies maintained by other newspapers in this period in not reporting unnatural crime. The threat posed by the sensation of the 'Stella and Fanny' case to British masculinity, and therefore Britain's status as a nation, had demonstrated to the new generation of *Times'* men, if not to Delane himself, the dangers of publicising and advertising the existence of unnatural crime.[99] When the trial collapsed in 1871, *The Times* registered its relief. If sodomy had been proven, *The Times* argued that the case

> would have been felt at home, and received abroad, as a reflection of our national morals, yet which, for that very reason, could not be hushed up after popular rumour had once invested it with so grave a complexion.[100]

It is clear from this commentary that, by the 1870s, cases of unnatural crime were inimical to a national sense of morality and adult masculine behaviour, to the extent that their existence could and should be 'hushed up'. Sex and Sexuality between men posed such a threat to British masculinity that any recognition of their existence was destabilising. Ignoring the existence of unnatural crime would have distanced British masculinity from continental European developments at this time. The Liberal Austrian government made a proposal to Parliament in 1867 to decriminalise sex between men and bring the Empire in line with arrangements in France, which had decriminalised this sexuality in 1805. The proposal was ultimately unsuccessful, but it fostered, in Austria, the tolerance of enquiry into the nature of sexuality between men, already established in France.[101] This may explain the lack of legislative clarification of the Buggery laws in Britain in these years. Questioning extant legislation too closely would constitute recognition of the existence of a phenomenon in British society of sexuality between men. In the 'Stella and Fanny' trial of 1871, much criticism was made of the 'newfound (sic) treasures of French literature upon the subject [of sodomy] which thank God is still foreign to the libraries of British surgeons'.[102]

Given this context, the relative lack of convictions in sodomy trials during the 1860s could be equated, in contemporary conceptions, to an absence of sodomy amongst British adult men. What appeared to concern *The Times* was that it should be a matter of supreme difficulty to convict a man, irrespective of class, of unnatural crime. This may explain the absence of argument in the publication for clarifications in the law or diminution of the rules of evidence in this period. Even when the public had judged participants in a sodomy trial as probably guilty, as in the 'Stella and Fanny' arraignment in 1870, the important point for *The Times* was that the courts had found the participants not guilty in 1871. As *The Times* stated at the close of the trial, 'the verdict of the jury should be accepted as clearing all the defendants of the odious guilt imputed to them'.[103] It is probable that, after 1872, *The Times*, responding to trends in popular journalism, conformed to other national newspapers and ceased confronting its readership with the existence of sex and sexuality between men. In continental Europe in these years and in France, Austria and Italy in particular, significant developments were being made to classify, clarify and categorise sexuality between men. In Britain, the legislature and the newspapers were, comparatively, silent on the subject. However, silence did not result in a diminution in sexuality between men in British society. The years of mainstream press silence on the existence of unnatural crime were also the years in which British writers clandestinely began to examine sexuality between men and society's hostility towards it. The sexual identities of John Addington Symonds, Edward Carpenter and other British homosexual writers of the period were shaped and self-made in the context of being British men reaching maturity in the 1860s and 1870s. Cocks argues that the culture of silence and the namelessness of homosexuality in Britain provided 'perverse opportunities' for these men to express homosexual desire, as a form of resistance to 'secrecy and negation'.[104] Indeed, the unwillingness of the press to reveal the existence or extent of the homosexual milieu in its cities provided much potential for sexual adventure, with the likelihood of purposive exposure by institutions of authority being remote.[105] However, in their quests to understand their senses of self through writing, these elite British writers looked enviously at cultures of masculinity either abroad or in the historical past, all of which gave the appearance of far greater tolerance of sex and sexuality between men than Britain. Symonds emigrated to Swizerland after 1877 to assuage the intense anxieties he felt about his sexual proclivities and the difficulties these created for him in Britain.[106] His most profound insights into 'inversion' and his first fully sexual affairs with men occurred after his self-imposed exile on the Continent. The most explicit analytical writings on the subject of homosexuality in Britain remained clandestine, unpublished or censored, shared at most by narrow groups of men who lived in fear of exposure; writings that, for all their intents and purposes, remained as silent as the silence of the newspapers.

Tacit awareness of sex between men and the 'types' of men that might engage in this form of sex was widespread in these years. This sexuality was inimical to masculinity as a social status in this country to such an extent that any public acknowledgement of its existence threatened society itself. In the interests of bolstering masculinity, the legislature was consistently resistant to clarifications in the law, even when confronted with prominent scandal. In a similar pattern, the newspapers, including *The Times* after 1872 and until the mid-1880s, rarely reported cases of unnatural crime involving British men. It is in this context that late nineteenth-century homosexual self-making in Britain was shaped and influenced, rather than in purposive developments in law and medicine to construct a pejorative homosexual identity.

4
Legislation

In the late nineteenth century, newspapers were not the only institutions reluctant to give publicity to the existence of sex and sexuality between men. Examination of the legislature, legislation and the Home Office in this period reveals considerable ambivalence and secrecy in this matter. Historiography in the medico-legal tradition has been dependent, to a significant extent, on analyses of developments in law and government policies for controlling sex between men. In the British paradigm, studies since Weeks' emphasise the importance of Henry Labouchere's infamous Amendment to the Criminal Law Amendment Act of 1885 in the construction of homosexual identity. Labouchere's Amendment, Clause 11 of the Criminal Law Amendment Act of 1885, stipulated that

> any male person who, in public or private, commits, or is party to the commission of, or procures or attempts to procure the commission by any male person of any act of gross indecency with another male person, shall be guilty of a misdemeanour, and being convicted thereof shall be liable at the discretion of the court to be imprisoned for any term not exceeding two years, with or without hard labour.[1]

Labouchere's Amendment, or Clause 11, is interpreted by historians such as Cohen and Weeks as a point of near-revolutionary change in the legal categorisation and punishment of male homosexuality. Cohen regards the formation of Clause 11 as a crucial shift in the legal definition of sexuality between men. He argues that the Clause represented a transformation in legal concepts, primarily because it conceptualised a statutory category that was 'wholly independent of ecclesiastical connotations'. Cohen emphasises the ecclesiastical basis of the Buggery Act of 1533, the legislation that served to proscribe acts of 'sodomy' in the nineteenth century. Cohen argues that the Buggery Act only specified 'the illegality of a limited range of sexual activities'.[2] Although Cohen acknowledges that Clause 11 contained 'no particular specificity save for the genital similarity of the sexual actors', he argues that the sexual actors were, through legislation, 'defined against a normative standard that deified the "purity" of the middle-class "household" '. Cohen goes on to argue that the definitions in law enshrined in Clause 11 stimulated a change in cultural perceptions of sexuality between men, stating that the 'cultural significance ascribed to such legal shifts necessarily lagged behind their legislative transformations'.[3] Cohen analyses the effects of Clause 11 in creating cultural perceptions of the homosexual through examination of two prominent homosexual scandal trials. He concentrates his attention, to some extent, on the 'West End Scandals', known better as the exposure of the Cleveland Street male brothel in 1889. However, most of his highly influential study is dedicated to the cultural implications of the prosecution of Oscar Wilde for gross indecency in 1895.

In Weeks' various studies of the historical construction of male homosexuality, which inform Cohen's arguments, Clause 11 is also represented as a fundamental departure and development in the legislative control of male homosexuality. Weeks at least acknowledges that Clause 11 did not simply '*create* hostility', but argues that the Clause 'helped shape a new mood, particularly in its operation'.[4] However, there are fundamental problems in the research and analysis of the developments in legal control of sex between men in nineteenth-century Britain. Significant recent specialist works, such as Cocks', challenge the assumptions inherent in Cohen's and Weeks' studies, that prosecutions of sex between men somehow exploded in proportion and meaning in the late 1880s. Cocks demonstrates that sodomy indictments in England increased significantly after 1800 and that the interpretation of sodomy in urban indictments meant, almost exclusively, sexuality between men throughout the nineteenth century. In his most recent study, *Nameless Offences*, Cocks argues that the emphasis on late nineteenth-century law distorts a much more consistent pattern of prosecution throughout the century. In addition, Cocks argues that the relationship between the law and homosexual identity formations was far more ambivalent than historians such as Cohen and Weeks claim.[5]

This chapter confirms Cocks' basic argument and critically examines the research and interpretation offered by Cohen and Weeks of the legislative changes surrounding sexuality between men. Both historians present their analyses of legal developments and their implications, in a highly mechanical framework of historical change. The only analysis of historical transformations that involve individual historical actors in these studies, is contained in the interpretations of the effects of legislation, such as Clause 11, in the writings of a small and highly elite group of 'homosexual' men in the late nineteenth century. John Addington Symonds and Edward Carpenter understood the difficulties created by Clause 11 for men who had sex with men. Oscar Wilde was to be spectacularly punished using Clause 11 in 1895. However, there is little or no sense of historical agency in Weeks' or Cohen's studies that would offer an insight into the highly incidental nature of the inclusion of Clause 11 in the Criminal Law Amendment Act of 1885. There is also little sense of the actions of individuals in policy making at the Home Office, the government department that had responsibility for interpreting and implementing changes in legislation. Cohen and Weeks present both the legislature and the Home Office as monolithic and faceless engines of purposive intent in the control of sex between men. This chapter, instead, analyses the conflict, chaos and ambivalence that existed amongst ministers and administrators at the Home Office in the late nineteenth century, in respect to control and punishment of sex between men.

Attention to the historical details of the legal and governmental arrangements for control and punishment of sex between men is important in this field. In both Weeks' and Cohen's studies, there are fundamental flaws in the chronology, accuracy and interpretation of legislative and policy developments pertaining to sex between men. These studies offer an analysis of purposive control of sex between men that is almost 'whiggish' in the presentation of its progress to the eventual construction of the modern male homosexual. Also, in *Sex, Politics and Society*, Weeks argues that the 'changing legal situation was intricately associated with the emergence of a "medical model" of homosexuality which helped provide theoretical explanation for the individualising of the crime'.[6] Weeks perpetuates this analysis through this and his subsequent works of historical sociology, published in repeated editions to date. Weeks' analysis is adopted, without criticism, in other, much broader historiographies of the period. For instance, Judith Walkowitz's prominent study, *City of Dreadful Delight*, adopts Weeks' interpretation of the effects of Clause 11 uncritically.[7] Walkowitz's study is substantially dedicated to examining the mass popular campaign that led to the creation of the Criminal Law Amendment Act in 1885. Of course, the Act and the campaign that led to its creation were only ever intended to protect girls under 16 from sexual coercion by men and Walkowitz's study concentrates upon this. The addition of Clause 11, without debate and at the final moment of the Bill's passage through parliament by the maverick Liberal MP, Henry Labouchere, is addressed by Walkowitz only in parentheses, reflecting the lack of attention given to the issue at the time of the campaign for the Act.

New evidence gathered from the late nineteenth-century Home Office files, adds to the recent historiography and challenges Weeks' medico-legal analysis. Far from being 'intricately linked' to 'medical models', the officials and politicians at the Home Office resisted any recognition or connection of crimes of sex between men with the new Continental sexological theories of homosexuality. A home-grown discourse of inversion was not tolerated.[8] Comparisons with European states at this time highlight the probable reasons for resistance in legal definitions or clarifications in Britain. In Austria, for example, the effects of debate in Parliament were far reaching – it was an Austro-Hungarian jurist who coined the neologism 'homosexual' to categorise the phenomenon in 1869. The persistent unwillingness to debate, legally classify or even officially acknowledge the existence or extent of sex and sexuality between men was inimical to any developments in scientific examination of this phenomenon amongst British men. Even if Weeks' historical analysis of a legal-medical construction of homosexuality were to be accepted, this pattern of development happened only in cultural contexts where the state became demonstrably less active in criminalising and punishing this phenomenon amongst consenting adults. Weeks argues that the British state created an increasingly purposive legal hostility towards the phenomenon of sex between men in the late nineteenth century. If this were the case, then this situation would have contradicted and excluded the fundamental arguments inherent in most nineteenth-century sexology, that homosexuality was a pathology and therefore could not be criminal. A more accurately contextualised analysis of attitudes at governmental levels towards sexuality between men is required.

In historiographies influenced by Weeks, concepts of sexuality between men and of 'types' of men who would engage in this kind of sexuality are presented as being barely formulated, before the mid-1880s. Matt Cook's recent work, *London and the Culture of Homosexuality 1885–1914* (2003), and Cocks' work, demonstrate that public awareness of sex and sexuality between men, in its many locations and guises, was a widespread, sophisticated, urbane but tacit knowledge in the 1860s and 1870s.[9] As we have seen, even *The Times* fell near-silent upon this subject between 1872 and 1885. However, there is much evidence to suggest that awareness of sexuality between men did not abate in these years. The incidence of sodomy indictments and trials actually increased after 1877, indicating a continued willingness to report incidents to the authorities.[10] Also, these were the years when the much examined 'homosexual' men, such as Symonds, Carpenter and Wilde, were exploring their senses of self, based on their sexual desire for other men.

Weeks and Cohen both present the Cleveland Street Affair in 1889 and the trials of Oscar Wilde in 1895, as the catalysts for awareness amongst the public of the existence of sexuality between men. These trials were both conducted using Clause 11 of the Criminal Law Amendment Act, 1885. But sex and sexuality between men was not a priority for legal clarification or for state control in these years, even in 1885. It was important, for the most part, for the institutions of authority to ignore this phenomenon. To do otherwise would give official recognition that this phenomenon existed amongst British men at all. Awareness of sexuality between men was widespread to the extent that mainstream newspapers and government officials refrained from reporting or assessing the existence of the crime in the metropolitan space of mainland Britain, for fear of undermining the status of masculinity.[11] An example of the imperative to ignore the phenomenon of sex between males, even when the crime involved corruption of youths, is revealed in a potential scandal that was brought to the attention of Scotland Yard by senior officials at the Post Office in 1877. The case involved the sexual corruption of three telegraph boys by James Smith, a City of London secretary with prominent social connections, over a period of some months. The case was referred to the Home Office for a decision as to whether a prosecution could be made. Adolphus Liddell, permanent under secretary at the Home Office, insisted that Smith not be put on trial unless there 'was a certainty of conviction'.[12] Liddell and his legal advisors were most concerned about the effects of a public scandal emanating from a lengthy trial involving a man of some social prominence with an uncertain outcome 'and such a scandal is much to be deprecated'.[13]

This correspondence reveals a certainty amongst Home Office officials that a crime had taken place. A. C. Hepburn, a Home Office civil servant who corresponded with Liddell on the case, stated that

> it is perfectly clear ... that the full offence was committed in every instance. ... Here is <u>a man, without doubt</u> – whatever may be the <u>legal evidence</u> obtainable – making it his business to debauch and corrupt young boys.[14]

This notwithstanding, there were concerns that there was a 'want of corroboration' on the part of two of the telegraph boys sexually assaulted by Smith. Nonetheless, Hepburn stated that a prosecution might be achieved, because 'a jury looking at [the boy's] youth might not discredit his story'. But Hepburn added that 'if there is to be no prosecution "without ... certainty of conviction" it is clear that ... there can be no prosecution'.[15] It is significant that the Home Office was prepared to ignore Smith's activities, if there was the possibility that the case could not be efficiently prosecuted. However, the officials eventually decided that the trial had to take place as the case involved extensive evidence of the sexual corruption of boys in Crown employment. In any case, the trial was not reported by the national newspapers and Smith was quietly incarcerated for a life sentence of penal servitude.

In spite of the reticence in reporting cases of this kind in the national newspapers, viewing the explosion of discussion in the newspapers of the Cleveland Street scandal as a new and unprecedented trope in 1889 is not substantiated by the evidence. In the examination of the broader context of the nineteenth century, discussion of crimes of sex between males in, at least, *The Times*, appears as a continuous, if somewhat muted, form of journalistic discourse. The level of public awareness revealed in the first few days of the 'Stella and Fanny' arraignment of 1870, indicates a degree of knowledge at least as sophisticated as that demonstrated in the reporting of the Cleveland Street scandal in 1889 and the trials of Oscar Wilde in 1895. The years of silence on the British aspects of this subject in *The Times* must, therefore, be seen as an aberration in the discussion of this phenomenon in this publication in the nineteenth century. The period of silence can also be regarded as probably the last episode in British political and journalistic history where discussion of sex between British men could be effectively suppressed by the few men who wielded power in these institutions and without legislation, ostensibly to preserve the status quo of gender relations.[16]

The period of press and governmental silence on this issue is concomitant with the first serious attempts to impose, through non-statutory departmental policies rather than legislation, a blanket of secrecy over a range of government action. Cocks detects a culture of increasing governmental and legal secrecy and press self-censorship after 1830 surrounding sodomy trials.[17] With the expansion of the Whitehall civil service after 1870,[18] government could no longer rely upon the spirit of 'honourable secrecy', supposedly prevalent amongst elite members of the administrative class in the earlier part of the century.[19] By the late 1870s, the Whitehall civil service was employing ever-increasing numbers of junior clerks from the lower white collar and manual classes. Although secrecy would not be imposed through legislation until the first Official Secrets Act of 1889, David Vincent's work regards the developments in departmental secrecy rules between 1870 and 1889 as forming the basis of this Act. In an era of ever-increasing democracy and press freedoms, senior government and administrative figures regarded it as imperative that government departments could effectively operate in a 'culture of secrecy'.[20] However, after the Great Reform Act of 1884, which greatly extended the male franchise, government departments found it increasingly difficult to impose secrecy through non-statutory means.

The years 1870 to 1889 can be regarded, therefore, as a period in which successive administrations attempted to impose secrecy in a range of matters, whilst regarding the realities of secrecy as not officially existing. It took a series of serious and potentially destabilising 'leaks' in matters of foreign policy, before British secrecy became an official reality in 1889. That tacit suppression of discussion or official recognition of sexuality between men operated in these years, in a culture that knew the existence of this phenomenon and feared its implications, may be regarded in the same light as the ambiguous arrangements for imposing secrecy before 1889. Home Office dossiers of sentencing policies for bestiality and sodomy between men were some of the first to be closed using the Official Secrets Act in 1889, along with foreign policy and military secrets. These dossiers contain material on this issue relating to the late 1880s and were closed in 1889 using the one hundred year closure rule, the most stringent tool of secrecy available to government. Another series of dossiers, containing material about prosecution of sex between men relating to the late 1870s, the 1880s and the 1890s, but compiled between 1892 and 1898, were finally closed using the one hundred year rule, in 1898. These dossiers, containing invaluable insights into late Victorian official attitudes towards the matter of sex between men, only became available for view in 1998. The secrecy surrounding this material is indicative of the imperative to keep the discussion of sexuality between men out of the public domain, utilising the rarely implemented one hundred year rule. The late Victorian administrations largely succeeded in this aim, as the bulk of this historically important material does not appear even, in recent historiography.[21]

Given the concealment of these matters, Henry Labouchere's Amendment to the Criminal Law Amendment Act, 1885 is best understood as a 'leak' or a breach of generally understood administrative secrecy. F. B. Smith, in his article on Labouchere's amendment published in 1976, points out that Clause 11, introduced without debate, late at night to a near empty house and at the last possible sitting in the House of Commons for the Bill, was rushed through the House of Lords for its third reading the following day and passed into law. Smith highlights that the broader aims of the Act had created enormous controversy for the embattled caretaker ministry in power in late 1885. By August 1885, the ministry was 'impatient to speed the Bill through its closing stages in committee, have parliament [dissolved] and address themselves to the coming general election'. Smith argues that 'in calmer times the Amendment would probably have been ruled out of order', but the urgency created by mass protests for the statutory imposition of a minimum age of consent for girls, meant that a wearied parliament was 'resolved to settle the age of consent controversy, come what may'.[22]

Both Cohen and Weeks connect the motives for Labouchere's amendment, without evidence, to the aims of the broader social purity campaign that led to the Criminal Law Amendment Act. However, Smith highlights that the subject of sex between men was never mentioned in the social purity campaign, either 'before or after the adoption of the clause'.[23] In his detailed examination of the career of the Bill through parliament, Smith demonstrates that Labouchere, along with other parliamentary members, was highly ambivalent about the tenor of the social purity movement and the associated parliamentary Bill. Throughout the long and difficult passage of the Bill during 1885, Labouchere had made frequent attempts to scupper the Bill. In July 1885, Labouchere had motioned to set the age of consent for girls at 21, a clearly preposterous amendment. Other similar amendments by Labouchere, equally unworkable, caused C. H. Hopwood MP, to point out to the house in debate on 31 July 1885 that

> he did not think [Labouchere's] action altogether with regard to this Bill was serious. It seemed to him that the Hon. Member was anxious, in this singular way, to show the Committee the absurdity of the whole of the Bill.[24]

Labouchere was a Liberal MP, but highly maverick in his parliamentary behaviour and firmly ensconced as a backbencher throughout his political career. Smith observes that moving Clause 11, with the motive of damaging the Bill, was entirely in keeping with Labouchere's parliamentary conduct of 'sheer ratty obstructiveness'. Labouchere made no reference to or defence of his amendment in 1885; his only comment the following day, was to rail against the secretive discussion of the Bill between the two front benches, arguing that it 'would have been better had the Bill been sent before a large and representative select committee'.[25] It is entirely possible that Labouchere had moved the Clause to achieve no more than force the government to reconsider the Bill in select committee.

In many respects, the inclusion of Clause 11 in the Criminal Law Amendment Act of 1885 cannot be viewed as a purposive attempt by the state to construct a pejorative homosexual 'type' through legislation. However, historians such as Cohen and Weeks emphasise the effects of this legislation, once implemented, on broader perceptions of a homosexual identity. Undoubtedly, the inclusion of Clause 11 did have some cultural effects. The legislation occasioned the first specified reports of unnatural crime in *The Times* since 1872. Montgomery-Hyde highlights that in July 1884, *The Times* had alluded to the existence of a libel trial in Dublin that was causing significant scandal for the Dublin Castle administration. The trial judge, 'in the interests of public morality' ruled that any publication of any part of this politically sensitive trial would be ruled in contempt of court.[26] This ruling was made in response to garrulous claims in the *United Ireland* newspaper in 1882 of links between Crown officials and a sodomitical brothel in Golden Lane. High-ranking officials implicated by the *United Ireland* in its revelations, sued the newspaper in 1883 and 1884. The officials involved had been acquitted of sodomy, but the one libel suit that made it to court collapsed. All the English and mainstream Irish newspapers did not report on the sodomy trials and shied away from reporting the exact nature of the libel trial, partly in response to the trial judge's ruling. Cocks argues that newspapers, such as the highly politicised and anti-British *United Ireland*, were also seen as 'illegitimate sources of knowledge and accusation' by mainstream publications, such as *The Times*, particularly at a time of extreme difficulty for those with the responsibility of implementing the government's coercion policies in Ireland.[27] Consequently, the existence and nature of the reason for the libel suit were only surmised, in much vaguer terms than had been the case in *The Times'* pages up to 1872. The decision of *The Times* to all but ignore the existence of this alarming series of trials was similar to its decisions to support the defence in the 'Stella and Fanny' trial in 1871. After the successful outcome of the libel suit for the editor of the *United Ireland*, readers of newspapers in mainland Britain, apart from subscribers to the ultra nationalist *United Ireland* and the *Freeman's Journal*, were spared the details of this potentially highly destabilising scandal. Readers of the ultra nationalist press, on the other hand, were encouraged to equate the vice exposed by the libel suit with British unfitness to govern Ireland. Analogies were made between the decadence and despotism of British rule in Ireland and the tolerance of 'unnatural vice' at the fall of the Roman Empire.[28] As this was a direct assault upon the masculinity of British officials, it is little wonder that British and moderate Irish publications chose to ignore the scandal. However, in October 1885, *The Times* decided to report a case in which the defendant was found guilty of the 'attempt to commit an unnatural crime' and had been prosecuted under the new Criminal Law Amendment Act.

The specific purpose of the Criminal Law Amendment Act had been effective prosecution of the perpetrators of the widely publicised scandal involving the prostitution of young girls. The scandal had been sensationalised by W. T. Stead's 'Maiden Tribute' articles in the *Pall Mall Gazette* and formed the basis for the mass Social Purity Campaign of 1885. The accused in this case were duly brought to trial at the Central Criminal Court on 22 October 1885.[29] But *The Times* reported on two trials, occurring immediately after the widely publicised social purity trial, from Carlisle Assizes, an unusual occurrence in itself. The trials, conducted on 29 October, involved two men convicted under the new legislation. In one trial, William Sarginson was convicted of indecent assault on a 12-year-old girl under the new Act, which fulfilled the popular purpose of the legislation. In another trial, Isaac Thirwall was convicted of attempted unnatural crime using the same legislation.[30] Investigative journalism had prompted the case for the Criminal Law Amendment Act and *The Times* clearly published the two cases from Carlisle to highlight the divergent implications of the legislation.

The inclusion of Clause 11 in the 1885 Act, had the effect of breaking press silence on the reporting of crimes of sex between men in *The Times*. However, following the article highlighting the implications of the Criminal Law Amendment Act, cases involving sexual coercion of boys appear to have attracted the singular attention of the newspapers in these years. *The Times* did not report another case of unnatural crime until June 1886. The occasion for reporting was the prosecution of Henry Moffatt, a clergyman, and Robert Fillingham, an undergraduate at Merton College, Oxford. These men were not accused of unnatural crime with each other, but of conspiring to sexually assault two 13-year-old boys. The boys gave, according to *The Times*, 'evidence of a nature that was unfit for publication',[31] but the case was also publicised in *Lloyds' Weekly Newspaper* and the newly instituted Sunday newspaper, *The People*. The reporting of the case in *Lloyds'* was minimal, but

The People reported more details of the trial. *The People* included no specifics of the sexual acts involved, but reported some of the prosecution evidence and the defence evidence, to make it clear that innocent boys were being defiled by their social superiors, ostensibly in a position of trust over them. *The People* and *Lloyds'* were clear, however, that Moffat and Fillingham were on trial for 'acts of indecency towards boys'[32] and that the defendants were being charged 'under the 11th "Outrages of Decency" section of the Criminal Law Amendment Act'.[33] The involvement of young boys in this case is an important distinction in the occasion for its reporting. Both *Lloyds'* and *The People* had followed the social purity campaign with intense interest and had been avid supporters of the concomitant legislation. As stated, the single emphasis of the campaign was the protection of girls under 16 from sexual preying by men. Although Clause 11 did not in any way offer this differentiation of childhood and consenting adulthood in the matter of sexuality between males, the legislation was presented in these publications as achieving the effect of offering protection to young boys as well as young girls.

It is important to emphasise the distinction between cases of sex between grown men and sex between men and boys in the period following the 1885 Act. The Act occasioned the reappearance of cases of unnatural crime in *The Times*, but the newspaper did not resume its pattern of reporting cases involving males of all ages that had been apparent in its pages throughout the nineteenth century up to 1872. Between 1885 and 1903, the relatively few cases of unnatural crime reported in its pages, if compared to the frequency of reportage in the 1860s, dealt with cases that involved the sexual preying of boys by grown men.[34] In 1887, *The Times* reported a case of unnatural crime from the Bristol assizes. The defendant, John Hamer, was convicted of the crime and sentenced to ten years penal servitude. *The Times* did not specify in this report the involvement of boys; in other cases, such as the Moffat and Fillingham case of 1886 and a case in 1891,[35] when boys were involved, *The Times* emphasised this element in the trial. The trial of John Hamer received the attention of the Home Office in a review of sentencing policies for crimes of sex between men made in 1892. In the dossier, Hamer was detailed as

> a well to do Bristol tradesman aged sixty-three. He made a great pretence of religion. He enticed a boy ... into his house by offering him sweetmeats and indecently assaulted him. He subsequently got the boy to sleep at his house when the full offence was committed.[36]

The Hamer case was not reported in the Sunday newspapers but like *The Times*, the only cases of unnatural crime that attracted the attention of the Sunday newspapers in the late 1880s and early 1890s were those involving the sexual preying of boys. The Home Office dossier of 1892 indicates that the majority of crimes of sex between males detailed in the report were cases involving adult participants, but the newspapers only reported on unnatural crime that involved men and boys. The Moffatt and Fillingham trial attracted press attention for this reason. Also, the Cleveland Street scandal of 1889 attracted the attention of these publications for similar reasons. The Cleveland Street scandal exposed the sexual exploitation in a West End male brothel of young telegraph messenger lads, one of whom was under 16 years of age. The exposure of this scandal undoubtedly gained momentum in all the newspapers because of the connection between the male brothel and some of its clients, who were of the highest social and political standing. But the attraction for the press was, initially, the corrupting of telegraph boys by their elders. It is significant that the trial in 1877 of James Smith, which also involved the sexual corruption of telegraph boys, did not attract press attention but the 1889 scandal did. After 1885, the focus of *The Times* and the Sunday newspapers on crimes of sex between men and boys, rather than cases involving adult men, would have been entirely in keeping with the emphasis of the campaigns during 1885 for the protection of young girls, even though neither the campaign nor the Act specified the need for protection of young boys.

The case of John Hamer, reported in *The Times* in 1887, highlights another significant problem with the interpretation in historiography of the legal significance of Clause 11 after 1885. Hamer's sentence of ten years penal servitude and the Home Office reference to the 'full offence', clearly indicate that he was convicted of anal penetration using the 1861 Offences Against the Person Act. The 1861 Act had removed the capital indictment for sodomy, but had retained the archaic Buggery Act of 1533 as the basis for legislation. The 1861 Act stipulated that sentences for convictions of sodomy should be life imprisonment with penal servitude. In addition, the Act stipulated the minimum sentence, which must be no less than ten years penal servitude.[37] Convictions of 'gross indecency' using Clause 11, on the other hand, carried a maximum sentence of two years imprisonment, with or without penal servitude. Cohen argues that Clause 11 criminalised 'same-sex practices between men generally, "in public or private" … [superceding] the earlier legal injunction against a specific kind of act', that is, sodomy. Cohen interprets the clause as a near-revolutionary departure in British jurisprudence, arguing that it specified a 'class' of offender, 'over and against previous notions that held "sodomy" to be a potential, [sinful] capacity ... inherent in all'.[38] Cohen, Weeks and other historians argue that Clause 11 somehow replaced earlier arrangements for criminalisation of sex between men. In the historiography, the 1885 legislation is presented as creating a new and hostile 'mood' and willingness to indict and effectively prosecute this form of criminal sexuality, in a culture where the crime had hitherto been perceived as a rare, barely understood and 'sinful' phenomenon. However, the inclusion of Clause 11 in the 1885 Criminal Law Amendment Act did not supersede the legality, meanings or use of the Buggery laws.

The Buggery Act remained the basis of legislation for prosecuting acts of anal sex between men until 1967. When sex between two men in private was decriminalised for men over 21, the Sexual Offences Act of 1967 did not distinguish between anal sex and other forms of sexual contact between men.[39] It is arguable that this legislation, in 1967, was the first in English law to distinguish a 'class' of men who had sex with other men.[40] The 1967 legislation accommodated the sexual lifestyles of men who, as long as they conducted their various and consenting sexual acts in private and the sexual encounter numbered no more than two persons, would not be prosecuted.[41] The introduction of Clause 11 in 1885 did ensure a legal catch-all of sexual acts between males. However, in 1885, British legislation did not create a specified legal category of a 'class' or type of men who would have sex with other men. Instead, legislation criminalised, through the Buggery laws and Clause 11 in combination, a cascade of sexual acts perpetrated by any man, ranging from anal penetration of other males (and bestiality and the anal penetration of women) to mutual masturbation between males. It is a misinterpretation of the legislative arrangements before 1885, to conclude that it was not possible to prosecute all sexual acts between men in all locations. As we have seen, the interpretation of sodomy was stretched to include even acts of mutual masturbation. Even more compelling evidence for the historical continuity, rather than the transformation, of patterns of indictment and prosecution of sex between men in the nineteenth century is contained in the details of the Offences Against the Person Act of 1861 and in the statistical breakdown of nineteenth-century indictments and convictions for sodomy, attempted sodomy and gross indecency. Cocks' careful statistical tabulation of annual judicial returns is adopted throughout.[42]

Between 1868 and 1872, the last years that *The Times* reported on cases of unnatural crime between British men before its self-imposed silence on the subject, judicial returns indicate that there were 200 indictments for sodomy, resulting in only 42 convictions, or 21 per cent. Between the years 1874 and 1879 judicial returns indicate that there were 238 indictments for sodomy. Of these, only 95 were convicted, or 40 per cent, substantiating the arguments for the difficulties in securing convictions in this crime and the unwillingness of the authorities to convict in cases of this crime. It is also interesting that the years of silence in *The Times* not only witnessed an increase in indictments, suggesting a continued willingness amongst urban populations to report the crime to the authorities, but also a slight increase in convictions. It is possible that convictions were slightly easier to secure in these years, as trials were not publicised in the newspapers. However, the judicial returns also categorised indictments and convictions for attempted sodomy, a lesser offence than the charge of full sodomy. The offence of attempted sodomy existed throughout the nineteenth century, reiterated in Peel's Offences Against the Person Act of 1828 and the Offences Against the Person Act of 1861. The 1861 Act stipulated a maximum sentence of three years, with or without penal servitude, for the crime. An examination of the category of attempted sodomy in the 1861 Act is important, as the details of the category is neglected in the historiography. The definition of sodomy in the Act retained the ambiguities of the Buggery Act, 1533, but Clause 63 stipulated that

> whosoever shall attempt to commit the said abominable crime [of buggery] ... or of any indecent assault upon any male person, shall be guilty of misdemeanour.[43]

It is clear that the courts had available to them a veritable catch-all before 1885. However, it was left up to the courts to interpret the meaning of 'indecent assault'.[44] Also, it is interesting that the Attorney General, in the 1871 'Stella and Fanny' trial in Westminster Hall, chose to indict the defendants with full sodomy. After the scandal of the press coverage of the arraignment, the Attorney General had no choice other than to commit the defendants to trial. An indictment and trial for attempted sodomy might have proved more successful in securing a conviction, but, as seen in Chapter 3, it was not in the interests of the government to achieve a conviction in this high profile case, involving as it did, the posthumous reputation of a member of the governing party.

In the reportage of unnatural crime in *The Times* before 1872, only a minority of cases involved the lesser charge of attempted sodomy. This notwithstanding, the returns for attempted sodomy between 1868 and 1872 show that there were 359 indictments, resulting in 201 convictions, or 56 per cent. The returns between 1874 and 1879 show that there were 402 indictments for attempted sodomy, resulting in 242 convictions, or 60 per cent, indicating that attempted sodomy was a more common form of indictment than full sodomy. The prosecution rates were higher than for full sodomy, but it was also a relatively difficult offence to prosecute.

It is significant that judicial returns for gross indecency did not begin until 1893, indicating that Clause 11 was thrust upon an unsuspecting and unprepared judiciary. This challenges historiographical assertions that an explosion in prosecutions is detectable after 1885.[45] There are no judicial returns for convictions for the year 1897, but in the years 1893–96 and 1898, there were 161 indictments for sodomy, 314 indictments for attempted sodomy and 323 indictments for gross indecency. The convictions resulting from these indictments were 66 for sodomy, or 41 per cent, 199 for attempted sodomy, or 63 per cent, and 180 for gross indecency, or 56 per cent. If the statistics for 1874–79 and 1893–98 are baldly compared, combining all categories, then there were 640 indictments and 237 convictions in the earlier quinquennium, or 37 per cent, and 798 indictments and 445 convictions in the later, or 56 per cent. At face value, the comparison of indictments and convictions between the periods do not even indicate an explosion in indictments and prosecutions after 1893, when judicial returns began for cases of gross indecency. Instead, the statistics indicate a steady, but relatively gradual increase of indictments for sex between males apparent for the years before 1879.[46]

If these statistics are set against the changes in urban demography in the second half of the nineteenth century, then the increase in urban indictments for sex between men appears as proportional to the huge increases in rates of urban living. In 1851, 51 per cent of a population of 17 millions was living in urban areas. By 1901, this proportion had increased to 77 per cent of a population of 33 millions.[47] Also, the proportion of convictions in the later period is higher than in the earlier, but not markedly so. Interestingly, the indictments for attempted sodomy in 1893–98 brought a higher proportion of convictions than indictments for the new category of gross indecency. All the categories for 1893–98 demonstrate that it still remained a matter of some difficulty to convict men of crimes of sex with other men.

Of course, there are difficulties in interpreting these statistics at face value. The main inherent difficulty is the near impossibility of differentiating with accuracy between indictments for bestiality and sexual acts between men in the categories of sodomy and attempted sodomy throughout the century (or, for that matter, for most of the twentieth century). As Cocks demonstrates, sodomy was interpreted in urban indictments to mean almost exclusively sex between men.[48] A. D. Harvey's recent short study of bestiality in late Victorian England argues that bestiality was a present, but rare crime in the period.[49] Also, an examination of Home Office records gives some indication for the proportion of sodomy convictions that pertained to sex with animals. The Home Office attempted, in 1892, to differentiate between prosecutions brought for sex between men, and sex by men upon animals. The Home Office officials experienced difficulties with this exercise, stating that 'the calendars do not always give particulars enabling a distinction to be made whether the crime was committed with mankind or beast'. Nonetheless, out of the 87 convictions for sodomy and attempted sodomy in 1891, the only year examined by the Home Office in this exercise, only eight convictions were stipulated for sex or attempted sex with an animal. The majority of other cases included in the Home Office exercise stipulated that the crime involved sex between men.[50] This means that approximately 7 per cent of convictions for sodomy and its attempt were for bestiality in 1891. It is impossible to discern the proportion of the 169 indictments that year for sodomy and attempted sodomy that involved cases of bestiality. But cases of bestiality almost invariably involved young, first offenders and the perpetrators were often described as imbecile.[51] These circumstances suggest that indictments for cases of sex with dumb animals, involving young and imbecile defendants with at least one witness to the event, had a higher probability of achieving convictions than the often fraught and ambivalent circumstances surrounding convictions for sex between men. With some caution, one can infer from the evidence that bestiality constituted probably no more than a small proportion of indictments for sodomy and attempted sodomy in the late nineteenth century.

In this analysis, it is argued that the level of indictments for sex between men was high in the 1870s and the 1890s, and that the increase in indictments between these years was relatively gradual. The increase in sodomy indictments between 1868 and 1879 reflected a trend in increased urban indictments for the crime that is detectable from 1800. The incidental imposition of Clause 11 onto the Criminal Law Amendment Act of 1885, has to be regarded as not much more than an accelerator to the trend of higher levels of urban indictments for crimes of sex between men in the nineteenth century and not a revolution in jurisprudence. The statistics for the 1890s do indicate some reduction in the levels of indictments for full sodomy and attempted sodomy. Given the probable low levels of bestiality and the absence of cases of anal penetration of women in the Home Office analysis of 1892, it is probable that the legal effect of Clause 11 was the indictment of sexual acts between males that had previously been tried under the sodomy categories extant before 1885. It is probable that indictments for sodomy and its attempt were, after 1885, reserved for acts or attempted acts of anal sex between males[52] and included the rare occurrences of bestiality, with the new gross indecency category absorbing other sexual activity between males hitherto tried under the categories of sodomy and attempted sodomy. Convictions remained relatively difficult to secure in all categories of criminal sexual acts between males in the 1890s, defying the Cohen analysis of a sudden and new awareness of this crime after 1885 and a concomitant explosion in the proportion of social opprobrium and criminal prosecutions.

It is therefore arguable that, in spite of the developments in 1885, legal definitions of a type of male who would engage with sex with other males were no less ambivalent than before the introduction of Clause 11. However, Weeks argues that the Home Office attempted to 'distinguish the various forms of buggery, which in practice meant a separation of bestiality from homosexual activity, which was being more closely defined as an individual trait'.[53] Weeks presents the chronology of this development as evolving in the 20 years following the Offences Against the Person Act of 1861. In Weeks' analysis, the introduction of Clause 11 in 1885 is presented as the attempt 'more directly' to control sex between men that had been developed at the Home Office. Weeks makes this analysis based on a single series of Home Office files. This file series, which contained the opinions of judges on sentencing policies for sodomy, was not compiled until 1888 and closed for a century until 1989. The judges were exclusively concerned in this exercise with the status quo of sentencing difficulties in 1888. A later series of dossiers, compiled between 1892 and 1898, closed until 1998 and not examined by Weeks, do contain references to trials conducted in the 1870s and 1880s. However, all of this material was compiled retrospectively in policy documents by the Home Office, or contained in files for individual petitions for pardon, in the 1890s. None of the Home Office files examined in this chapter make explicit reference to trials conducted before 1877. This makes Weeks' chronology and analysis of Home Office policy in this area inaccurate and misleading.

The Home Office, the Director of Public Prosecutions (DPP) and the Treasury Solicitors, were the government departments with the ostensible responsibility for the prosecution of crimes of sex between men. However, examination of their archives reveals a paucity of policy information on this issue in the mid-nineteenth century. There is no reference to any kind of policy material regarding this matter from the late 1840s until 1871. As Cocks states, between 1780 and 1850, government departments only occasionally intervened in high profile cases and the police were rarely involved in sodomy prosecutions.[54] Even after this date, when police arrests for sexual indecencies between men increased, the vast majority of cases were reported to the authorities by private individuals. Importantly, there was no specific policing policy of actively investigating the crime, unlike contemporary Paris.[55] Cocks argues that the thousands of sodomy indictments brought between 1780 and 1850 represented thousands of individual circumstances, rather than the results of any systematic government policy. However, the considerable body of material in the DPP archive relating to the trial of *Regina v. Boulton and Others*, or the infamous 'Stella and Fanny' Westminster Hall trial of 1871, can be regarded as a development in government policy.[56] These files contain the opinions of the Attorney General and the trial transcript itself. The Attorney General's deliberations in this instance were particular to this trial. The trial involved the reputation of an eminent political figure and did not apply to the conditions of the many other sodomy and attempted sodomy trials in the period, involving men of no social importance. It is understandable, given the lack of material in the archives, that the 'Stella and Fanny' files have attracted the attention of historians. The emphasis placed by many historians on this material alone, has, unfortunately, distorted the analysis of awarenesses and cultural meanings attached to sexuality between men in the 1870s. Clearly, this material has been interpreted with a lack of attention to the broader historical context.

Similarly, Weeks' emphasis on a single Home Office series of files results in a misinterpretation of state control of sex between men and the shaping of a pejorative homosexual identity in the late nineteenth century. Weeks' presentation of his historical evidence asserts that a pattern of development in the Home Office then translated into legislation in 1885. This 'fits' the argument for the legal construction of the homosexual category in late nineteenth-century Britain, which in turn crystallised notions of this category in the public imagination in the late 1880s and the 1890s. However, the examination of much broader evidence indicates that perceptions of sexuality between men were much more developed amongst urban populations throughout the second half of the nineteenth century than this historiography suggests. Men indicted for sex with other males destabilised prevailing notions of what was considered necessary for an adult male to acquire masculine status, irrespective of class. The centrality of masculinity as status and a social responsibility to gender relations, fostered cultural vilification and abhorrence of behaviours that threatened the fragile dominance of masculinity in social and class structures. It is arguable that developing structures of masculinity in nineteenth-century Britain were all pervasive in creating widespread notions of aberrant and rare types of men that would have sex with other males. Men indicted, exposed in the press and prosecuted, lost their masculine status, irrespective of their class. This is probably why the state went to great pains to secure a not guilty verdict in the 'Stella and Fanny' sodomy trial in 1871. A guilty verdict would have posthumously rendered Lord Arthur Clinton as lower than the lowest orders of men in social status. The conviction of Simeon Solomon, the pre-Raphaelite artist, of attempted sodomy in 1872, offers material evidence of the effects of such a conviction. Although not publicised in the newspapers, the Royal Academician was never able to work successfully again and died, in spite of his family and social connections, in the workhouse.[57] Similarly, Oscar Wilde so threatened British masculinity that he was forced to live in exile after his release from prison and died in poverty in Paris.

The awarenesses demonstrated before 1885 of sexuality between men and its guises are indicative of a pervasive and tacit cultural knowledge. The levels of indictments for the crime in the nineteenth century indicate that urban dwellers were willing to use the justice system to punish these outrages against what was considered masculine. The justice system and the law, on the other hand, demonstrably lagged behind or attempted to ignore this cultural development. The majority of unnatural crime cases that made the pages of *The Times* before 1872 had been brought to the attention of the authorities by members of the public. The metropolitan police had been active in bringing the 'Stella and Fanny' scandal to trial, much to the embarrassment and discomfiture of the Attorney General and the DPP. But even the Cleveland Street male brothel scandal of 1889 only came to light when the Post Office, employers of the telegraph boys, reported to the police the amounts of money the boys were carrying, suspecting them of theft.[58] During the Cleveland Street investigations by the police, Jack Saul, an adult male prostitute employed at the brothel, attested that in his long 'career', the police had 'never interfered' with him, adding that 'they shut their eyes to more than me'.[59]

Neither more nor less concerned with protecting and bolstering the requirements of masculinity amongst British men than the public, the authorities attempted to resist clarification or investigation of the crimes of sex between men. To allow clarification would have offered official recognition that the phenomenon existed amongst British men at all. Then why, for the first time in 1888, did the Home Office attempt to distinguish between crimes of bestiality and sodomy between men? Even if it is accepted that Weeks misinterpreted the chronology of Home Office policy formations, the Home Office exercise could be interpreted as emanating from the changes in legislation in 1885. However, this conclusion would misinterpret both the motives and purposes behind the Home Office exercise and the unanimity at the Home Office on this issue at the time. The 'Opinions of Judges on Sentences for Buggery' (1888), commissioned in secret by the Conservative Home Secretary, Henry Matthews, was not, primarily, an exercise in clarification of crimes of sex between men. Crimes of gross indecency, the offence stipulated by Clause 11 in 1885, did not receive consideration. The question posed by the Home Secretary was whether there was a consensus amongst judges that the 'sentences of ten years to life penal servitude is too harsh … for bestiality'.[60] Since 1861, sentences of between ten years and life of penal servitude had been passed on convicts for crimes of anal penetration of males and sexual penetration of animals. The punishment of imprisonment with penal servitude, suffused with notions of reformation of the convict, had been developed since the 1830s for a range of crimes. By the mid-1830s, the British state had effectively overturned its notorious 'bloody code' of the eighteenth century and could punish felons with either penal servitude or transportation for all but seven capital felonies, which included sodomy. With the removal of the capital charge for sodomy, in all its forms, in 1861, punishment for this crime was also included in the reformatory penal system. However, the wisdom of the efficacy of penal transportation, predominantly to Western Australia, was called into serious doubt by the mid-nineteenth century, not least by the law-abiding colonists in that land. The use of transportation had largely dwindled by 1853, but intermittent penal transportation persisted until 1867, when it was finally abolished. By the 1870s, penal servitude was regarded as the only acceptable alternative to transportation for a range of crimes.[61] However, by the late 1880s, the system of penal servitude, involving hard labour and very long periods of solitary confinement, came under increasingly organised criticism and parliamentary examination.[62]

The convict prisons, directly and uniformly managed by Sir Edward Du Cane, chair of both the Prison Commission and the Convict

Directorate since 1869, became notorious for the harsh treatment of prisoners. Du Cane frequently kept the Home Office in the dark about serious mistreatment of prisoners, only to be embarrassed by revelations by journalists, such as Arthur Morrison and reform organisations like the Howard Association. The civil servants at the Home Office and the indomitable Du Cane, were locked in a seemingly interminable row in the late 1880s and 1890s and there was serious concern within the Home Office 'about the independent and autocratic style of his management'.[63] The very public furore between Du Cane and the Home Office resulted in the 1891 Penal Servitude Act, which stipulated that sentences of penal servitude were only applicable 'for any period not less than three years and not exceeding five years'.[64] The row culminated in the Royal Commission of 1895, at which the Home Office civil servants were principal witnesses and which resulted in Du Cane's retirement. In evidence, the Home Office had collected extensive dossiers of prisoners mistreated under the Du Cane system of penal servitude between 1877 and 1895, and had conducted reviews of which prisoners should be punished under the system.[65] The Royal Commission recommended that juveniles should not be committed for penal servitude and encouraged the organisation and expansion of juvenile reformatory schools, a move that eventually led to the development of the Borstal system for juvenile offenders in the first decade of the twentieth century.[66]

It is in this context that the 'Opinions of Judges on Sentences for Buggery' in 1888 is best understood. The Home Office garnered opinions from the judiciary, on the grounds that males convicted of bestiality were often adolescent, 'imbecile' and first offenders and therefore could not possibly benefit from the system.[67] One of the judges, Justice Hawkins, opined that the penal servitude system was probably too harsh for offences of bestiality. He commented that 'for the most part that crime [bestiality] is committed by young persons, agricultural labourers, etc., out of pure ignorance'.

However, Hawkins revealed his opinion on the crime of sodomy between men:

> The crime of sodomy with mankind stands upon a different footing and deserves ... much more serious consideration. ... and even with regard to that abominable crime, much, I think, might be said in favour of limiting the minimum punishment of ten years penal servitude to persons over a certain age.[68]

There was much public criticism about the system of penal servitude, for confirming 'young offenders in a criminality that was rapidly becoming fixed'.[69]

It is clear that Justice Hawkins reflected public criticism in his opinion of prosecutions for young offenders convicted of sex with animals and sex with other males. The huge public campaign against the penal incarceration of young offenders in adult prisons had been based upon 'the criminological thrust towards selective and differential treatment on the basis of assessed physical, mental and moral deficiency [and] unanimously emphasised special treatment for the younger prisoner'.[70] Much of the judicial opinion expressed in the 1888 buggery dossiers emphasised a desire for relative clemency for the young offender, reflecting developments in positivist criminology that recommended that criminal youths could lead 'law abiding lives if subjected to education and training'.[71] Crimes of bestiality, almost invariably committed as a first offence by the young and 'ignorant', could be punished with shorter sentences. In these dossiers, men convicted of sex with animals were regarded by the Home Office officials as 'imbecile' and possibly 'lunatic'. It is of historical importance that adult perpetrators of sodomy 'with mankind' were, under no circumstances, to be considered under this category. The judges and the Home Office were prepared to accept, up to a point, the development of a scientific criminology, separating the consideration and treatment of youth crime. However, the adult perpetrators of the crime 'with mankind' were to continue to be considered common felons and be punished, when convicted, using the full weight of the law.

The opinions of Justice Hawkins and the other judges who contributed to this Home Office review do not amount to a legalistic construction of the homosexual category. Instead, the opinions reflected the judges' preoccupation with the perpetrators of certain kinds of sexual acts. Acts of mutual masturbation and other forms of male on male sexual intimacy not amounting to anal penetration or its attempt were, by 1888, penalised more leniently using Clause 11 of the Criminal Law Amendment Act. It was the act of anal penetration of males that exercised the judges to exclude this form of sodomy from the more lenient treatment being considered for punishing bestiality, predominantly a crime of youth. Within the category of sodomy between males, the judges were also prepared to consider some leniency in sentencing for boys involved in the crime. It is interesting that the judges appear, by the 1880s, to reflect wider developments in social concerns for the delineation and protection of childhood. Of course, the public campaigns only ever articulated the need to protect girls from sexual coercion in 1885 and the case for special arrangements to reform criminal boys in the late 1880s and the 1890s. The case for protecting boys from sexual preying by men was not articulated in either campaign, but the need to do so was implicit in the scant resurgence of unnatural crime reportage in the press after 1885 and its focus on cases involving men and boys.

The change in judicial attitudes towards sentencing youths involved in unnatural crime cases is indicated by the Home Office evidence. In the prosecution of James Smith in 1877, it is clear that the case came to the attention of the authorities when Post Office officials reported disturbing evidence from their telegraph boys. Smith had shown the telegraph boys implicated in the case, an Italian book of photographs that contained pornographic images of men. Some of the boys talked about this at the Post Office and their superiors reported the case to Scotland Yard. One of the boys arrested by the police, George Wright, was advised by his counsel to 'turn Queen's evidence'. During the trial, he gave details of numerous sexual encounters with Smith, including full sodomy. However, the judge, Justice Manisty, sentenced the boy to ten years penal servitude as well as sentencing Smith to life penal servitude. It is not at all clear from this case whether the boy had been anally penetrated by Smith, or whether Smith had also been penetrated by the boy, but the boy was deemed as guilty of the crime as his adult partner. After the trial, the judge did appeal to the Home Office on Wright's behalf for mitigation of the sentence, arguing that 'the boy Wright has aided the authorities to bring the man Smith to justice'.[72] Wright soon had his sentence mitigated and there was much concern expressed between the judge and the Home Office about the sexual corruption of telegraph boys in the case.[73] However, it is significant that in 1877 the judge felt that he had to convict and sentence Wright so heavily and then conduct mitigation proceedings in confidential communication with the Home Office after the trial. In the Moffatt and Fillingham case, reported in the newspapers in 1886, there was no question that the two boys who gave evidence were also to be charged with gross indecency. Also, in the Hamer case in 1887, there was no indication in this trial for full sodomy, that the boy who gave evidence was also charged and convicted. However, it is clear from the Home Office policy dossiers for 1892–98, that boys under 17 were being convicted of sodomy with males in these years. But the Home Office officials were at pains to ensure in this exercise that no boys convicted of sodomy had been committed by the courts either for sentences greater than 14 months or for sentences involving penal servitude.[74]

Nonetheless, the judges and the Home Office ministers stoutly resisted any legislative clarification of the Buggery laws. Justice Hawkins recommended that the punishment of young offenders in all categories of this crime 'might well be amended by leaving the punishment discretionary with the judge'.[75] Application of judicial discretion and differentiation in sentences for cases of bestiality and sodomy was thrown into disarray by the implementation of the Penal Servitude Act of 1891. The reasons for conducting the policy exercise between 1892 and 1898, ordered by Henry Matthews in April 1892 and continued by Herbert Asquith, the Liberal Home Secretary after the 1892 general election, were twofold. The 1861 Offences Against the Person Act, which stipulated between ten years and life penal servitude for convictions of sodomy, was now at odds with the new Penal Servitude Act, which legislated that sentences of penal servitude should be for no less than three years and no more than five. This legal anomaly notwithstanding, the Home Office had, since the late 1870s, also received several and repeated petitions for remission of life sentences of penal servitude on behalf of men incarcerated for sodomy with males. Some of these individual petitions received powerful and influential support. For instance, Martin Martinelli, a sailor and a subject of the Austrian Empire, was incarcerated for life penal servitude in 1878 for sodomy with a 16-year-old cabin boy on board a British merchant ship. His petition for remission received repeated support from the Austro-Hungarian embassy and ambassador in the late 1870s, the 1880s and again in 1891 after the passing of the Penal Servitude Act. In one of the letters sent to the Home Office in 1879, the Austrian Embassy was in no doubt, in diplomatic terms, that the 'court only arrived at this decision after a conscientious and forensic examination [of the facts] of the very serious accusation made against [Martinelli]'. However, the embassy official questioned whether 'the life sentence is one of exceptional severity', highlighting that 'in Austria, a tribunal could not impose such a severe sentence'.[76]

In 1892, the Home Office was under considerable pressure from individual petitioners, not least from the Austrian embassy, to mitigate the sentences imposed before the 1891 Act. Rather than attempt a revision of the buggery laws, the Home Office was at pains to come to some accommodation of petitioners for those already convicted before the Act. The Home Office also went to considerable lengths to persuade the judges not to pass sentences on new sodomy convicts that were unduly harsh or contravened the Penal Servitude Act and thereby avoid the pressure of need for legislative clarification of the buggery laws. The difficulties inherent in this exercise were highlighted by Godfrey Lushington, permanent under secretary of state since Liddell's death in 1885. Lushington commented that there was

> an unusually wide divergence of opinion evidently [existing] amongst the judges as to the light in which these offences are to be regarded and the severity with which they are to be punished. The anomalies are so great that it is very desirable to mitigate them.[77]

The Home Office officials discovered that, in spite of the judicial review conducted in 1888 and the stipulations of the Penal Servitude Act in 1891, certain judges were persisting in passing sentences of ten years penal servitude or more for cases of sodomy between males. Some of the sentences had been passed against the adult perpetrators of sodomy with boys, reflecting the broader developments in concerns for protection of youth expressed by the judiciary in 1888. The memo which highlighted these anomalies sought the advice of the Lord Chief Justice. In its address to the Lord Chief Justice, Henry Matthews, the Home Secretary acknowledged that

> the offence of sodomy is one which presents more variety in the degree of guilt [than bestiality]. It may be accompanied by corruption of youth, or by abuse of authority, or by deliberation or contrivance, all of them aggrieving [sic] circumstances.

Matthews reminded the Lord Chief Justice of a sodomy case, which he tried 'the day before the Penal Servitude Act came into operation'. The defendant was sentenced to ten years penal servitude for sodomising a boy but the sentence was mitigated to five years in accordance with the new penal servitude rules. Matthews added that

> this recommendation appeared to afford some guide to the treatment which might be properly applied in other cases which preceded the Act. But I observe that in two subsequent cases a sentence of ten years has been passed.

Matthews outlined the cases he referred to. One referred to the incarceration of a sailor who had sodomised a 15-year-old apprentice and appreciated that the crime was 'no doubt committed several times' with the youth. But in the second case, involving 'Canham', a labourer aged 28 and 'Baker', a barman aged 32, Matthews expressed concern that the judge convicted both men caught in the act of anal sex for ten years each. Matthews had enquired of the trial judge as to the aggravating circumstances in this case. The judge replied and was quoted by Matthews as stating that he did not feel 'that there was anything unreasonable in the old statutory minimum as applied to a bad case of real sodomy'. The case was a matter of concern for the Home Office, not least because Baker committed suicide after the trial rather than face ten years penal servitude. Also, Matthews highlighted that similar 'subsequent cases ... which received much milder treatment were [also] cases of real sodomy'.[78]

Matthews was relieved of post with the change of government in August 1892 but his task in this area was continued by Herbert Asquith, the new Liberal Home Secretary. Senior Home Office Officials expressed in memos the hope that some legal clarification might be forthcoming from the new Home Secretary. However, the desire for amendments to the law, motivated by civil servants' sense of administrative efficiency, was not to be satisfied by Asquith. Asquith recommended, as a solution to the problem, the mitigation of sentences for sex upon animals using the Royal Prerogative. Asquith based his formulation on the sentences that had been imposed by judges for this crime since the passing of the Penal Servitude Act in 1891. He stipulated that 'all sentences for bestiality or attempts exceeding six months should be brought before the Secretary of State for consideration'. Asquith recommended that boys under 15 be incarcerated, without penal servitude, for no more than six months and boys between 15 and 21 for no more than nine months. But for crimes of sodomy between males, Asquith stipulated that

> there does not appear to me to be at present any sufficient reason for laying down special rules for the reconsideration of sentences in cases of sodomy or attempted sodomy.[79]

In spite of the complaints of Home Office officials about extending the application of the Royal Prerogative far beyond the intention of its use, it is clear that Asquith, like his predecessors, would rather have lived with the irritation of the Home Office officials who dealt with the administrative chaos of sentencing for sodomy, than risk a political scandal through attempting to clarify the Buggery laws. This state of affairs continued far into the twentieth century.[80] A Home Office memorandum in this series from August 1895 commented that, three years after the sentencing review, 'the sentences for [sodomy] are infinitely various'. The memorandum also highlighted that '[Justice] Day is probably the only judge who now adheres to the former practice of giving twenty years or life sentences of penal servitude'.[81] It is evident that by the end of the nineteenth century, the men of the legislature – and the Home Office – tolerated wide discrepancies in the matter of punishment of sex between males to avoid clarification and public debate of this matter. It does appear that, by 1895, all the judges apart from one were manipulating the existing legal framework to comply with legal changes in prison sentencing. This had the effect of keeping discussion of sodomy out of the public domain. It must be remembered that this contrivance was kept secret from the late nineteenth-century public and, for that matter, the public until the late twentieth century.

Emphasis on the legislative and policy developments surrounding the 1885 Criminal Law Amendment Act are not the only legal factors in Weeks' analysis of the construction of the homosexual. A significant theme developed by Weeks in his later studies is the connection between legislation 'concerning male homosexuality' and legislation controlling female prostitution in the late nineteenth century. In Weeks' important analysis, he argues that 'all homosexual males as a class were equated with female prostitutes' in the period. Weeks makes this argument based on the perspective of the Wolfenden Committee in the late 1950s, which was set up to investigate male homosexuality and female prostitution. Weeks traces the 'juncture of the two concerns' in the 1950s to legislative developments in the late nineteenth century. Weeks bases his analysis of the connection between female prostitution and male homosexual identity on the juxtaposition of legislation 'concerning male homosexuality' with legislation 'designed to control female prostitution', such as the 1885 Criminal Law Amendment Act and the 1898 Vagrancy Act.[82] However, as Walkowitz demonstrates, the campaign that led to the Criminal Law Amendment Act of 1885 concentrated exclusively on the scandal of female child prostitution, not female prostitution in general. The campaign, argues Walkowitz, 'exaggerated the role of children in the social economy of prostitution'.[83] Newspapers, such as *Reynolds News* dubbed the proposed legislation as 'Our Daughters' Protection Bill' and the campaign's sympathies lay 'wholeheartedly with the working-class paterfamilias whose property – his daughter – had been expropriated by the idle rich'.[84] The campaign 'forced the passage of age-of-consent legislation'.[85]

The 1885 Act raised the age of consent for all girls to 16 and did give the police additional powers to prosecute streetwalkers. As stated, Labouchere's Clause 11 was probably added on to this legislation as a wrecking amendment, but inadvertently ended up on the statute books. However, it was the emphasis on child protection in the broader legislation that resulted in the beginnings of official, but secret and often conflicting, delineation of punishments for sex between men and boys and sex between grown men. The newspapers also demonstrated some interest in cases of unnatural crime between men and boys after 1885. But this was the single detectable implication of the juxtaposition of the Criminal Law Amendment Act with Labouchere's Amendment in the aftermath of the legislation. Importantly, Labouchere's Amendment prompted no campaigns whatsoever for the sexual protection of boys from men, similar to that mounted for the sexual protection of girls. Sympathies expressed about protection of boys in Home Office secret correspondence were confined to the particular officials and ministers. Ultimately, discretion in such cases rested with the judge and the Home Secretary. In addition, 'all male homosexuals' were not, in any respect, defined as 'a class' in legal arrangements following Labouchere's Amendment.

Weeks' analysis is also highly problematic in connection with the aspects of the Criminal Law Amendment Act of 1885 that ostensibly controlled female adult prostitution. Bristow, Mort and Walkowitz argue that the Criminal Law Amendment Act stimulated vigilance committees to ensure the enforcement of the Act and forced the police to crack down on solicitation and brothel keeping.[86] However, as F. B. Smith confirms, there was no recognition by the organised campaigns after the Act became law that all sexual acts between men had been criminalised. The amendment was not even mentioned in the 'detailed narrative of the passing of the Bill in the *Annual Register 1885*'.[87] Nor did the Act result in a campaign against 'all male homosexuals as a class', in spite of the zeal of vigilance committees 'imposing a single standard of chastity on men and women'.[88] Also, the effectiveness of the 1885 Act in controlling female prostitution proved very limited, as specific sexual acts had to be proven under this legislation.[89]

It was not until the 1898 Vagrancy Act was introduced, that some attempt was made to achieve effective control over the activities of female prostitutes. The notorious Contagious Diseases Acts of the 1860s, which had allowed the authorities in garrison towns to enforce medical examinations on women suspected of prostitution, had been repealed in 1883, following a vigorous campaign. Repeal had given female prostitutes a form of recognition and state tolerance, not necessarily affected by the Criminal Law Amendment Act in 1885. However, female prostitution remained a perceived problem in 'civic discourse'.[90] Some control of female prostitution was achieved by the 1888 Vagrancy Act. But, as Home Office officials complained in the drafting of the 1898 Bill, the existing legislation could only control 'riotous and indecent behaviour by a prostitute'. The Home Office memorandum highlighted that 'these offences are all offences by women only, and by common prostitutes only'.[91]

There was recognition amongst the Home Office officials drafting the 1898 Bill that singling out women prostitutes did little to tackle the perceived problem of prostitution. This state of affairs also ran the risk of public protest. The repeal of the Contagious Diseases Acts campaign, led by Josephine Butler, had created a 'feminist discourse ... constituted as a politicised language ... in which one could discuss sexual danger'.[92] The Home Office acknowledged that if the legislation was to be meaningful in combating prostitution, then pimps had to be criminalised as well as the prostitutes. Examination of the difficulties in legal categorisation of the pimp, or 'souteneur', is important in the context of control of male prostitution. Legislating for criminalisation of the souteneur proved a challenging legal task for the drafters of the Bill. The Home Office officials identified that the law, as it stood, could not prosecute the souteneur, because the souteneur was not guilty of 'definite acts ... of sexual immorality'. Instead, the problem posed to law by the souteneur was 'not that he commits acts of immorality himself, but that he allows himself to be supported by such acts committed by others. It is not easy to find parallels in the Criminal Law for legislation aimed at conduct of this kind'. The Home Office decided that 'the analogy of the Vagrant's Act' was an obvious potential route to effective prosecution of the souteneur as it was 'especially aimed at a disorderly way of living'. The civil servants at the Home Office recognised that there was 'much difficulty about framing a definition of a souteneur suitable for placing him in this class'. Nonetheless, the Home Office persisted with the Vagrancy legislation to make pimping illegal. The new legislation gave the courts the powers to force a suspected souteneur to 'give a satisfactory account of his means of subsistence'. If the suspect could not do this, then the souteneur could be charged with being 'an idle and disorderly person'.[93]

The Home Office had similar difficulties in the drafting of a formulation that would criminalise both female and male prostitution. One Home Office official[94] pointed out in secret memoranda that

> everyone knows what solicitation by a prostitute means ... but what is meant by a man habitually ... importuning or soliciting for immoral purposes is very difficult to say. The words can scarcely refer to a man importuning a prostitute, for the importunity comes from the other side. Neither can it refer to a man importuning a well conducted woman.[95]

These words could be interpreted as ignorance at the Home Office as to the existence of male prostitution. But this legislation was drafted after the Cleveland Street Scandal of 1889 and the trials of Oscar Wilde in 1895, all involving the presence of male prostitutes. Another letter in this series advised that 'I should include men. ... we have a good deal of solicitation of old men by lads at this time'.[96] The Home Office had great difficulty in providing a separate clause in law that classified the well-known existence of the male prostitute. As the arraignment of the 'Stella and Fanny' trial had demonstrated in 1870, the milieu of the male prostitute had been tacit knowledge throughout the second half of the nineteenth century. Nonetheless, acknowledging the existence of the male prostitute in law would have been tantamount to official recognition of the existence of this milieu. In the final formulation, the officials and their legal advisors provided a clause that was not gender specific or classificatory in its interpretation of importuning. The law criminalised

> every person who, in any street, thoroughfare or public place ... habitually or persistently importunes or solicits any other person or persons for immoral purposes .... The concourse ... of numerous persons ... in ... any public place for immoral purposes shall be deemed a public nuisance and any person who for immoral purposes loiters in or frequents any such concourse or place of resort, shall be deemed an idle and disorderly person.[97]

The Home Office regarded the final formulation as 'the outcome of the notion of the equalisation of the sexes'.[98]

The 1898 Vagrancy Act was also the 'outcome of the notion' that a phenomenon like male prostitution should not be given classificatory recognition. The French penal code only criminalised sex between adults and children. Consensual adult sexual relations, including those between men, were legal in France, as long as they were conducted in private. However, as Greenberg argues: 'decriminalisation by no means eliminated all prejudice, or even legal repression'.[99] The police in Paris had the powers to repress public immorality, including male prostitution. Official repression of male prostitution in Paris fostered the tolerance of medical examination of male prostitutes in police custody. Tardieu's medico-forensic study *Etude Medico-Legal sur les Attentats aux Moeurs*, published in France in 1857, had been based on years of rectal examinations conducted on male prostitutes in police custody. The work gave medico-legal recognition to the existence and the prevalence of male prostitution in Paris.

In Britain, on the other hand, no legal category of male prostitute existed in this period and certainly no medico-legal study of male prostitutes was conducted.[100] Weeks may be correct that the spirit of the Vagrancy Act of 1898 demonstrated the desire to control and repress the activities of the male prostitute, as well as the activities of the female prostitute and the pimp. However, the 1898 Vagrancy Act did not demarcate 'all homosexuals as a class' any more than Labouchere's Amendment had done in 1885. It is impossible to discern from the Calendar of Prisoners or the Judicial Returns the prevalence or the presence of male prostitution in British society following the passing of the 1898 Vagrancy Act. Male prostitutes and souteneurs were charged under this legislation with being idle and disorderly persons. Repeated offenders were charged with being rogues, vagabonds or incorrigible rogues, gradated according to the number of offences committed.[101] There was no differentiation in the category of convict between male prostitutes and souteneurs. Nor, for that matter, were these kinds of vagrants differentiated from other types of idle and disorderly persons, such as beggars and dossers. In British legal records, categories of male prostitutes and pimps were not differentiated until 1954.[102] The legal categorisation of male prostitution in the mid-1950s was commensurate with a long-resisted acceptance in Britain of the medical analysis of homosexuality. These developments were also concomitant with the setting up of the Wolfenden Committee, which led to eventual decriminalisation of sex between men on the grounds that if the phenomenon were somehow a sickness, it could not be criminal.[103] It is arguable that the legal and medical construction of homosexuality in Britain described by Weeks dates from the 1950s, not from the late Victorian period. The British legislature and British society had stoutly resisted the developments in legal and scientific classification of homosexuality that had prevailed in other states, such as Germany and the United States. In doing so, the British could foster ideals of masculinity and manliness, in which the phenomenon of sex between men was perceived as exceedingly rare, compared with other societies.

There is little to suggest in the legal framework for prosecuting sex between men that the British legislature, in the late nineteenth century, purposively constructed through law a concept of homosexual identities. Labouchere's amendment to the Criminal Law Amendment Act in 1885 did not, as historians have claimed, create a legal definition of a homosexual type that then, in turn, constructed notions of this type amongst the general public. The general public, or at least significant sections of urban dwellers demonstrated, throughout the second half of the nineteenth century, a well-developed and tacit understanding of the guises and locations of this sexuality. These males offended and threatened developing perceptions of what was required to attain full adult masculinity. The legislature perpetuated, throughout the second half of the nineteenth century, an archaic, highly inefficient and ambivalent legal framework for prosecuting sex between males. The importance of protecting and bolstering masculinity as central to gender and class structures meant that it was not in the interests of the British state to enquire too deeply or to prosecute this crime efficiently. Even the legislation controlling males soliciting males in 1898 only classified the guilty as vagabonds and rogues, along with pimps, dossers, beggars and female prostitutes. Legal clarification and classification of sexuality between males would have revealed and publicised that this sexuality existed at all.

Clarification would have possibly lent official recognition, albeit negative and criminal, that this form of sexuality was a widespread, individuated and even collective phenomenon amongst British men, as it appeared to be, thanks to the new science of sexology, amongst German, French, Italian and Austrian men. Of course, this sexuality did manifest itself throughout the period and, if the evidence were irrefutable, the state had to act. But it remained a matter of some difficulty to achieve a conviction in trials, even after the introduction of Clause 11 in 1885. In spite of the difficulties in achieving convictions, the public demonstrated willingness, throughout the period, to use the judicial system to punish sex between men, when encountered. Once prosecuted, these males lost the ability to maintain full masculinity. In the late nineteenth century, this would have meant a devastating loss of status, irrespective of class.

After 1885, the state had, at its disposal, a cascade of criminal sexual acts proscribed by legislation that could be applied to any male who forced the authorities, through being caught in a sexual act with another male, to conduct criminal proceedings. Beyond this, the state recoiled from further clarification of this criminal phenomenon. British legislation in this respect is remarkable for how little it was altered throughout the nineteenth century. The alteration in 1885, which simply reiterated the criminality of sexual acts that were already potentially punishable by law, was created more by accident than design. However, this legislation did not have the near-revolutionary effects claimed by historians in this field. Instead, the legislation acted as an accelerator to the already high rates of indictment for crimes of sex between males. Also, the legislation provoked the press into reporting cases of unnatural crime, after a period of silence on the matter that had been maintained for 13 years. But the focus of newspaper reporting was quite different from the patterns detectable before 1872. The newspapers were, predominantly, interested in cases that involved sex between men and boys. Although the legislation did not differentiate in this matter, the protection of childhood appears to have interested these publications far more than reporting potentially destabilising cases of sex between consenting adult males. This new concern with protecting boys is also detectable in secret Home Office sentencing policies for the period. However, unlike the concomitant and highly articulate campaigns for the protection of girls from sexual coercion, the similar need to protect boys did not feature in the discourse. Protection and delineation of boyhood in the matter of sex between males is detectable after 1885, but the need to do so remained ambivalent and imprecisely defined. This ambivalence remained in prosecuting sex between males for almost all of the twentieth century.

Throughout the period, legal definition of sexuality between men was a matter that the state preferred to ignore and was not a priority for legal clarification. Policies to distinguish between crimes of bestiality, sodomising of boys and sodomy between men, were only conducted when the Home Office was forced to do so. Campaigns for reform of punishments for juvenile offenders and reform of the penal servitude system in the late nineteenth century did not conceptualise or articulate the need to reform the laws which made sex between all males illegal. However, these campaigns and the concomitant legislative changes forced an unwilling Home Office, almost in parentheses, to bring some cohesion to the chaos of sentencing apparent in the punishment of anal sex between males and sex between males and animals. These changes, kept secret by the state until very recently, resulted in extraordinary powers being given to the judges and the Home Secretary in the matter. Men prosecuted for anal sex with each other were completely at the mercy of the sensibility of the judge and could be incarcerated for time ranging from months, years, or life. The judges and the Home Office were happier to accept the chaos of unfair, uneven treatments and a bewildering array of petitions for mitigation of punishment, than risk an internationally embarrassing public debate by clarifying the clearly unworkable buggery laws in parliament. By 1900, British masculinity was being deliberately projected, by both political parties, as the pre-eminent moral exemplar throughout the expanding Empire and in comparison to its Continental neighbours. Also, masculinity as a social status had increasingly become an aspiration for and expectation of, enfranchised working-class men. It would have been unthinkable, in this context, to question this image by indulging in the kind of debate that would be needed legally to clarify or classify a homosexual 'type' or 'class'.

5
Resistance

As we have seen, historians of homosexuality have argued, until recently, that developments in sex psychology and the power of this new discipline in the late nineteenth century were central to the construction of modern homosexual identities. Oosterhuis' important study takes this analysis even further, pointing out that homosexual identities in this period could only be formulated through direct interaction with sex psychologists, such as Krafft-Ebing. Krafft-Ebing and his male, homosexual correspondents lived in the Austrian Empire, German Reich and France. In these nations, there was a grudging social acceptance of the psychiatrist of the sexual and the milieu of the homosexual. The homosexual and his world remained marginal to the bulk of respectable European society. However, the works of Krafft-Ebing and others in his field were published in repeated editions and Krafft-Ebing received a large correspondence from homosexual men throughout Continental Europe. The works of Continental sex psychologists, which examined sexuality between men were not, however, tolerated in Britain. This chapter examines the culture of resistance in Britain to Continental works of 'inversion theorisation'. Resistance to such ideas also prevented the development of inversion theorisation as a domestic scientific discipline. The culture of resistance in Britain problematises arguments for the purposive medico-legal construction of homosexual identities in this period. With one or two notable exceptions, Krafft-Ebing received no correspondence from Britain in this period.[1] Also, the works of Krafft-Ebing were available only in limited pirated editions and, when regarded at all by the medical authorities in this country, were considered to be little more than scientistic pornography.[2]

Since Weeks' publications, historians have tended to argue that nineteenth-century sexology worked, in conjunction with developing legal repressions, to construct a pathologised and criminal perception of the male homosexual. An examination of British cultural attitudes to the matter of sex and sexuality between men in the period reveals that even pejorative analysis of this phenomenon could not be countenanced in public discourse. As late as 1909, this sensibility was prevalent in a review in the *British Medical Journal* of Edward Carpenter's highly anaemic apologia for same-sex relationships, *The Intermediate Sex*, first published in 1906. The review excoriated the work and recommended that 'urnings' ought to

> emigrate to some land where their presence might be welcome, and thus serious people in England might be spared the waste of time reading a low-priced book of no scientific or literary merit, advocating the culture of unnatural and criminal practices.[3]

The *British Medical Journal*, undoubted organ of medical authority in this period, clearly regarded the subject of sex between men as not only not fit for serious enquiry, but the perpetrators of the vice had no place British society.

Following Foucault's refutation of the 'repressive hypothesis', historians of nineteenth-century sexuality in Britain have given emphasis to the large volume of discursive texts on matters of sexuality available in 'The West' in this period. Although this historiography has done much to collapse 'Victorian' sexual stereotypes, in *The Facts of Life: the Creation of Sexual Knowledge in Britain, 1650–1950* (1995), Roy Porter and Lesley Hall highlight that 'there is a risk of setting up new and equally misleading generalisations' in historicising sexuality in the period.[4] Scientific commentary upon general matters of the sexual, even tracts which concentrated only on the procreative aspects of sex, had an uneasy and perilous existence in late nineteenth-century Britain. Also, Porter and Hall argue that the 'widespread sexual anxieties and inhibitions' that prevailed at the time 'should not be minimised'.[5] Their study has done much to chart the difficulties in developments of 'sexual science' in Britain in the late nineteenth and early twentieth centuries, albeit in a truncated account of the broad range of developments in this country. This chapter concentrates on the specific and extreme difficulties associated with the publication and public discussion of scientific interpretations of sexuality between men in Britain and the reasons for a culture of resistance to these kinds of developments. The use of the term 'culture of resistance' in this context is important. Resistance, in a Foucauldian sense, suggests an outpouring of sexualised discourse against a cultural backdrop of ignorance and silence – in other words, a will to knowledge. However, in examining the perspective of the Victorian British in the matter, resistance is more appropriately illustrative of the attempts to suppress an explosion of continental discourse, particularly in the field of inversion theorisation. Taking account of these difficulties is important in examining sexuality between men in Britain, particularly in the light of the Oosterhuisian interpretation of (homo)sexual identity formation in the late nineteenth century.

The peculiarly British problem with this matter attracted the incisive commentary of George Bernard Shaw. In 1898, Shaw stated that he had been concerned with the hostility in Britain towards a predilection 'which involved no danger whatever to society'. Many years earlier, Shaw's attention to the harshness of treatment in Britain 'to the subject' had been attracted by 'the passing of a sentence of twenty years' penal servitude on a harmless elderly gentleman'. This so shocked Shaw's sense of 'common humanity' that he 'made an attempt to get the press to protest'. He experienced nothing but hostility from journalists. As we have seen, the national newspapers recoiled from even commenting upon the bare facts of trials for sex between men between 1872 and 1885. Shaw's plea, based upon 'common humanity', was highly unlikely, in an atmosphere of press silence upon the subject, to result in a campaign for relaxation or public discussion of British law on the matter. Shaw discovered why his call for a press campaign was unsuccessful, stating that he

> discovered that the fear of becoming suspected of personal reasons for desiring a change in the law in this matter, makes every Englishman an abject coward. ... and professing in public and in print views which have not the slightest resemblance to those which he expresses in private conversation with thoughtful and educated men.

Shaw had great difficulty countenancing the hypocrisy that pervaded British society on this 'subject'. Shaw's letter confirms that in public, it was impossible for men to express anything other than ignorance of the phenomenon or the deepest condemnation and personal distancing from it. But in private and amongst elite and educated circles, tacit understanding of the phenomenon was apparent. This dichotomy in values observed by Shaw of his contemporaries is significant. It illustrates the ability of the government, the press men and the reading public to subsume and 'forget' the widespread and sophisticated knowledge of sex and sexuality between men, as demonstrated at the arraignment of

'Stella and Fanny' in 1870.[6] Shaw, ever the maverick and counter-cultural radical in his own time, found it unconscionable that educated British men could tolerate this hypocrisy, to the extent that sex between men could be punished so severely and without protest. He demonstrated that hypocrisy in this matter had resulted in cruel and unusual treatment for those unfortunate enough to be prosecuted, particularly when the sentence was compared with the 'trifle' of the 'punishment of a man who batters his wife almost to death'.[7] However, even Shaw refrained from naming the 'subject' to which he was referring.

The occasion for Shaw's outburst, albeit in a highly marginal publication called *The Adult*, was the prosecution for obscene libel and banning of Havelock Ellis' work *Sexual Inversion* in 1898. Both *The Adult* and the process of banning Ellis' work will be examined in this chapter. Shaw railed against the hypocrisy of there being

> no authoritative scientific book on the subject within the reach of Englishmen and Englishwomen who cannot read French or German. ... in Germany and France the free circulation of such works ... has done a good deal to make the public understand that decency and sympathy are as necessary in dealing with sexual as well as with any other subject.[8]

Shaw's reflections on 'the subject' indicated that the British public could not tolerate any discussion, either scientific or otherwise, about sex and sexuality between men. Ellis' biographer, Phyllis Grosskurth, regards the near-total clampdown on Ellis' work as resulting from the furore of the Oscar Wilde trials in 1895 and his release from prison in 1897.[9] This prominent and scandalous series of events undoubtedly had their effects in the year that Ellis decided to publish; however, too much emphasis on the Wilde scandals alone detracts from the culture of resistance to works like *Sexual Inversion* throughout the mid-to-late nineteenth century in this country. The phenomenon of banning scientific works like *Sexual Inversion* in Britain has to be regarded as a 'culture of resistance'. Hostility to inversion sexology was not simply a matter of resisting the flood of new Continental ideas from streaming into British society and culture. Had it been so, then a Foucauldian analysis of the phenomenon could conclude that Victorian Britain was little more than an example of cultural ignorance and silence that discourse attempted to resist. But Britain in the nineteenth century should, ostensibly, have been at the forefront of an understanding of and a scientific approach to a phenomenon like sexuality between men. After all, British philosophical and scientific thinking had stimulated widespread enquiry in the West into other contentious matters of the sexual.

English philosophical works, such as T. R. Malthus' *Essay on the Principle of Population*, published in 1798, rationalised and problematised, for the first time, procreative sexuality and the need to limit population numbers. Although Malthus made no comment upon sex between men, his problematisation of sex suggested to some the need to control conception by artificial means. In this analysis, which accepted the pleasure of sex and the need to control the birth rate, non-procreative sexual phenomena, like masturbation and sex between men, merited examination.[10] These implications of the Malthusian analysis of artificially controlling procreativity and procreative sex, found little expression in this country in the first half of the nineteenth century. As Porter and Hall state, in this period 'birth-controlling voices were a tiny and precarious minority'. Medical treatises on new-found problems of sexuality abounded in these years. Yet the tendency in most of these texts was to pathologise a range of sexual activity, including masturbation and excessive intercourse. Significantly, the phenomenon of sexuality between men received no mention in the context of this discourse. Undoubtedly, the problems of excessive procreation underlined by Malthus received attention in Britain, but British culture resisted the development of practical solutions to prevent conception and toleration of non-procreative heterosexual activity. Instead, medical and quasi-medical advice manuals increasingly promulgated a culture of 'self-command' and 'abstinence', even within marriage.[11]

Later in the century, Charles Darwin's groundbreaking study, *The Descent of Man and Selection in Relation to Sex* (1871) opened the way for the study of the sexual as a 'natural' phenomenon, distinct from its pathological treatment by medical interpretations for much of the century. This approach to the study of the sexual, and sexuality between men in particular, did not gain acceptance in Britain until well into the twentieth century. However, Darwin's analysis was used by continental sexologists to 'prove that heterosexuality was a natural norm for higher forms of life and that perversions like homosexuality were necessarily abnormal'.[12] Darwin's thinking was significant in the ideas and methodology of Krafft-Ebing's work.[13] Krafft-Ebing, Magnus Hirschfeld, Carl Westphal and other sex psychologists were heavily influenced by the concept of 'psychophysical intermediacy' in the work of Karl Ulrichs.

In the 1870s, Ulrichs, a German jurist who campaigned for greater toleration of sex between men, used Darwin's ideas to argue that sexual intermediacy, or homosexuality, was a naturally occurring phenomenon and created in foetal development. Darwin regarded masculinity and femininity 'not as static properties, but as malleable functions that depended on the contribution any given trait made to the survival and reproductive success of the organism'.[14] Ulrichs and others used the concept of gender mutability to argue that the human species could create an abnormal, but naturally occurring, biologically intermediate type. In doing so, these sexologists also created the polarised notion and category of 'heterosexuality' as the union of the 'fully male and the fully female'.[15] Ulrichs and others used evolutionary theories of intermediacy to argue for the suspension of criminal punishment for sex between men, as the intermediate was a naturally occurring, abnormal phenomenon.

This notwithstanding, the uses of Darwin's theories in the matter of sexuality between men received no attention, development or discussion in Britain in this period. Undoubtedly, the Continental thinkers who adapted Darwin's theories to the new discipline of inversion theorisation, had also had a century of German philosophical tradition to build upon. These traditions in German thinking had fostered a forensic approach to the question of sex between men during the nineteenth century.[16] However, it was the ideas of Darwin that provided the analytical departure for theories of inversion. The reluctance of British culture to adopt the implications of its rational theorists, scientists and polemicists is well established by historians. For example, ideas of the contractual political state espoused by Locke found far more resonance and expression in France and the United States than they ever did in Britain in the eighteenth and much of the nineteenth centuries.[17] In the name of stability and preservation of social order, British society resisted and often ignored the literal interpretations and application of the ideas of its political philosophers that had underpinned revolutions and counter-revolutions in France and other Continental states throughout the century. The history of fundamental political and social upheavals and revolutions and the pervasive presence of the military in continental states during the nineteenth century might also explain why, to some extent, these societies had less difficulties in absorbing philosophical and scientific thought that led, amongst other things, to a tolerance of inversion theories in the late nineteenth century. Conversely, British political masters throughout the nineteenth century pointed to the dissolute morality and propensity to insurrection on the Continent, and cited superior British morality, including the sexual, as the reasons for the continued and unique stability and prosperity of the British nation in the period.[18]

By the mid-century, however, it was statistically demonstrable through the census that Britain was not only expanding in population at an exponential rate but had also become the first predominantly urban society. Much concern was expressed at the time and for the remainder of the century about this explosion in population and change in social demography. In 1854, a neo-Malthusian doctor, George Drysdale, published the radical text *Elements of Social Science, or Physical, Sexual and Natural Religion: an Exposition of the True Cause and Only Cure of the Three Primary Social Evils: Poverty, Prostitution and Celibacy*. The novel interpretation of Malthus' philosophy inherent in *Elements* has been examined by Porter and Hall and in detail by Michael Mason and J. Miriam Benn. Drysdale was part of a small group of radical free thinkers in the mid-nineteenth century, who deplored the lack of analysis and discussion of sexual problems in medical journals. Drysdale's work propounded the view that non-procreative sexual activity between men and women was healthy and normal and that procreation should be limited, not by abstinence, but by use of contraceptive methods. The link between Drysdale's work and the proscribed campaigns for family limitation in the 1870s is well established by historians.[19] However, Drysdale also briefly examined the phenomenon of same-sex relationships. This aspect of Drysdale's work and its significance has not been examined by historians. Its inclusion in *Elements* represents unique commentary on this subject and is of importance in the assessment of knowledge of sexuality between men (and, for that matter, between women) in Britain in the period.

Elements was published in repeated editions between 1854 and the First World War.[20] In *Elements*, Drysdale explored the existence of sexuality between men in the context of an examination of prostitution, taking the 'opportunity of saying a few words on the subject of *unnatural vices*'.[21] Drysdale explained to his readership that the unnatural vices were 'very common in Paris, in London and other large cities'. However, there was a fundamental problem in examining the unnatural vices as, in British society 'a subject like this is generally held to be an unspeakable one, as if it would soil both him who talks of it and those who listen'. Drysdale railed against men of knowledge from shying away from examination of unnatural vices. He had

little sympathy with this rose-water morality; which cannot bear to scrutinise the deeds of our fellow beings, nor even hear of things which are daily done and suffered. Such scruples are as alien to the heart of the true moralist, as it would be for the true physician to shun the infectious disease.

Drysdale went so far as to accuse his contemporaries of: 'an inherent weakness and effeminacy of the mind' for 'the very dread of approaching such subjects'. He regarded his educated fellow men as becoming like women upon this subject. The minds of women, according to Drysdale, were 'so underdeveloped ... unreal and effeminate', because they were 'debarred from studying the phases of vice ... in the moral world'.[22]

Although Drysdale was convinced that the vice of 'sodomy, or the intercourse of two persons of the same sex' was common enough between men, the secrecy surrounding the subject meant that his exploration was a venture into *terra incognita*. Significantly, sodomy exclusively meant, for Drysdale, penetrative anal sex between males. In his brief exploration of the subject, he did not allude to practices of bestiality in his description of the unnatural vices. Also, sexuality between women received separate treatment by him in the section on unnatural vices and this 'class' was described by him as 'tribades'. Drysdale highlighted the incidence of sodomy in prisons, but also indicated, from his experience as a physician, its prevalence in the venereal hospitals. Drysdale described men with

> gonorrhoea or chancre of the anus, which the patients, when pressed hard, either confess, or tacitly admit to have been contracted by these unnatural practices; although at first they always deny that the disease has such an origin, and ascribe it to an unclean water closet, &c.

Drysdale also made a brief and somewhat confused allusion to the phenomenon in the writings of Voltaire and Rabelais, amongst the ancients and more recent monarchs. He acknowledged his own lack of knowledge on the subject and his examination was a 'demand [for] a much more earnest treatment, than either jesting allusions or impotent avoidance of the subject'. However, Drysdale had his own theories as to why sodomy was so prevalent in contemporary society. He insisted that prurient, but stringent, morality with regard to all but uxorious sex was the creator of a range of sexual problems, including unnatural vices. Drysdale stated that

> the whole subject of unnatural vices ... requires to be regarded in a very different light, from that, which is usual at present. ... The present harsh views of sexual morality give ... an underhand and

degraded position to all unmarried intercourse, which is very favourable to the growth of the unnatural propensities.[23]

Drysale, who advocated 'due exercise [of the generative organs] from the time of their maturity'[24], clearly regarded the prevalence of sodomy as being due to the restriction of sex and sexuality to a strictly uxorious and procreative expression. Drysdale did not advocate or approve of sodomy and other unnatural sexual practices between men, regarding them as 'evils of such gravity [that] point to a serious want of reverence for nature'.[25] This notwithstanding, Drysdale argued that a society that had, through moral rectitude, created the propensity for sex between men, should critically re-examine its attitude towards the vice, if only to understand and help eradicate it. Advocating a philosophy of free 'normal sexual love', Drysdale suggested that

the true mode of eradicating these unnatural vices, is not to regard with horror ... those who indulge in them; but with a loving and reverential spirit to examine into their nature, and remove their causes by the light of a true physical religion. ... As long as ... all unmarried love is regarded in a harsh and degrading light ... so long will ... unnatural vices flourish, and it will be out of human power to suppress them.

Drysdale argued that the climate of fear and harsh punishment surrounding sex between men

provokes people into the commission of the acts it reprobates. ... The moral guilt ascribed to such acts, which many people regard with as much horror as they do murder ... is quite out of proportion ... and this unsound physical basis shakes ... the moral superstructure.[26]

Drysdale provided, in effect, a reverse and counter-cultural analysis of the pervading attitudes towards sex between men and its perpetrators. Although his work was successfully published, *Elements* provides evidence of the contemporaneous unacceptability of all sexuality, except procreative uxorious intercourse. Drysdale's *Elements* spawned work advocating contraception and family limitation, such as the tracts published by Charles Bradlaugh and Annie Besant in the 1870s. However, these and other works were the subject of legal prosecution and suppression. Porter and Hall argue that *Elements* avoided prosecution because it was 'chiefly a philosophical, medical and political justification for the artificial limitation of families rather than a birth-control tract as such'.[27] Similarly, Drysdale's analysis of unnatural vices provided the philosophical justification for enquiry into the subject, rather than any kind of detailed examination of the phenomenon. Unlike the spread of birth-control literature influenced by its publication, *Elements* had no effect in stimulating either a change in societal attitudes towards sex and sexuality between men, or a tolerated domestic scientific enquiry into the phenomenon. It is significant that in the 1905 edition of *Elements*, Drysdale's analysis of British society's problems with the subject and the plea for enlightened enquiry remained unabridged.[28]

One of the main aims of Drysdale's work was to improve the discussion of sexual problems in medical journals. However, *Elements* was ignored by the medical journals and lambasted in lay journals for its blasphemy and immorality.[29] British medical journals are notable in the second half of the nineteenth century for a near absence of discussion on the subject of sexuality between men, particularly in comparison to Continental European or American productions. In the United States, the Surgeon General's Office had, from the early 1880s, undertaken cumulatively to index by subject all medical journal articles published in all countries. This vast undertaking, conducted alphabetically by subject and published piecemeal as each alphabetical section was completed, took nearly two decades to compile. The work formed the basis of the internationally recognised but American organised *Index Medicus* in the first decade of the twentieth century. The *Index-Catalogue of the Library of the Surgeon-General's Office* catalogued sexuality between men, in 1892, as sodomy.[30] The *Index-Catalogue* listed 51 medical journal articles addressing the subject. The earliest article listed dated from 1828; however, all but five articles were published after 1863 and the majority listed were published between 1876 and 1891. Significantly, only one article was written and published in the English language and this article was published in Philadelphia, USA, in 1886 by an American doctor, reporting on an 'epidemic of gonorrhoea contracted from rectal coition'.[31] The remainder were entirely Continental European publications. The articles were predominantly in either French or German, with three published in Italian. Other American articles, not indicated in the *Index-Catalogue*, such as those carried in the Missouri publication, *The Alienist and the Neurologist*, discussed sex and sexuality between men in the context of broader 'perversions' in sexual matters.

A rare exception to this pattern of excluding or ignoring the subject of sexuality between men in British medical journals is contained, albeit very briefly, in an article carried in the *Medical Times and Gazette* in 1867.

The anonymous article, entitled 'Aberrations of the Sexual Instinct', offered a compendium of aberrant sexuality for use by the medical man. The article fell far short of what Drysdale would have regarded as an adequate medical analysis of the sexual. Nonetheless, the article merits examination because it highlights the chasm in thinking between philosophical tracts such as Drysdale's and the British medical establishment. The article declared what it regarded as the normal sexual instinct:

> The propositions laid down in the Marriage Service of the English Church seem to embody the common sense of the matter, wherein they state that marriage is ordained for three purposes – (1) the procreation and the due education of children; (2) the avoidance of incontinence; (3) the mutual society ... of the married pair. Any union of the sexes in which provision is not made for fulfilling every one of these purposes may be proved contrary to natural law, using that word in its widest sense.[32]

The author intended from the outset to establish that uxorious sexuality, preferably the English and Anglican manifestation of this state, was to be the universal and scientific benchmark of normality for British doctors. The article listed and detailed a variety of aberrations for examination, most of which affected women. The pathologisation of women in this context is not surprising. As Ornella Moscucci argues, in medical thinking in this period, women had become

> by definition, disease or disorder, a deviation from the standard of health represented by the male. ... Not only did woman's biological functions blur into disease, they were also the source of a host of psychological disorders.[33]

The sexual aberrations listed in the article included masturbation, sexual incontinence amongst women, especially amongst 'women of the Celtic race' transplanted to towns, infanticide, family limitation within marriage, being unmarried, being 'free lovers', 'spiritualists', 'Bible Communists', 'Mormons', and 'androgynism', which the author interpreted as 'the intrusion of one sex into the other's province'. Most of the author's 'evidence' of androgynous aberrations emanated from the United States, where women were, apparently

> thrown ... into a thousand restless agitations; ... into public hysteria; ... table-rapping; ... anti-wedlock societies; ... theories about natural

marriage, free-love, ... anti-offspring resolutions, ... sectarian poly-
gamy ... [and] community of wives.

The author ascribed these phenomena in America to the scarcity of
women in American society, but felt it wise to warn British doctors
about them. Even though Britain had 'a superabundence of women',
similar propensities were being experienced amongst British women, for
the diametrically opposite assumption of 'a want of husbands'. In the
midst of this author's lengthy and misogynistic catalogue of sexual
'aberrations' was a reference to sexuality between men. Unlike other
aberrant categories, which mostly affected women, the author was elusive about the male aberration he was referring to and avoided detailed
description:

> To complete this summary of selfish sensualities, we need only
> allude, in passing, to those dark crimes which, as the law says, are not
> to be named of Christian men, and which are shortly catalogued in
> the Epistle of the Romans, Casper's 'Medical Jurisprudence', Gall and
> Spurzheim's 'Phrenology'. They illustrate the dangers of unchaste
> thought, even without unchaste act.[34]

The article advised the British doctor of references to contemporary
Germanic medical commentary on the unnameable subject, with priority
given to Saint Paul for guidance in this matter. The article gives evidence
to a fundamental avoidance of this subject amongst British medical
men, at a time when the broader fields of British surgical and diagnostic
methods, hospital design and administration, and nursing methods
were at the forefront of international medical developments.[35] It is clear
that British doctors, unlike some of their Continental counterparts,
resisted developing philosophical and scientific analyses that might
have fostered medical enquiry into sexuality between men.

This anomaly in professional thinking amongst British doctors was
highlighted by a review article in the *Journal of Mental Science (JMS)* in
1871. First published in 1859, the journal represented the professionali-
sation and specialisation of psychiatrists, or 'alienists'[36] as psychiatric
practitioners called themselves in this period, as distinct from other
medical doctors and medical practice. *JMS* also carried articles on developments in asylum practice and management. The journal was edited
from its inception by Dr Hack Tuke (1827–95), a London physician who
established himself as a renowned specialist in mental disease in the second half of the nineteenth century.[37] In 1871, the journal ran an article

reviewing the quality of German 'Medico-Psychological' literature and included in the review a reference to Carl Westphal's *Die Contrare Sexual Empfindung*, published in Germany in 1869. Wesphal's work, translated by *JMS* as 'The Inverted Sexual Proclivity' was the first work to define 'contrary sexual feeling' as a psychological illness and formed the basis for a century of homosexual pathologisation by psychiatrists.[38] *JMS* did not indulge in an extensive review of Westphal's work, but attempted to attract the interest of psychiatrists by highlighting one of Westphal's case studies, which was

> that of a man who, habitually, from love of it, dressed in women's clothes. In him the only anatomical foundation for this choice was that the testicles easily ascended into the inguinal canals. His face had a slightly feminine appearance.[39]

The timing of this review in Britain is significant. Westphal's work had been in print, in Germany, for three years and had been ignored by the British medical journals, including *JMS*. Also, Westphal's work was of the first importance in introducing the concept of 'inversion' amongst French and German doctors.[40] The review article regarded the work of Westphal and other German alienists, who wrote on subjects such as 'chorea', 'paralytic dementia' and other diseases of the nerves and the brain, as far superior to anything in the field in Britain:

> It need hardly be said that the scientific analysis of the symptoms and *post mortem* appearances is excellent to an extent which only Germans can often reach.[41]

This commentary upon the relative backwardness in Britain in the field of the alienist, especially in the examination of the sexual, and the encouragement given by *JMS* to British alienists to examine Westphal's work, is best understood through the widespread media attention paid to the 'Stella and Fanny' arraignment of 1870 and the Westminster Hall trial of July 1871. The *JMS* review was published in October 1871, three months after the notorious 'Stella and Fanny' trial. As editor, Tuke clearly realised that, after such widespread publicity given to the cross-dressed defendants in the trial, the subject of cross-dressing in men, at the very least, had briefly entered the public domain. Also, an examination of the fate of the usefulness of the 'physical' signs of sodomy in the 'Stella and Fanny' trials suggests why *JMS* chose to highlight Westphal's work and its emphasis on the psychological approach to the question of

sexuality between men. As seen in Chapter 3, the Bow Street arraignment in 1870 revealed widespread but tacit knowledge of sexuality
between men and its various guises. The trial in 1871 also demonstrated
the capacity of the British mainstream press and the legal authorities to
suppress this painful knowledge and present a public discourse of 'ignorance' of the matter. This was achieved to such an extent in 1871 that
the coverage of the trial served to demonstrate to the world that 'Stella
and Fanny' were rare and vilified occurrences amongst British men. This
presentation of masculinity in Britain was enhanced by the medical
evidence given at the trial.

The evidence of medical men in the trial has been examined by
almost every historian in this field. The lack of medical expertise in the
field of sexuality between men has been used by historians, especially in
the Weeks/Foucault tradition, to demonstrate that sexuality between
men and 'homosexuality' were barely understood in society at this time.
However, examination of the broader context of the trial reveals a
sophisticated and widespread, but tacit and anxious knowledge of sexuality between men and 'types' that might engage in this kind of unnatural vice.[42] Ivan Crozier argues that the 'Stella and Fanny' trial did not
'construct the legal conception of homosexual identity'. The trial constructed, according to Crozier, a discourse on sodomy for the medical
profession in a legal setting 'by dealing entirely with the physical signs
attendant on whether or not anal penetration had taken place'.[43] The
case was repeatedly published in Taylor's *Medical Jurisprudence* well into
the twentieth century and Crozier emphasises that seven medical
practitioners gave evidence at the trial. However, the presence of the
'Stella and Fanny' trial in Taylor's did not construct a discourse for medical men in this context. Rather, the 'Stella and Fanny' trial served as
a warning to medical men not to meddle or comment in legal cases
concerning sex between men.

Historians have tended to emphasise the ignorance expressed by
Dr Paul, chief medical witness in the 'Stella and Fanny' trial, about the
'clinical details' in examination of a prisoner suspected of sodomy.
However, close examination of the trial transcript reveals that a medical
examination of this nature was most unusual in these kinds of trials. In
the numerous trials for unnatural crime reported in *The Times* between
1861 and 1872, no mention is given to the necessity of a medical examination to establish evidence. All other trials in the period relied on the
evidence of one or more witnesses to 'penetration'. Similarly, in trials
reported after 1885, when *The Times* resumed interest in some of
the cases of unnatural crime in the courts, no references were made to

the admission of medical examination as evidence. Arguably, the 'Stella and Fanny' trial was unique in this period for its involvement of medical men at all.

The presence of medical evidence in the case was something of an accident in decision making at Bow Street police station when Boulton and Park, or 'Stella and Fanny', were arrested. Under cross-examination at the Westminster Hall trial the following year, Dr Paul revealed that he had examined the defendants without a magistrate's order. Paul was evasive in his answers, but the defence barrister, Mr Digby-Seymour, pressed the point: 'had you received any magistrate's order or any authority to make this examination?'.[44] It transpired that the station sergeant had asked Paul to examine the prisoners, to 'ascertain their sex', given that they were arrested in women's clothes. It was Paul himself who decided to 'ascertain something more' in the case by also conducting rectal examinations of the defendants. Paul's medical findings were then included in the Bow Street arraignment that followed Boulton and Park's arrest and were key factors in the prisoners being refused bail.

When pressed during the trial in 1871, Paul revealed that the additional examination was 'an idea from my own reading'. Paul's reading had consisted of Taylor's *Medical Jurisprudence*, studied over 20 years prior to the medical examination of Boulton and Park.[45] This text, first published in the 1840s, elusively defined sodomy as 'the unnatural connection of man with man'. Taylor also noted that sodomy was 'commonly sufficiently proved without medical evidence'.[46] Paul had also admitted in the trial to reading the works of Tardieu and brought a copy of the work to the proceedings. Tardieu had published, in France in 1857, his forensic study, *Etude Medico-Legal sur les Attentats aux Moeurs* [Medico-Legal Study of Crimes Against Public Morals] and the work was published in repeated editions. His study, based upon years of rectal examinations conducted on male prostitutes in Paris, claimed to identify the 'pederast by telltale signs, such as a funnel-shaped anus in the receptive partner'.[47] When pressed, Paul revealed that he had only read Tardieu after his examination of Boulton and Park. The court was told that Tardieu's study was 'the work of a French surgeon ... relating to these unpleasant matters and specially devoted to them'.[48] When asked by the defence how he became aware of such a work, Paul answered that he had read the work following 'an anonymous letter that I had received'.[49]

The use of medical evidence in the manner demonstrated in the 'Stella and Fanny' trial was unique in its time, to the extent that the case remained infamous for decades after. The reason why there was so much

in the way of medical evidence was the persistence of the defence council in demonstrating to the court the arbitrary and unusual incidence of
a medical examination in cases of this kind. The other medical practitioners that gave evidence, summoned by the defence council, concluded that sodomy could not be categorically proved by physical
examination. Two of the surgeons, Mr Gibson, Surgeon to the Gaol at
Newgate and Mr Frederic le Gros Clark, examiner at the University of
London and the Royal College of Surgeons, had been summoned as an
expert, independent witness. They had been ordered to examine
Boulton and Park six weeks after their arrest. The purpose of this was to
corroborate Paul's medical evidence, and they found that their examinations showed no conclusive evidence of sodomy. This evidence,
examined in some detail by Crozier, suggested in a legal framework and
setting that sodomy was sufficiently rare amongst English men for there
to be a lack of expertise in this field. As Crozier argues, the trial

> did much to suggest that sodomy was a rare thing in Britain, again
> tacitly juxtaposed with the immense amount of Continental knowl-
> edge on the subject, supposedly due to the wider existence of such
> practices across the channel.[50]

In other words, to allow doctors to develop diagnostic tests for the
'signs' of this culturally well-understood phenomenon, would have constituted a public admission that this disturbing sexuality existed
amongst British men at all.

By the end of the trial, Paul's medical evidence of sodomy had, in the
face of other expert witnesses, collapsed. Dr Paul appeared, in the face of
such eminent surgeons, as a humble and not very well-read surgeon to
a police station, who acted upon his own authority and with malicious
intent to conduct an inappropriate and unfounded medical examination. His attempts to use Continental medical literature to defend his
actions after the examination, appeared, at the trial, as a rather desper-
ate attempt to lend scientific authority to his decision. In the Lord Chief
Justice's summary, Paul was lambasted for 'studying foreign works upon
this subject' and singled out for particular opprobrium for involving
medical testimonies at all in the trial:

> He goes to Bow Street; he is desired by the police to examine these
> men; he is told to examine them simply with reference to their sex;
> but it occurs to him that he will examine them for something more;
> he will see whether they are in the habit of practising this vice and he

desires them to expose their persons to him, when he had no more authority to call upon them to undergo this revolting examination than if he had caught a man in the street and asked him to unbutton his breeches and let him see what was behind.[51]

Paul, who had started the trial as the prosecution's expert witness, ended the trial with his moral character seriously in question. The Lord Chief Justice questioned Paul's own propensities and 'desires' in this matter, for consulting Continental works on the subject and initiating an unauthorised 'revolting examination'. Paul was warned in the summary:

> In future ... know better than to take upon himself without the direction of a magistrate, and without the direction even of the police, the responsibility of enquiring into such a thing as this.

The Lord Chief Justice added that, had the defendants not been 'effeminate young men' but 'a man having the strength and energy to do it, he would not have escaped summary punishment for proposing so revolting a thing'. In this statement, the top common law judge in the kingdom appeared to endorse physical assault of a Crown surgeon, should a similar examination be suggested in future cases.[52] It is little wonder, following this trial, that this kind of evidence did not appear in subsequent sodomy cases in the period. The Lord Chief Justice's comments also enshrined in English case law a notion of the inviolate and impenetrable nature of a man's body, irrespective of his social status or the crime of which he was suspected. This ruling appears especially poignant at a time when the Contagious Diseases Acts of 1864, 1868 and 1869 had empowered the state to enforce the medical examination of the bodies of women suspected of prostitution in garrison towns.

The evidence of one of the surgeons during the trial also suggests why knowledge of the physical signs of sodomy, should they have existed at all, was rare amongst British practitioners. Mr Richard Barwell, surgeon to Charing Cross Hospital, was called to give evidence because he had treated Park for a sore in the anus in early 1870. Barwell attested that Park's condition was not a venereal disease of the rectum. Here, he was contradicting his own evidence, which the surgeon had given at the arraignment in 1870. Barwell had, apparently, confused Park for another man he saw in the outpatient department of Charing Cross hospital that day. That man, who was not named in the trial, was attending the outpatient department for a 'gonorrhoeal discharge, as he himself called it, from the anus'. Barwell never examined or treated this man, because

> he confessed so cynically to the act of sodomy that I drove him away. He confessed how he had got this sore so cynically ... almost boastfully or jauntily ... that I would have nothing to do with him.

And Barwell had this patient, with a venereal infection, thrown out of the department. It is remarkable that, in the years following the Contagious Diseases Acts, a surgeon of considerable standing would refuse to treat a patient with venereal disease, on the grounds of moral indignation. Barwell had assumed at the arraignment that this patient was Park, or 'Fanny', due to the furore surrounding his arrest. However, when he saw Park at the trial, Barwell remembered that the defendant was, in fact, his other male patient that day with a malady of the anus. Barwell remembered Park as 'quiet' and making no allusions as to how he might have contracted a sore in his anus. We will never be able to tell whether Park was, in reality, the man whom Barwell indignantly refused to treat in 1870. It is possible that, like the newspaper reporting, this prominent surgeon managed to 'forget' that the patient that caused him such outrage in 1870 was actually Park. This would have had the result of discrediting Paul, a mere police surgeon, and achieved the inadmissibility of medical evidence and therefore the desired 'not guilty' verdict in the trial. This notwithstanding, Barwell's refusal to treat or examine the nameless, self-confessed 'sodomite' on the same day as he examined Park, was accepted by the court without demur or question. The acceptability of ignorance amongst British medical men on the subject of sexuality between men is contained in the Attorney General's often quoted summary:

> Fortunately, there is very little learning ... upon this subject in this country; there are other countries in which ... learned treatises are written. ... Fortunately, doctors in England know very little about this matter.[53]

The Lord Chief Justice added that the lack of knowledge amongst the surgeons, with the exception of the reprehensible Paul, meant that

> that vice [sodomy] has not yet tainted the habits of the men of this country – for that thank heaven. Therefore the medical men here cannot give you ... what perhaps medical practitioners in other and less happy countries in that respect could give.[54]

If viewed from the perspective of medical practitioners, this landmark trial and the treatment of Paul would have created a climate of fear amongst British doctors in attempting to study the physical manifestations of sodomy. In editions of Taylor's following the trial, the subject was headed by the warning that 'decency suggests that these [cases] should be left unnoticed, but claims of legal medicine necessitate a brief reference to them'.[55] A cursory examination of the fate of Dr Paul would have warned British surgeons not to meddle in these matters in this country. Crozier may be correct in his assessment of the trial constructing a medical discourse in a legal setting that concentrated exclusively on the physical aspects of sodomy. However, the incidental nature of the place of medical evidence, submitted unauthorised by a lowly police surgeon in this trial, served as a precedent to warn doctors away from involving themselves in crimes and cases of this nature. No other trials for sodomy in the period used medical evidence and the advice in Taylor's on this matter remained unabridged for the remainder of the nineteenth and much of the twentieth century.[56]

Given this context, it would have taken an extremely foolhardy surgeon to even contemplate a study of the physical signs of sodomy in men in England. The Lord Chief Justice had legitimated the use of physical assault against any surgeon who examined a man's rectum for this purpose and had ruled that this kind of examination was inadmissiable as legal evidence. However, the ruling of the Lord Chief Justice mentioned nothing about the scientific examination of a man's mind in the exploration of this subject. It is quite possible that the timing of *JMS*'s review of Westphal's work, in October 1871, reflected this new and distinct possibility for British alienists. This notwithstanding, the review in *JMS* did not stimulate an enquiry amongst British practitioners, or result in a home-grown discipline of inversion theorisation. With the exception of pirated, inaccurate and intermittent translations of *Psychopathia Sexualis*, no works were available in English on the subject. To this date, Westphal's article of 1869 remains untranslated into English: access to his work is still limited to scholars who can read German. The work of Continental sexologists continued to be reviewed by *JMS* throughout the century. However, reviews were scanty and frequently inaccurate. The occasional review of Continental inversion theories in *JMS* did not even indicate that the subject in question involved sexuality between men.[57] It appears that although British alienists had, through reading *JMS*, some awareness of the existence of Continental sexology and inversion theorisation, all resisted developing these ideas into a recognised scientific discipline in Britain.

The exception amongst British doctors in this respect was, of course, Havelock Ellis. Ellis was, as recent historians have demonstrated, difficult to categorise in the field of medical practice. In the late nineteenth century, he was notable, particularly in the milieu of the new socialists in the 1880s and early 1890s, for his ideas on 'literary, medical and sociological topics'.[58] Most contemporary works of psychology, sociology and history accord Ellis with the professional epithet 'sex-psychologist' or 'sexologist' and Ellis is regarded as firmly belonging to the 'modernisers' in the analysis of the sexual.[59] However, Ellis never practised either medicine or 'alienism' in any conventional sense. His medical qualification consisted of a licence to practice from the Society of Apothecaries, which, as Grosskurth states, was 'a somewhat inferior degree which always rather embarrassed him, although he strenuously defended its validity'.[60] In his autobiography, written in 1939, Ellis claimed that he undertook medical training because he wanted a doctor's education, rather than a doctor's life.[61] The sum of Ellis' 'medical' practice was a three-month post as superintendent of a hydropathic establishment at Harrogate, where his duties consisted of advising 'the patients on the waters and [presiding] at table'.[62] Ellis used this time to finish his first book, a radical political tract called *The New Spirit*. Published in 1890, *The New Spirit* encapsulated the ideas, naïve optimism and sense of the new that pervaded radical thinking at the time. Ellis regarded the 'manifestations of the new spirit abroad in the world [as being] the growing sciences of anthropology, sociology and political science; the increasing importance of women; the disappearance of war; the substitution of art for religion'.[63] It was Ellis' political beliefs and his contact with radical thinkers, such as Carpenter, Shaw, Symonds, Edith Lees, Olive Schreiner and others, that suggested to him the possibility of a work such as *Sexual Inversion*, rather than his practice as a medical man.

Ellis was persuaded to embark upon the work for *Sexual Inversion* in 1892 by Symonds. This collaboration, which Ellis was to regret as a 'mistake' many years later, was stimulating for Ellis because he

had found that some of my most highly esteemed friends were more or less homosexual (like Edward Carpenter, not to mention Edith).[64]

The 'Edith' referred to in this statement was Ellis' own wife, Edith Lees, who had sexual relationships with other women. In spite of the influence of his literary and political 'homosexual' friends and relations, Ellis insisted that *Sexual Inversion* was to be a work of medical and scientific analysis:

> I do not wish to put myself in opposition to the medical psychologists. ... to do so would in any case be bad policy: I simply wish to carry their investigations a step further.[65]

The dangers for Ellis in conducting anything other than a strictly medical and scientific analysis of the subject in Britain were highlighted by his friend and correspondent, the radical feminist thinker Olive Schreiner:

> I hope you won't get mixed up with any of these inverted peoples' affairs. People may not understand you are studying these things merely scientifically.[66]

In spite of his rejection of medical practice, Ellis remained personally enamoured of medical analysis in questions of the sexual. From 1890, he had contributed articles on matters of the sexual to *JMS*. These eventually formed Ellis' anthropological and biologically deterministic work *Man and Woman*, which concentrated on secondary sexual characteristics and was published in 1894. Also, Ellis was respected by Hack Tuke, the editor of *JMS*. In his *Dictionary of Pathological Medicine* (1892), Tuke included Ellis' article 'The Influence of Sex on Insanity'.[67] Ellis was to retain his contact with *JMS* until the end of his life, serving as a distinguished and eminent reviewer of sex-psychological work until the eve of the Second World War. However, Ellis' venture into the enquiry of sexuality between men after 1892 resulted in a clash with Tuke. When Ellis eventually attempted, in 1895, to get *Sexual Inversion* published by Williams and Norgate, whose reputation was based upon publication of scientific works, the study was rejected by Tuke, who was reader to this publishing house. Grosskurth attributes Tuke's rejection of *Sexual Inversion* to the furore created by the trials of Oscar Wilde during that year. But Tuke was the editor of the article that had advertised the existence of Westphal's work in the months following the 'Stella and Fanny' trial in 1871 and should, ostensibly, have allowed *Sexual Inversion* to be published. It is probable that in the ensuing 24 years, Tuke had developed severe reservations about the effects of allowing inversion theorisation its place in British alienism. Tuke told Ellis that he feared that the work 'could not be confined to the specialists and might contaminate the wider public'.[68] Tuke also warned Ellis that 'there are always the compositors!'

Tuke had been a close friend and confidant of Dr John Symonds, a prominent physician. Both doctors had much in common, including the knowledge that their sons, John Addington Symonds, eminent litterateur, and Henry Scott Tuke, famous Cornish painter, desired men.[69] In spite of cordial relations between Tuke senior and Symonds junior after the death of Dr Symonds, including visits by Tuke to Symonds' retreat in Switzerland, Tuke had 'always refused to discuss the subject of inversion with Symonds'.[70] In 1871, Tuke had been the editor of a new and innovative branch of medical journalism which admired the rigour and analysis of Continental psychologists. However, by the 1890s, Tuke was regarded as one of the most eminent academics of psychiatric enquiry in Britain. The disagreeable knowledge of the propensities of his son and the tendency of Symonds to use the works of inversion theorists to justify his desires had no doubt combined to produce a reactionary stance in the, now elderly, alienist. Symonds had died in 1893 and his widow and literary executor went to considerable lengths to preserve his posthumous reputation from the odious taint of his sexual desires. Should the propensities of Symonds, even posthumously, or those of Tuke's son be unveiled in the public eye, then Tuke's reputation would have been exposed to considerable risk. By 1895, Tuke had the responsibility of his status to consider. The connection between Tuke and the Symonds' was common knowledge. If it transpired that Tuke had given his assent to the publication of *Sexual Inversion*, with Symonds' co-authorship intact, then his reputation would have undoubtedly collapsed.

Ellis' efforts and difficulties to get *Sexual Inversion* published appear as a litany of the opprobrium and scandal associated with the subject of same sexuality in British society in this period. Ellis' difficulties with the publication also demonstrates the culture of resistance in Britain to toleration of inversion theorisation, or any learned commentary on the matter of sexuality between men. *Sexual Inversion*, in the form of its first edition, was a work of co-authorship between Ellis and Symonds. Symonds had provided a historical analysis for the text, similar to his essay 'A Problem in Greek Ethics', privately printed in 1883, and Ellis had provided the medical and scientific analysis of inversion. After Symonds' death, Ellis felt 'loyally bound' to use his work. Ellis was determined to publish the work in Britain. In correspondence with Edward Carpenter on the matter in 1894, Ellis stated that he was 'not anxious to publish it in Germany – where it isn't required, but that may pave the way for English publication'.[71] Nonetheless, the work was published in Germany, with both Ellis' and Symonds' names as the authors,[72] but caused 'no particular stir',[73] as the work, in the context of German science, was neither controversial nor innovative. Ellis then attempted to publish in England in 1897. After the rejection of the work by Williams and Norgate in 1895, reputable publishers were hard to find. A friend of Ellis' recommended the services of Roland de Villiers, who had just set up a new, small publishing house. De Villiers' firm, the Watford University Press, wished to establish for itself a reputation for publishing scholarly works with narrow appeal. The Watford University Press proved willing to publish the first English edition of *Sexual Inversion*. However, Symonds' literary executor, Horatio Brown, intervened in the publication. Brown had been initially enthusiastic about the posthumous publication of Symonds' contribution to this work, but Symonds' widow, who had never read the manuscript for herself, garnered other opinions of the work, including that of Herbert Asquith, Home Secretary until 1895. All of Catherine Symonds' advisors on the matter opined that the publication of *Sexual Inversion* would do irrevocable damage to her husband's posthumous reputation and that of his family and descendants. Brown duly bought up all the existing copies of the first edition from de Villiers in July 1897.[74] Almost all of them were destroyed.

Ellis worked rapidly to produce a second edition, with the authorship and most of the work by Symonds removed. The Watford University Press published this revised work in early 1898.[75] All seemed to go well, but attempts to sell copies of *Sexual Inversion* resulted in its seizure by the police and the arrest of the vendor in May 1898. The vendor was George Bedborough, a maverick, well-educated character, who was a member of the Legitimation League and editor of the radical journal, *The Adult*. Although the Watford University Press was at some pains after Bedborough's arrest to dissociate itself from Bedborough and the Legitimation League, the firm published *The Adult* and Bedborough had been selling the firm's publications from the front room of his home. A copy of *Sexual Inversion* had been inadvertently sold to John Sweeney, a detective inspector from Scotland Yard.[76] In 1904, Detective Inspector Sweeney wrote his memoirs, *At Scotland Yard*, which included a detailed recollection of the arrest and prosecution of Bedborough and the suppression of *Sexual Inversion* as a work of obscene libel. *At Scotland Yard* proved to be a popular book, as another edition was published in 1905. The memoir is historically important, as it gives a detailed account of the policy and actions of the police towards the publication of works like *Sexual Inversion*. Sweeney's purchase of *Sexual Inversion* was not an accident, but the culmination of two years of police surveillance of the Legitimation League and the activities of the Watford University Press.[77] The Legitimation League campaigned for the legal rights of illegitimate children, but by 1898, was also associated with the promotion of 'free love', adultery, unconventional coupling between men and women and 'anarchy'.[78]

The Legitimation League merited police attention because, in Sweeney's view, the organisation posed a dangerous threat to society. The police first became involved with the organisation in 1896 when

> a certain young lady, Miss Edith Lanchester, had been confined to a lunatic asylum on the certificate of her parent's medical advisers. Miss Lanchester was said to be a believer in the doctrines of the Legitimation League, such belief constituting a sufficiently dangerous mania ... as to necessitate Miss Lanchester's seclusion.[79]

The League mounted a vigorous campaign in the newspapers for the unfortunate Miss Lanchester's release, which attracted the attention of the authorities. Sweeney attended the League's meetings for two years undercover. In 1898, Sweeney believed he had enough evidence that the League constituted a serious threat to order and morals to bring the organisation to the attention of the Director of Public Prosecutions (DPP). The DPP agreed and was 'anxious to protect the public from all the objectionable features of an open and unashamed free-love movement in its midst'. However, Sweeney and the DPP were also concerned to 'abstain from interference with legitimate freedom of speech'.[80] Nonetheless, close scrutiny was maintained on the League meetings, where some of the meetings were 'incendiary' and on *The Adult*, which was 'outspoken to an extreme degree'. When Sweeney came across the second edition of *Sexual Inversion* on sale in Bedborough's home, he knew that the police had enough evidence to prosecute and close the organisation down. Sweeney described *Sexual Inversion* as

> a book which I cannot possibly describe here. ... the book has been condemned as obscene, and there was nothing whatever in the mode of publication to suggest that it deserved a better fate.[81]

Sweeney regarded the Watford University Press as dangerous and disreputable, because it threatened to flood the country with 'books of the "Psychology" type'. Sweeney argued that, had Ellis' work been a serious work of science 'he would have submitted it to one of the many high class publishers of medico-scientific literature'.[82] Unbeknown to Inspector Sweeney, Ellis' had tried to get *Sexual Inversion* published by a reputable scientific publisher and had failed. An examination of the Watford University Press' catalogue for 1899 does show, that between 1897 and 1899, before the firm transferred its activities to the Continent, it did attempt to publish limited, pirated editions of works of Continental sexologists. However, the works were available by mail order only and were very expensive.[83]

Grosskurth's biography of Ellis, which remains the most detailed and authoritative study of Ellis' life to date, takes some pains to extricate Ellis and his reputation from that of the Watford University Press and the activities of *The Adult* and the Legitimation league. No other historian has examined Ellis' participation with these organisations in the detail given by Grosskurth's biographical treatment of these events and her magisterial study is cited in all subsequent studies of Ellis.[84] For Grosskurth, Ellis' entanglement with these organisations was an accident of circumstances and, when Ellis' agreed to publish with the new Watford University Press in 1897, 'the books [de Villiers] proposed to publish seemed eminently respectable'.[85] However, an examination of *The Adult* reveals that Ellis not only published commentary on sex education in the journal, but that his close friend, Edward Carpenter and his wife, Edith Lees, were also literary contributors to the publication.[86] Ellis and his immediate circle were fully aware of the activities of the League and *The Adult* before Bedborough's arrest. At that time in Britain, Ellis' work and its subject matter were no more acceptable, and probably a good deal less acceptable, than the nefarious activities of the Legitimation League. Grosskurth, writing in the 1970s in North America and respectful of Ellis' ideas and totemic reputation amongst American psychologists, placed him and his work on a more reputable pedestal than the writings and activities of his contemporaries in the Watford University Press and the Legitimation League. However, it was the presence of Ellis' work *Sexual Inversion* that, after two years of close surveillance, finally gave the police and the DPP the evidence they needed to prosecute and shut down these organisations. Sweeney recollected with considerable pride his role in the arrest of Bedborough and the suppression of *Sexual Inversion*. Sweeney regarded the subject of the work as one that 'the law of England has decided wisely enough cannot be discussed in books'. By arresting Bedborough, the police and the government were able 'at one blow [to] kill a growing evil in the shape of a vigorous campaign of free love and Anarchism'.[87] Sweeney informed his readership: 'I may claim some credit' for the successful suppression of an organisation that, if tolerated, would have resulted in 'the growth of a Frankenstein monster wrecking the marriage laws of our country, and perhaps carrying off the general respect for all law'.[88]

The arrest and prosecution of Bedborough for selling *Sexual Inversion* in May 1898 became a *cause celebre* for *The Adult*. Bedborough had been the editor of *The Adult* since its inception in June 1897. The publication had been part-sponsored by the Legitimation League and served as a forum for discussion of its issues, amongst other 'important phrases of sex questions which are universally ignored elsewhere'.[89] Nonetheless, *The Adult* has, surprisingly, attracted little attention from historians.[90] Admittedly, the publication enjoyed only a very limited circulation, confined mainly to Legitimation League members and thinkers on the margins of the late Victorian intelligentsia. However, through the Bedborough trial, the existence of *The Adult* was brought to the attention of the public. As the editorial of the August 1898 issue commented: 'one of the immediate effects of the Bedborough prosecution was the doubling of the circulation of *The Adult*. For which inestimable blessing we are duly thankful'.[91] The Bedborough trial also occasioned the commentary of Shaw in its pages, in defence of the free publication of *Sexual Inversion* and Ellis' reputation. In addition to this, the attention given to the Legitimation League and *The Adult* by Sweeney's popular memoirs, reminded the public in the first decade of the twentieth century of the existence of the publication and the reprehensibility of its aims and contents.

In the first year of its existence, *The Adult* and its editorship under Bedborough appeared determined to attract attention and challenge British proprieties in publication. Between June 1897 and Bedborough's arrest in May 1898, the publication was variously titled as *The Adult: The Journal of Sex: Discusses Marriage, Divorce and All Sex Problems* and *The Adult: A Journal for the Advancement of Freedom in Sexual Relationships*. As Anderson states, despite the 'titillating promise' of the journal title and some of its articles, such as 'Some Sex Problems Considered' and 'The Sexual Enslavement of Men', contributions to the publication tended to be very earnest treatments of their subjects, 'dry in content and ponderous in tone'.[92] Notwithstanding its claims to address 'all sex problems', *The Adult* did not address or carry articles about sexuality between men until Bedborough's prosecution and the suppression of *Sexual Inversion*. In the name of press freedom, *The Adult* and its contributors mounted a campaign to provide funds for payment of Bedborough's defence lawyers, announcing that the Watford University Press had 'opened a defence fund with a donation of fifty guineas'.[93] Although the sale of *Sexual Inversion* was the main indictment in the obscenity trial, certain editions of *The Adult* were also indicted as obscene publications, including contributions by Carpenter and Ellis. With the loss of its editor and the distinct possibility of the journal being closed down, it is little wonder that *The Adult* mounted a vigorous campaign in defence of the publication of *Sexual Inversion*. As well as inviting donations and commentaries for the defence of *Sexual Inversion* as a publication, *The Adult* also published a running transcript of the trial throughout its proceedings.

It is clear from most of the commentaries that the defence of *Sexual Inversion* in *The Adult* was based more upon the principles of freedom of scientific enquiry and freedom of expression, than anything to do with its contents. In *Sexual Inversion*, Ellis described and explained inversion in men in scientific terms but never ventured into possibilities of treatments or cures. Ellis did not address the subject of 'treatment' for inversion until the 1936 edition of *Studies in the Psychology of Sex*. In this edition, he recommended that the role of the psychiatrist in the field of male inversion was best served by enabling 'an invert to be healthy, self-restrained and self-respecting'. In achieving this, Ellis argued that psychiatrists would 'have often done better than to convert him into the mere feeble simulacrum of a normal man'.[94] Ellis accepted, and had always accepted, the 'essential nature' of the invert and his desires and *Sexual Inversion* in 1898, served as a scientific analysis of this opinion. However, commentary in *The Adult* during the Bedborough trial defended the publication of *Sexual Inversion* on the grounds that Ellis' work offered a cure for eradicating sex between men. The editorial of *The Adult*, in an appeal for support and funds for the defence, commented that

> an appeal is hereby made to all lovers of free enquiry, free discussion and free publicity. ... 'Sexual Inversion', written by Dr Havelock Ellis ... is the first of a projected series on the 'Psychology of Sex', a subject which is investigated freely on the Continent. ... It is written in a spirit of scientific detachment. It throws light on certain abnormalities, with a view to their rectification; it is unpleasant in the same way that a treatise on cancer is unpleasant.[95]

Other commentators in the publication defended the existence of *Sexual Inversion* in a similar vein; 'the state should subsidise, not suppress, the spread of knowledge so beneficial to her citizens'. This anonymous commentator reminded the readership that the state had sent Oscar Wilde to prison for the 'exercise of sexual perversion'. The commentator's

defence of the publication of *Sexual Inversion*, and criticism of the incon-
sistencies of the 'state' in this matter, was based upon the assumption
that Bedborough was selling a cure for this perversion:

If one man is punished for sexual perversion, and another man
is punished for circulating a book showing how to eliminate sexual
perversion – for the best way to eliminate it is to impart a scientific
knowledge of the nosological [sic] principles upon which it is based –
can inconsistency and fatuity further go?[96]

Clearly, these commentators had not read or had not understood the
contents and aims of Ellis' work. Others, notably Shaw, demonstrated an
understanding of Ellis' analysis and a sense of compassion and toleration towards the phenomenon of sex between men. Nonetheless, all the
commentators were being true to their sexually radical, counter-cultural
and maverick credentials in accepting the existence of a publication like
Sexual Inversion at all. Even those who thought that a work like *Sexual
Inversion* equated with a cure for perversion were prepared to comment
upon and acknowledge its existence. What marked them out from the
legal and medical authorities and from most of British society was this
preparedness to discuss the matter, even in pejorative terms. The acceptance of 'free love' by the men and women of *The Adult* confined these
people to the margins of their society. Their rejection of strictly uxorious
sexuality, promotion of 'free love' and campaigns for the legal rights of
illegitimate children and unmarried coupling deeply threatened society,
to the extent that the police authorities kept them under very close
scrutiny. During the Bedborough trial, the Legitimation League was
condemned by the court as obscene and a 'conspiracy against marriage'.[97]
Even amongst the liberal 'free lovers', sexuality between men represented
a phenomenon to be eradicated. The purpose of *Sexual Inversion*, to
many of the 'free lovers' of *The Adult*, was that in ideal future societies
the perversion would not exist, and the unpleasant necessity of scientific
enquiry in British society of the 1890s would have achieved its 'aims'.

Throughout the trial, *The Adult* maintained a positive and upbeat
commentary on its outcome, convinced that, in the modern era, a work
of science could not be prosecuted or suppressed. The journal informed
its readership that

since the prosecution the author [of *Sexual Inversion*] has received a
large number of sympathetic letters from the leading physicians and
specialists of the world, amongst which there is not one that does not
speak with strong disapproval of this prosecution.[98]

International opinion notwithstanding, the trial prosecution and proceedings appeared determined to secure a conviction in the case and
suppress *Sexual Inversion*. Bedborough was indicted with selling the
work, which was described by the indictment as containing 'wicked,
lewd, impure, scandalous and obscene libels'. Bedborough was advised
by his defence barristers to plead guilty, on the grounds that he was an
agent in selling the book, but had no part in its compilation. In his
judgement, the Recorder, Sir Charles Hall, stated to Bedborough that

> you have acted wisely in so pleading to these counts, for it would
> have been impossible for you to have contended with any possibility
> whatever that this book and ... this magazine [*The Adult*] were not
> filthy and obscene works.[99]

The Adult had attempted in August 1898 to persuade Ellis to publish the
international scientific testimonials for his work. Ellis did not do so until
after the trial and, even then, his defence of his work was privately
printed in the United States. Ellis was probably wise to refrain from this
action during the trial and publishing his defence in Britain. The court
had already decided that *Sexual Inversion* was an obscene publication:

> It is impossible for anybody with a head on his shoulders to open the
> book without seeing it is a pretence and a sham, and that it is merely
> entered into for the purpose of selling this filthy publication.[100]

By pleading guilty simply to selling the book, for which he was fined
£100, Bedborough saved the court the trouble of putting the contents of
Sexual Inversion and its author on trial as well. Had he pleaded not guilty,
then the courts would have been forced to discuss explicitly the
contents of *Sexual Inversion*, which would have opened the possibility of
such a trial being reported scandalously in the newspapers. Grosskurth
demonstrates Ellis' extreme discomfiture throughout these proceedings
and argues that he wished for the entire 'controversial matter' to conclude
as quickly as possible and with the minimum of damage to his reputation.
Grosskurth argues that Bedborough's actions during the trial were not
heroic, but 'neither, for that matter, was Ellis'.[101]

Bedborough's and Ellis' acquiescence in their acceptance of the judgement of obscene libel for *Sexual Inversion* without contest is best understood through the prevailing attitudes amongst the judiciary and the
government towards discussion or recognition of the existence of sexuality between men in British society. As seen in Chapter 2, in 1896, the

Lord Chancellor, Lord Halsbury, had attempted to introduce a bill to parliament. Halsbury's Publication of Indecent Evidence Bill would have criminalised the publication of details of trials for sex between men. In proposing the Publication of Indecent Evidence Bill, Halsbury had the support of the Prime Minister, Lord Salisbury, who stated to the House of Lords that

> it is a well-ascertained effect that the publication of details in cases of that kind has a horrible though undoubtedly direct action in producing an imitation of the crime.[102]

The Bill never became law; it was opposed by the Lord Chief Justice, the Master of the Rolls and the Liberal opposition, on the grounds of press freedom. However, the Bill was reflective of legal and governmental attitudes towards the matter of sexuality between men. The stimulus for Halsbury's Bill was undoubtedly the journalistic furore created by the trials of Oscar Wilde in 1895. But the Wilde trials simply forced leading members of the government to articulate, for the first time, a sensibility that was prevalent throughout the late nineteenth century. Halsbury claimed that 'fathers of families' would welcome this legislation as newspaper reports of unnatural crimes did 'infinite mischief' to the correct governance of the household. Halsbury's proposed legislation was 'the most explicit example of a far wider inhibition on the written word' on this matter in the period.[103] Halsbury's proposal is also explicit evidence of the inability of British society to tolerate even newspaper commentary on cases where the law severely punished the perpetrator of unnatural crime.[104] The unnatural crime had to be punished in secret, in the Lord Chancellor and the Prime Minister's view. In this context, the optimism of the journalists at the *The Adult* for the exoneration of *Sexual Inversion* on the grounds that it was a work of science appears rather naïve. If leading members of the government and the judiciary could not tolerate the reporting of the punishment of the perpetrators of unnatural crime, then they would have had even greater difficulties in tolerating the publication of *Sexual Inversion* which, if read carefully, regarded inversion as a natural aberration of the sexual instinct. *Sexual Inversion* could readily be utilised by the invert to understand and accept his propensity; this would have been anathema to the government and society of the day.

Nonetheless, the successful prosecution of Henry Bedborough and the suppression and destruction of nearly all but a few copies of the second edition of *Sexual Inversion* was greeted with dismay and disbelief by *The Adult:*

> The prosecution and conviction of 'Sexual Inversion' as obscene is one of the greatest scandals of the century, and is an attack upon the liberty of scientific research.

As stated, *The Adult* had remained confident throughout the trial that authorship by Ellis and the scientific approach he adopted in the study would rebut a prosecution of obscene libel. The anonymous article writer 'Justitia' proposed some of the reasons why the prosecution had, after all, been successful:

> This first volume had for its special subject matter the question of sexual abnormality, a difficult and obscure problem which has hitherto received no scientific attention in England. Among the scientific writers on the continent it is otherwise. ... it is worthwhile to reflect for a moment on the reception which a study of this nature meets in England.

'Justitia' reminded his readership of the relative freedom experienced in England in nearly every other matter:

> All the world knows that in England we enjoy a large measure of political and religious freedom of debate. It is commonly admitted ... that we are far ahead of many foreign governments. In certain countries ... we find a harsh and violent veto on all criticism of the administration.

In England, liberty and freedom evaporated if an attempt was made to discuss the sexual, particularly sexual aberrations:

> In moral matters, even when discussed in a purely scientific spirit, England acts, or shows signs of acting, precisely as an autocratic ... government acts with regard to freedom of the press in political questions.

'Justitia' highlighted the existence of

> a body of narrow and bigoted men [who] would like to institute a sort of inquisition in this country. At every moment it seeks to prohibit the discussion of this or that.

This 'body' included the judiciary, the Prime Minister, the DPP, the Lord Chancellor, the Home Office, the police, the national newspapers, the medical professions and the legislature. 'Justitia' expressed perceptive concerns for the implications of the prosecution of *Sexual Inversion*:

> It has often [been] attempted to ... vilify art, to gag literature [in England]; but now, what is infinitely more serious, [England] attempts to gag science. This is surely a dangerous movement. It is for the man of science who has made a special study ... to dictate whether matters dealing with sex and morality, however unpleasant and startling, should be investigated. ... Dr Havelock Ellis ... has studied a grave problem. His book is written in technical language, and is addressed only to thinkers.

'Justitia' concluded that it was 'for science alone, not law, to determine the limits of her province'.[105]

The concerns of *The Adult* were well founded. Ellis eventually had to publish his banned work in the United States. In spite of numerous editions published repeatedly until the Second World War, copies of Ellis' work, which incorporated *Sexual Inversion*, could only be obtained in Britain by subscribing privately to the publishing house in the United States. In 1913, Ellis replied to a British correspondent, who was exasperated at the exorbitant price of *Studies in the Psychology of Sex* for shipment from the United States:

> It is quite true that the price of my studies, since they are not for indiscriminate circulation, is £2.19.0.[106]

A significant quantity of Ellis' correspondence in his later years was taken up with replies to people in Britain who experienced severe difficulties in obtaining copies of his work. Indeed, his *Studies in the Psychology of Sex*, accorded with reverence and totemic status amongst twentieth-century American psychologists, were not published in Britain until 1936.

The suppression of *Sexual Inversion* in 1898 created extreme difficulties for the Watford University Press and for publication of sexual scientific works in general in Britain. The Watford University Press announced in a statement in December 1899, which has, since then, been archived in the British Library's pornographic catalogue collection, that future scientific works would be published and distributed from Paris and Leipzig. The firm announced its intention 'not to stock [these works] again in Great Britain'. In many respects, Ellis, Bedborough, *The Adult* and the Watford University Press, through their capitulation, reinforced the culture of resistance in Britain to inversion theorisation. The firm defended its reputation and responsibilities in the matter of distribution of works of the nature of *Sexual Inversion*: 'these indicted works have never been offered to the public nor to any but medical men. ... these scientific works ... should not be placed in the hands of the young or of the general public'. The statement went on to inform its clients that 'the French and German scientific press comment on this new outrage in the severest terms'. The firm cited the protest of Dr Charles Féré, French author of *The Pathology of the Emotions*, on the outcome of the trial:

> This grotesque seizure of scientific publications would have been seen here as an extraordinary piece of naïveté. But in England, where even science is subjected to the tyrannical value of that hypocritical spirit which dominates everywhere, a protest by the medical profession against these continued outrages seems appropriate and necessary.[107]

No public protest was forthcoming from the medical profession in Britain against these 'outrages'. Ellis did, however, privately print an article in New York in 1898, commenting on the trial and defending the scientific grounding of his work. Ellis stated that

> every medical journal in half a dozen countries which has reviewed the work has without exception judged it favourably, and not one has suggested that I have been guilty of the slightest impropriety. ... it has been repeatedly remarked that an English tone of reticence distinguishes this book from other works on the same subject by continental writers.[108]

English reticence in tone notwithstanding, it is clear from the evidence surrounding the suppression of *Sexual Inversion* that British society effectively resisted and was intolerant towards any form of inversion theorisation in this period. Continental observers found this culture of resistance in this respect in Britain remarkable, particularly if compared to the relative freedom of expression accorded to inversion theorists in Continental states, such as France, Germany and Austria. Ellis commented with bitterness and some embarrassment that his work could and would not be tolerated in Britain:

> I regret that my country should be almost alone in refusing to me the conditions of reasonable intellectual freedom. I regret it the more

since I deal with the facts of English life, and prefer to address English people.[109]

The culture of resistance to inversion theorisation in Britain was to persist effectively until after the First World War. Indeed, attempts to establish societies and university disciplines in the broader fields of psychology in Britain encountered great difficulties in the first decade of the twentieth century. By 1900, Continental universities such as Paris, Leipzig, Vienna and many others, had well-established chairs of psychology. In Britain in the late nineteenth century, attempts to establish institutional psychological enquiry met with indifference and failure.[110] Even the foundation of the British Psychological Society at the 'Godless College', or University College, London, in 1901, could boast of only ten members in the first few years of its existence. As Lovie states, the Society experienced 'near-death experiences' in its first few years and even by 1918, had only 100 members.[111] In the first half of the twentieth century, the disciplines of psychiatry and psychology in North America and Continental Europe were significantly influenced by the ideas of Ellis and Sigmund Freud. In these same years, British psychiatry, almost uniquely, ignored the ideas of Ellis and Freud, dismissing them as 'an unhealthy interest in the workings of the mind'.[112]

In many respects, Britain and its scientific community in the nineteenth century must be regarded, over and above Continental states, as having the potential to originate the scientific analysis of sexuality between men. British philosophers and scientists fostered and created, to a significant extent, the intellectual conditions for a science of inversion theorisation. The writings of Malthus in the 1790s problematised procreative sex for the first time. In the 1850s, Drysdale extrapolated the ideas of Malthus in new directions. Drysdale's work promoted the examination of methods of artificial contraception and admitted the possibilities of pleasure and fulfilment to be experienced through non-procreative sex. The Malthusian basis of Drysdale's philosophy, which problematised excessive procreativity, suggested to Drysdale that same-sex sexuality also merited serious study and examination, on the rational grounds that they were forms of non-procreative sexual phenomena. Admittedly, Drysdale believed that same-sex relationships existed because of the strict and pervasive insistence upon procreative, uxorious sex in British society. But his work promoted the idea, as early as 1854, that a dispassionate and rational examination of same-sex sexuality could and should be conducted. Similarly, the ideas of Darwin in the early 1870s stimulated and expanded an already extant scientific enquiry of same-gender sexuality in Continental Europe, especially in Germany, Austria and France. Darwin's thinking on the biological mutability of gender fostered an expansion in examination of same-gender sexuality on the Continent and provided the analytical basis for the discipline of inversion theorisation.

In the major states of Continental Europe, scientific examination of same-gender sexuality developed in environments where it and the homosexual milieu it examined were, more or less, tolerated and accepted. To be sure, the milieu of homosexuals and the scientific community that examined them were confined to the major cities, such as Paris, Berlin and Vienna and disapproval was expressed on moral grounds in mainstream newspapers. As Féré argued in the late nineteenth century, the 'hypocritical spirit' in matters of sexual morality was dominant throughout Europe. However, this did not translate into suppression of or resistance to the examination or publication of theories about same-sex sexuality, in particular the problem of sexuality between men. The states of Continental Europe had histories of political convulsions and frequent militarisation of their metropolitan spaces in the nineteenth century. It is possible that these conditions meant that, in societies that had intermittently collapsed, such as France, and in which domestic martial cultures were often apparent, inversion theorisation was not perceived to pose a challenge to social and gender structures.

In Britain, however, the patterns of social and political stability were quite different. After the Napoleonic Wars, British society distanced itself from events in Europe. Britain was undoubtedly martial in the nineteenth century, but wars were conducted in distant lands or exotic imperial territories. The presence of the military in mainland Britain was minimal, if compared to Continental countries. In addition, recruitment to the British Army was, after 1815 and until 1916, voluntary. Tucker argues that the army was held in low regard by British society in this period and that conscription was an 'evil word'.[113] On the other hand, in Continental countries, particularly the German-speaking lands, conscription was an indelible feature of life and the experience of every adult male, for at least part of his life.[114] Mass conscription, particularly in Imperial Germany, was seen as integral to a sense of civil society. In other words, Continental societies had an alternative masculine social status achievable through the army, that was valorised on a par with heading a family and regarded as a much more tangible expression of social belonging than participation in politics and the franchise.[115] In this context, Isabell Hall argues that the state and the profession of medicine had unique access to the moral and physical state of its men, and therefore an interest in defining unacceptable sex amongst men.[116]

George Mosse argues that the aesthetic of the beautiful male and the camaraderie and *bund* of men became central to public discourse and public art. In such a society, forensic analysis of the physical signs of sodomy and pathologisation of the invert served to separate this vilified type from the ideal, beautiful, martial male.[117]

In Britain, social stability was founded upon marriage and the governance of the male head of household, rather than by the presence of a martial culture. National institutions, such as the government, judiciary and the professionalised discipline of medicine, saw it as their duty to preserve and maintain the authority of 'fathers of families' as the cornerstone of British society. In this conception of masculine authority, the existence of sexuality between men was inadmissible. In the mid-to-late nineteenth century, British doctors, when they discussed the subject at all, projected an Anglican, strictly uxorious and procreative sexuality as the scientific benchmark of sexual normality. For British doctors, no further examination of this conception of normality and sexual health was deemed necessary. Continental enquiry into sexuality between men, if allowed to enter Britain, threatened to question the domestic authority and uxorious morality of British men – how could British men maintain their fragile authority over their wives and children if it were admitted that men in Britain had sex with other men? Sex between men in Britain had to be seen as extremely rare and confined to certain reprehensible and outlandish types. To allow scientific enquiry into this reprehensible and domestically disruptive masculine trait might reveal that sex between men was more widespread than supposed.

The medical professions, the judiciary, the police and the government went to considerable lengths to suppress and resist any form of learned discussion of the matter of sexuality between men. Historiography in this field has argued that medicine and the law constructed, in apparent harmony, a pejorative category of the male homosexual in these years. This may be the case, up to a point, in states such as the nineteenth-century German or Austrian Empires. However, in Britain, the medical professions and the judiciary colluded to ensure that not even the articulation of a pejorative concept of 'the homosexual' existed. The rulings on the inadmissibility of 'physical signs' of sodomy as evidence in the 'Stella and Fanny' trial of 1871 ended any potential for British surgeons to conduct a scientific enquiry of this nature. Also, the Lord Chief Justice had permitted the physical assault of any doctor who attempted to conduct such a study. After this case, the body (and in particular, the rectum) of the British male was considered to be inviolate.

Continental science was, at this point, departing from the study of the physical signs of sodomy and developing neurological, biological and psychological analyses of the phenomenon of sexuality between men. British alienists were aware, as early as 1871, that much potential resided in the psychical analysis of this phenomenon. Indeed, after the 'Stella and Fanny' trial, the examination of the mind remained the only recourse left to British doctors wishing to examine the phenomenon. But analysis of this kind was not forthcoming from British alienists.

The notable exception was Havelock Ellis and his work, *Sexual Inversion*. When Ellis published *Sexual Inversion* in Germany in 1896, the work was considered to be neither controversial nor innovative. But when Ellis attempted to publish his work in Britain, he met with a wall of resistance from the medical professions, the police and the judiciary. Late nineteenth-century Britain was notable for its freedoms of political expression, a national trait admired even by British counter-cultural radicals who were deeply critical of their society. Nonetheless, in matters of the sexual and, in particular, the matter of sexuality between men, Britain proved to be one of the most hostile, intolerant and repressive cultures in the Western world. Sexually radical ideas such as free love and unmarried coupling were deemed by the authorities to be subversive to society to the extent that they merited suppression and eradication. However, it was the presence of a work like *Sexual Inversion* in the midst and milieu of sexually radical organisations, that provided the evidence and the catalyst for the authorities to act. The analysis in *Sexual Inversion* offered the potential for the inverted male to attempt to accept and understand his propensities. A work of this nature was deeply threatening to British social and gender structures and stability. British culture had great difficulty in even acknowledging the punishment of sex between men in its newspapers. *Sexual Inversion* was regarded by the authorities as the anathema in a radical milieu that was already promulgating a critique of British marriage.

Historians since Foucault's refutation of the 'repressive hypothesis' have done much to dispel the stereotypes of 'Victorian' sexual prudery. These histories demonstrate that there was a veritable explosion in sexual discourse, including the matter of sexuality between men. However, in the field of sex between men, discourse was an almost entirely Continental European and, to some extent, American development. British culture and society stoutly resisted such developments within its shores and effectively repressed attempts to conduct a public scientific discussion of the phenomenon. Discussion of the phenomenon certainly happened in Britain, but it was an intensely private, marginal and covert pursuit. In the late nineteenth and early twentieth centuries in Britain, inversion theorisation and even the broader concepts of psychology were viewed with intense suspicion and as alien developments to be repelled and resisted.

6
Lives

Contrary to what many historians claim, legislative developments in late nineteenth-century Britain did not construct a legal category of 'the male homosexual' or 'all male homosexuals as a class'. Similarly, science and medicine in Britain did not construct a pathologised category of 'the homosexual'. These disciplines distinctively eschewed attempts to develop inversion theorisation and rejected Continental developments in this field. This notwithstanding, historians have emphasised that the legal-medical classifications of male homosexuality prevalent in Britain in the 1950s originated in the late nineteenth century. The concept of homosexual pathology or abnormality amongst many British doctors in the 1950s can be traced to nineteenth-century developments in sex-psychology. This concept amongst British psychiatrists and a grudging acceptance of the ideas of Freud and Ellis, was a development of the years following the Second World War.[1] This book has attempted to demonstrate that the pejorative medico-legal construction of modern male homosexual identities was a Continental European and North American development, stoutly resisted in Britain. Nineteenth-century British society could not contemplate permitting discussion of the phenomenon, even in pejorative terms, for fear of giving it credence and admitting that the phenomenon existed amongst British men at all.

This chapter examines the sexualised self-making of Edward Carpenter (1844–1929) and John Addington Symonds (1840–93). The ideas expressed by these authors on sexuality between men are contextualised with the implications of expression of this phenomenon in Britain. Historians in the late 1970s and 1980s interpreted the lives and homosexual identities of Carpenter and Symonds for the first time. Carpenter and Symonds feature prominently in Weeks' collaborative early work with the socialist historian, Shiela Rowbotham. In *Socialism and the New Life* (1977), Rowbotham and Weeks examine the lives and homosexuality of Carpenter and Symonds and their connections with the sex psychologist, Havelock Ellis. Carpenter and Symonds also feature in Weeks' subsequent studies of homosexual identity formations in Britain. However, the construction of homosexual identity presented by Weeks contextualises both Carpenter's and Symonds' formation of identity in an apparent milieu of near-revolutionary legal and medical categorisation and purposive oppression of male homosexuals in Britain. Both Carpenter and Symonds engaged thoroughly, though clandestinely, with the developments in Continental sexological inversion theorisation. Symonds was the co-author of Ellis' *Sexual Inversion* (1897) and Carpenter was the author of *The Intermediate Sex* (1906), the first published work in Britain to discuss the matter of same-sex sexuality in any detail.[2] Ostensibly, the sexual identities of Carpenter and Symonds, expressed in their writings, appear to allude to a construction of modern male homosexual identities in the context of British society in the period. This certainly seemed the case to gay-politicised activists and academics in the late 1970s. Indeed, Carpenter enjoyed something of a renaissance of interest in these years. His homosexuality attracted the attention of the Gay Liberation movement in the late 1970s. At that time Carpenter was, as the playwright Noel Greig states, a forgotten character. 'I first stumbled upon Edward Carpenter in 1977 – as a foot-note', he recalled.[3] Greig was researching material for his important series of *Gay Sweatshop* plays which demonstrated that modern gay identities had antecedents.[4] Three volumes of Carpenter's writings were planned for publication by the Gay Men's Press and a substantial biography was written in 1980.

Carpenter's revival as a historical icon of Socialist gay identity was, however, somewhat short lived. His literary productions continue to attract the attentions of literary critics. In histories of homosexuality, he has commanded little recent attention. The historiography which does examine Carpenter has tended to either emphasise his writings on homosexuality or his involvement with the early Socialists. Both of these approaches are important in any evaluation of the man. However, Carpenter was notable in his time for his critique of the strictures of marriage in Britain and of the status of men and women in Victorian society. His thoughts in this direction have commanded the attentions of feminist historians, mostly in the late 1970s and the 1980s. Nonetheless, little attention or analysis has been directed towards Carpenter's own sense of masculinity.[5] This chapter examines the extent to which his writings on marriage and sexual 'intermediacy' were expressions of his own deep discontent with prevailing structures and perceptions of masculinity in Britain. Also, Carpenter's fashioning of his own sense of self, centred on his sexual desires for other men, is assessed here. Carpenter was undoubtedly influenced by the inversion theories of sex psychologists.[6] However, in the context of Carpenter's Britain, this was an alien and prohibited source of inspiration and guidance.[7] Carpenter was also strongly influenced by oriental mysticism. His journey to Ceylon in 1891 formed a pivotal juncture in his life, in terms of his understanding of his desires for other men. In the context of Britain's Indian Empire of the 1890s, it would have been seen as highly questionable that a British man embrace native and alien culture and belief systems. Carpenter jettisoned the values of Anglicanism and Christian, British masculinity in favour of an oriental idiom that, indirectly, facilitated his sexual propensities. His self-making was not, as historians claim, the 'construct' of medico-legal developments in Britain. Instead, the indiscriminate criminality of a cascade of sexual acts between men and an overbearingly moral and uxorious public limitation to sexuality, stimulated Carpenter to look beyond Britain for guidance, criticism and meaning for his discontent.[8]

John Addington Symonds' reputation did not experience a revival in interest, in contrast to that of Carpenter's, in the late 1970s. Symonds and his thoughts on homosexuality certainly feature in modern historiography; his involvement with Ellis' study *Sexual Inversion* guaranteed his place as an historical actor in the upsurge of interest in the history of homosexual identities. However, in the milieu of political gay identity formations in the late 1970s, Symonds appeared firmly as belonging to another age. He was married, socially prominent and committed to the Victorian bourgeois lifestyle and its aspirations, his life striking an anxious balance of intense loyalty to his wife and family and exploration of his sexual desire for men.

Symonds is presented by historians of homosexuality in the context of late-Victorian Britain. However, he spent most of his life, from the late 1870s, in self-imposed exile in Switzerland. He rarely made visits to Britain, though his prodigious published works and articles of literary and artistic criticism, were published in Britain and ensured his reputation as one of this country's most eminent scholars. With the exception of his collaborative and posthumous contributions to *Sexual Inversion*, his writings on sexuality between men were, unlike Carpenter's, never published. His writing in this direction was, during his lifetime and long after his death, shrouded in secrecy and shame, much of it locked in an archive for decades. In a culture of gay political consciousness in the

1970s which set out to 'smash the caricatures and become themselves',[9] it is little wonder that Symonds provided scant historical inspiration. His life has attracted only one modern biographer, Phyllis Grosskurth, who published in 1964.[10] As Grosskurth states, Symonds' reputation had 'slipped into semi-oblivion' in the modern world.

Symonds' life and his ideas merit serious re-examination. His collaboration with Ellis should, ostensibly, place him firmly within the discipline of sex psychology that constructed modern homosexuality. However, closer examination of Symonds' ideas in this milieu reveal him to be the most articulate and incisive critic of the scientific approach to the phenomenon of sex between men. It must also be recognised that although Symonds and Ellis collaborated, the two men never actually met.[11]

Symonds provides us with his own sense of discontent and exasperation at the moral strictures and asceticism that dominated public conceptions of British masculinity and femininity of his day. His personal recollections are full of incidents that illustrate the particular difficulties of sexuality between men in Britain. Of course, these ideas were not published in his time. His contributions to *Sexual Inversion* were emendated by Ellis after his death in 1893.[12] Even this revision of Symonds' critique could not prevent the publication being condemned in 1898 as pornographic and a work of obscene libel.[13] When examined in their unabridged forms, Symonds' studies formed a critique of nineteenth-century British and European attitudes towards sex between men, that recognised the cultural specificity of this phenomenon. Much of Carpenter's work on sexuality between men, particularly before 1914, appears in comparison as highly eccentric to modern views. Carpenter had an almost naïve belief in the potential of science to explain the causes and the 'special nature' of uranianism, or sexual intermediacy. Symonds, on the other hand, formulated a critique of his own society that not only recognised the inability of the British to tolerate discussion of sex between men, but also provided perceptive concerns about the implications of inversion theorisation on the Continent. In many respects, Symonds' historicist approach to the phenomenon retains some of its analytical resonance today.

In any historical assessment of Symonds' and Carpenter's sense of sexual 'identity', it must be remembered that both men, to differing degrees, went to great lengths to preserve their reputations as literary men in Britain. Neither experienced prosecution for same-sex acts. Symonds' memoirs examine the lengths he went to avoiding sex with men in Britain, for fear of exposure. The memoirs give detailed accounts of how he sublimated his desires in this direction. However, Symonds' sex life with men flourished when he exiled himself and his family to Switzerland.[14]

Carpenter experienced some uncomfortable excoriation for his ideas following the publication of *Homogenic Love* in 1906. *Homogenic Love* was published as a chapter, entitled: 'The Intermediate Sex' in Carpenter's book *Love's Coming of Age*. The notions of 'uranianism' in this work are highly anaemic and apologetic. The mainstream press ignored the 1906 edition. Nonetheless, *Love's Coming of Age* was popular enough to be republished in 1909 and attract the attention of critics. Reactions to the 1909 edition were intense in hostility. The *Yorkshire Post*, conscious of Carpenter's prominence in socialist politics in the city of Sheffield, published letters which lambasted the work. The letters were written by M. D. O'Brien, outpoken critic of socialism and a resident of Sheffield. O'Brien took issue with the 'disgusting, loathsome and socially destructive vice' described by Carpenter in *Love's Coming of Age*. Interestingly, O'Brien's criticism of Carpenter's work was centred on its possible deleterious effects on the status of masculinity in the region. The letters questioned whether Carpenter's work was 'calculated to make Sheffield's citizens better husbands, better fathers or better sons'.[15] Also, the *British Medical Journal*'s *(BMJ)* intense disapproval of Carpenter's work in 1909 served notice on 'urnings' to 'emigrate to some land where their presence might be welcome'.[16]

Carpenter's public prominence in this field has resulted in historians giving considerable attention to his work. In this chapter, the ideas of Symonds and Carpenter will be addressed chronologically. Carpenter's work on intermediacy was the first published work to attract widespread attention in Britain in 1909. However, Symonds' studies on sexuality between men were written before Carpenter's. Also, Carpenter admired Symonds greatly and was somewhat in awe of his scholarly reputation. According to C. Tsuzuki, Carpenter's biographer, when Symonds died in 1893, Carpenter 'felt that he was fated to succeed Symonds in the defence of homosexuality'.[17] Symonds' engagement with and subsequent rejection of scientific theories of inversion, was the end point of a life-long examination of his own proclivities for men. Symonds' thoughts on the status of sexuality between men in his own society are contained predominantly in three extraordinary documents, 'A Problem in Greek Ethics' (privately printed in 1883), 'A Problem in Modern Ethics' (privately printed in 1891), and his *Memoirs* (written in 1889 and locked away in the London Library until 1976).[18] In addition, Symonds' copious correspondence was published in three volumes in 1967, 1968 and 1969.[19]

John Addington Symonds

John Addington Symonds was aware from youth of the implications of
sex and sexuality between men in his own society. Examination of this
is historically important. His memoirs give a personal and insightful
account of the problems associated with sexuality between men in
British society and the class to which he belonged. Also, the memoirs,
written in 1889, are an essential analytical adjunct to the ideas expressed
in 'A Problem in Greek Ethics' and 'A Problem in Modern Ethics'.
Symonds' memoirs, published by Phillis Grosskurth in 1984, are used
here to evaluate Symonds' better-known work on sexuality between
men, his own sense of manhood and the prevailing expectations of masculinity in his time.[20] Symonds' intense anxieties about his desire for
men are best understood by examination of his class and cultural background. He was the son of a Bristol physician of national prominence
and reputation. Dr John Symonds governed his son's life and moral
outlook until Symonds married in 1864 at the age of 34. Symonds' obe-
dience to his father's wishes appear remarkable to the modern reader.
His mother had died when he was only four years old and his father
remained a widower. Symonds' memories of his youth and adulthood
until his thirties were dominated by the authority of his father.
Dr Symonds was earnest and had become socially very well connected
during his life. As Grosskurth states, the 'dedicated pursuit of the intellectual life' amongst his family 'might have provided Matthew Arnold
with a sterling example for the middle classes to emulate'.[21] Symonds
was brought up from a very early age in a milieu where 'friends were
cultivated ... interests were edifying, and ... pleasures were purposeful'.
Although a sickly child, this did not protect him from being sent to
Harrow School at the age of 13. Symonds detested his experience at
Harrow.[22] His memoirs provide us with a remarkable insight into the
sexual immorality prevalent at the school in the 1850s:

> Every boy of good looks had a female name, and was recognised as
> a public prostitute or as some bigger fellow's bitch. Bitch was the
> word in common usage to indicate a boy who yielded his person to
> his lover.[23]

Symonds commented that 'the Harrow system in my time was a bad
one .... the little state of Harrow was rotten to the core'.[24] He found it
remarkable, in retrospect, that the sexual culture of the school was so

contrary to prevailing mores in British society. He described the sexual culture amongst the adolescents in the studies and the dormitories as

> incredibly obscene. Here and there one could not avoid seeing acts of onanism, mutual masturbation, the sports of naked boys in bed together. ... my school fellows realised what I had read in Swift about the Yahoos.

Certain boys in the school were given sexualised nicknames, such as the *notissima fossa* (the most infamous trench) or Bum Bathsheba. Symonds somehow managed to resist sexual contact at school. This was not simply a disclaimer to protect his reputation. The memoirs are candid about his sexual desires and encounters with men throughout his life. Years later, Symonds' intimate friends at school, who all rigidly conformed to an uxorious sexual standard expected of them in adulthood, told him emphatically

> that they thought I'd passed through the school without being affected by, almost being unaware of, its peculiar vices. And yet those vices furnished a perpetual subject for contemplation and casuistical reflection to my inner self.[25]

Symonds remembered his sense of moral rectitude at encountering sex at school; 'I felt sure that these vices were pernicious to our society', he noted.

Symonds entered Balliol College, Oxford, in 1858, an experience he recalled as one of intense relief following the sexually foetid atmosphere of Harrow. He thrived in the atmosphere of intellectual freedom at Balliol and developed the passion for Ancient Greek literature that was to shape his life and literary career. However, Symonds' time at Balliol was clouded by problems concerning Harrow School. In addition to encountering the sexual culture between the boys there, he was party to the knowledge that the headmaster, Charles Vaughan, had been conducting a sexual affair with one of the senior boys. Symonds had been the recipient of Vaughan's physical overtures at the age of 17, though never himself sexually assaulted by Vaughan. In 1859, at Balliol, Symonds was arguing about the 'unrecognised passion between male persons' in Greek literature with his mentor, Professor John Connington. Like many of his pedagogical contemporaries at Balliol, Connington 'repudiated' the interpretation of love between men in Greek literature. A 'turn in the argument' forced Symonds 'to blurt out what [he] had so long concealed about Vaughan's story'. Connington warned him that 'such things ought not to be lightly spoken of'. Symonds convinced the professor that he could 'support what [he] had said by evidence, and that [he] was certain of the facts'. Symonds had some of the letters from Vaughan to the schoolboy in his possession. Connington took no action himself, but convinced Symonds that he should approach his father. When Symonds did approach his father, with Vaughan's letters and his own Harrow diaries, Dr Symonds 'took as little to convince … as it had been to convince Connington. The evidence was plain and irrefragable'.[26] Vaughan was, privately, persuaded by Dr Symonds to retire. By his own admission, the quiet removal of Vaughan from office influenced Symonds' sense of morality and masculinity. It highlighted the problems his sexual desires were to create for him. Also, the Vaughan incident is indicative of the potential for scandal of the most serious kind created by sexuality between males at the beginning of this period.

Dr Symonds did not approach the authorities and Vaughan was never prosecuted for his sexual misdemeanours. Instead, Dr Symonds wrote to Vaughan, revealing that he had full knowledge and proof of his sexual misdemeanours with one of the schoolboys at Harrow. Dr Symonds promised not to make public exposure of Vaughan, provided he 'resign the headmastership of Harrow immediately and sought no further advancement in the Church'. After a little prevarication, during which Dr Symonds made it clear that he was serious in his intent, Vaughan's wife, a member of the aristocratic Stanley family, visited Dr Symonds to plead on behalf of her husband. Symonds states that Mrs Vaughan prostrated herself in front of his father, admitting that 'her husband was subject to this weakness, but it had not interfered with his usefulness in the direction of the school'.[27] From this statement, it is clear that the worldly Mrs Vaughan was aware of her husband's propensities, but was prepared to tolerate them for the sake of public maintenance of the couple's social status. Vaughan's advisors in the matter were not prepared to be so tolerant. These advisors were his brother-in-law, Arthur Stanley, and Hugh Pearson, Canon of Windsor and a close family friend. Together with Professor Connington of Balliol, Vaughan's advisors supported Dr Symonds in his insistence that Vaughan retire, rather than risk exposure of 'a matter of such grave importance to a great public school'. Vaughan retired in 1860. He conducted his departure into private life with 'consummate skill', arousing no suspicions. At the banquet given at Harrow on his retirement, Vaughan presented 15 years of headmastership as 'as much as a man's strength could stand and quite enough for the school he governed'.[28] These reasons were acclaimed by the public as honourable circumstances for retirement and the government offered Vaughan the choice of the See of Worcester or the See of Rochester. Vaughan initially accepted the senior preferment of Rochester, an audacious decision, given the circumstances, as it bestowed upon him a seat in the House of Lords. Nonetheless, Dr Symonds 'telegraphed, on hearing the news, that he must cancel the act of acceptance'.[29] Dr Symonds' demand was met and Vaughan cancelled his acceptance of the See.

Vaughan's sudden abdication as Bishop of Rochester posed something more of a mystery to the public than his retirement from Harrow. Symonds confirmed that the matter was kept as secret as possible:

> No one knew the reason. ... the withdrawal of Dr Vaughan into private life, and his refusal of two Sees, were, however, so mysterious and so dramatic that the suspicions of worldly people awoke and we had some difficulty for several years to suppress the real history of the case.

Symonds was in no doubt as to the social furore that would have ensued had his father revealed Vaughan's activities at Harrow: 'it is singular that a secret possessed by several people' should have been closely kept 'while curiosity was still alive'. The implications of Vaughan's disgrace would have affected Harrow school, the established church and the government. Clearly, those involved in the conspiracy of silence were intent upon keeping this secret, and the reputation of these bastions of British masculinity, intact. Even Dr Symonds, the instigator of Vaughan's moral blackmail, kept his silence as long as the headmaster complied and retired from public life. In addition, Symonds' literary executor, in a note in the margin of the manuscript, took this episode as 'proof that J.A.S could not have intended his autobiography to be published *in extensio*'. Symonds kept the evidence that damned Vaughan in a package sealed by his father. Many of Symonds' private papers were destroyed after his death, including, undoubtedly, the evidence against Vaughan.[30] Also, Symonds was condemned as dishonourable by the small group of friends from Harrow, including the boy in liaison with Vaughan, for revealing Vaughan's activities to his father. These estranged friends never spoke to Symonds again. By the time Symonds wrote his memoirs in 1889, one of these schoolboy friends, Charles Dalrymple, was a Conservative Member of Parliament. Nonetheless, Symonds' 'dishonourable' indiscretion did not provoke a public scandal. Instead, a prominent member of the Victorian establishment was quietly removed for sexual misconduct with a boy. All those who removed him, or knew of the reasons for his removal, kept absolute silence, in order to preserve the reputations of the institutions touched by Vaughan.

A culture of secrecy and honour had been associated with the public schools and their alumni throughout the nineteenth century. As John Chandos states in his study of the public school system: 'despite their name', the public schools 'were not ... open places; little of what went on in them was intentionally revealed. ... only the initiates knew for certain what was the truth. ... They had long tended to be silent other than in private'.[31] Chandos states that 'sexual life of boys in public schools ... was seldom alluded to openly in print'. Even writers who could discuss adult sexual relations and prostitution 'avoided references to what they well knew existed' about the sexual culture of the public schools.[32] The power of the codes of silence surrounding the sexual activities in the public schools, underpins the pattern of silences about this phenomenon, in the legislature and government ministries of the nineteenth century.[33]

Chandos confirms that the truth of Vaughan's departure from Harrow was maintained as a close secret. Vaughan's refusal of preferment became, 'in the eyes of the world', a 'noble exemplar of Christian humility and disinterestedness in a Church of preferment-hungry prelates'. One panegyric described Vaughan as 'the one living instance of *nolo episcopari*, who refused bishoprics one after another to hold upon his quiet way'.[34] Vaughan became something of a sanctified figure, maintaining great influence in the Church of England in spite of his lack of office. He attracted acolytes, including Edward Benson, Archbishop of Canterbury, who deeply admired him for his apparent saintly otherworldliness. He was even commemorated for his services by the foundation of the Vaughan Library at Harrow School. Vaughan himself consented to the inconspicuous preferment of Dean of Llandaff in 1871, to the relief of a grateful and admiring nation. Dr Symonds had died earlier that year, so Vaughan evidently felt able to accept the position without his sexual proclivities being exposed.[35]

Given this context, Symonds' revelations to his father were indeed remarkable. However, the compact between father and son to blackmail Vaughan into retirement is best understood through Dr Symonds' social class and religious background. Dr Symonds came from a long line of doctors who, because of their Non-Conformist religious beliefs, were debarred from entering other professions in England by the University Tests Acts. The University Tests Acts excluded Non-Conformists and

Roman Catholics as undergraduates from Oxford and Cambridge Universities and the legal professions until the late 1820s. Until 1854, all teaching appointees at the ancient universities had to be in Anglican holy orders. The Anglican church maintained its monopoly in appointing only Anglican communicants to teaching posts at Oxford and Cambridge until the repeal of the last vestiges of the University Tests Acts in 1871.[36] Dr Symonds himself was not public school educated and went to Edinburgh University at the age of 16 to study medicine.[37] Edinburgh University was firmly outside the Anglican aegis and had been a magnet for English Non-Conformist undergraduates since the mid-eighteenth century.[38]

Grosskurth argues that in adulthood, Dr Symonds had eschewed much of the rigid sectarianism of his religious upbringing. He married a socially prominent Anglican and his son was a confirmed Anglican. In other words, the Symondses were social parvenus in the milieu of Harrow School and Oxford University. By the 1850s, these establishments were opening their doors to the sons of 'new men'. However, the sons of 'new men' had to disavow 'their backgrounds and their class' and submit to the culture of the ancient educational institutions.[39] In 1866, Symonds lambasted Harrow to his lifelong friend and confidante, Henry Dakyns. Symonds identified the incongruous social mix at the school and lamented the homogenisation imposed by the institution. He commented that the boys were

> drawn from the lower aristocracy & the moneyed classes for the most part; idleness, plethoric wealth, hereditary stupidity & parvenu grossness combining to form a singularly corrupt amalgam.[40]

Symonds implored Dakyns not to 'publish this letter abroad'.[41]

Symonds and his father clearly understood the culture of secrecy that emanated from these institutions, even in an era when the class basis of the participants was somewhat more diffuse than it had been earlier in the century. Dr Symonds' Non-Conformist upbringing influenced the 'sobriety with which he conducted every aspect of his life'.[42] His background and earnestness convinced Vaughan that the parent, who was something of a social outsider to Harrow, might be serious in his threats to expose him. It is significant that Vaughan had initially accepted the Bishopric of Rochester, in full knowledge of the blackmail hanging over him, and only refused the See when Dr Symonds promised to act upon his threat. Cocks argues that in the mid-nineteenth century, blackmail of this kind could be successfully contested by a man of Vaughan's social status and character. There was a general refusal to believe accusations of sodomitical practices levelled against a man of Vaughan's standing and public character. Blackmailers were, predominantly, of a lower social status than the accused.[43] It is probable that Vaughan judged that Dr Symonds would be risking as much, in terms of his *arriviste* social standing, as Vaughan himself, should his proclivities be made public on his acceptance of a bishopric and a seat in the House of Lords. By the 1850s, blackmail of this kind had become 'indelibly associated' with criminality and a 'lack of moral character'.[44] The incident was clearly a battle of wills which Dr Symonds won. There is no indication that Dr Symonds wished to take any direct or public action about the sexual culture of Harrow School other than quietly to remove its headmaster. Dr Symonds' preservation of silence and his treatment of the evidence that would have condemned Vaughan, indicated that Dr Symonds had no greater wish to discuss the matter of sex between males than any of his contemporaries. Symonds commented, in defence of his abhorrence of Vaughan and Harrow of the late 1850s, that he 'knew what serious harm the school was suffering from these customs, so ill-adjusted to the spirit of the times we lived in'.[45] This stance was undoubtedly influenced by his father, who was, in many respects, an embodiment of the 'spirit of the times'.

Symonds' confidence in his father over the Vaughan affair resulted in a new intimacy of trust between the two men. Symonds reveals in his memoirs that, from this point on, his father knew of his desires for other men. This may in part explain his father's reluctance to use the authorities to prosecute Vaughan. However, had Dr Symonds decided to go to the authorities, the concomitant arraignment would have involved evidence from some of the most socially prominent families in the land. A trial of this kind would have been a national spectacle, reported at least in *The Times*. A trial would have resulted in some kind of social opprobrium for all the parties concerned, not least for forcing the authorities to consider publicly the existence of this unmentionable vice amongst men in Britain.[46] Dr Symonds also ran the risk of facing criminal charges of blackmail, and a libel suit from Vaughan, should the courts judge that the evidence in his possession was insufficient to convict. On the eve of the 1861 Offences Against the Persons Act, a prosecution for sodomy was still a capital indictment and convictions were difficult to secure.[47] This notwithstanding, Vaughan must have been uncertain enough of the parvenu Dr Symonds, to be convinced eventually that this parent might just risk social obloquy and expose him. In the event, the method of Vaughan's departure ensured the effective removal of a pederast from a position of high office without any implications of disgrace for the institutions or families involved.

It is clear from Symonds' memoirs that Dr Symonds maintained a firm grip over his son's life after the Vaughan incident. If anything, Dr Symonds' authority over his son intensified after this episode. Symonds, who was 19 at the time of the Vaughan incident, would have been considered a young man and still subject to his father's authority. But the potential pitfalls of a sexual scandal gave Dr Symonds added reason to protect and intimately guide his son's actions. Symonds had had no sexual experience with other men and his desires were, at this stage in his life, notional. Nonetheless, there is no indication that Dr Symonds, an eminent physician, interpreted his son's nature in medico-scientific terms, even though forensic analysis of this kind was appearing on the continent.[48] Instead, Dr Symonds viewed his son's 'problem' in terms of what was considered to be acceptably masculine in their social class. Symonds recalled himself as 'an aberrant being, who was being tutored by [his] father's higher sense of what is right in conduct'. Symonds had taken his father's guidance in the matter of the Vaughan incident. His father's handling of the affair made it clear to Symonds that sexuality between men and the public admission of its existence was an impossibility in contemporary society. Soon after this episode, Dr Symonds made his son acutely aware that the inadmissibility of this propensity did not just affect men of social prominence in the 'spirit of the times' in which they lived. Symonds had fallen in love, at the age of 20, with Willie Dyer, a local Bristol boy aged 17. When Dr Symonds learned of the nature of the romantic friendship between the youths, he insisted upon 'a cautious withdrawal from the intimacy'. Symonds elaborated on his father's reasons:

> the arguments he used were conclusive. ... the possibility of Vaughan's story becoming public, and the doubtful nature of my own emotion, prudence pointed to a gradual diminution or cooling-off of friendship.

His father made him see, 'under the existing conditions of English manners', that an ardent friendship between the youths was impossible. Symonds recognised that the incongruity of the class of the two youths increased the risks of detection of the true nature of their friendship. Symonds did not conduct a sexual affair with Dyer. Nonetheless, the relationship was, for Symonds, passionate and imbued with sexual longing. With a youth of his own class, the intimacy could have been passed of as intense friendship between peers, and any possible sexual intimacy preserved from exposure by the culture of secrecy and silence amongst men of this class. Dr Symonds made it clear that if the truth of their romantic friendship became known, it would damage Dyer's reputation as well as his own. Dyer was the son of a Dissenting tailor. Symonds eventually capitulated to his father's wishes:

> I foresaw the possibility, if I persisted in my love for him, of being brought into open rupture with my family, and would involve my friend thereby in what would hamper his career by casting the stigma of illicit passion on our intercourse.[49]

The Vaughan incident and his father's reaction to his relationship with Willie Dyer had a profound effect upon Symonds' own sense of masculinity and class. Symonds was unequivocal about the social perils of his desires:

> The instincts of my blood, the conventionalities under which I had been trained, the sympathy I felt for sisters and brothers-in-law ... brought me to look upon myself as an aberrant being. ... I gave up Willie Dyer as my avowed heart's friend and comrade. I submitted to the desirability of not acknowledging the boy I loved in public.[50]

Symonds proffered a perceptive analysis of the plight he found himself in and the reasons for eschewing his affair with Dyer:

> We are, all of us, composite beings, made up, heavens knows how, out of the compromises we have effected between our impulses and instincts and the social laws which gird us around.

Symonds' recognition of the reprehensibility of his desires, or the isolated and perilous sense of self his desires engendered, were not constructed through developments in legislation or scientific analysis. Instead, Symonds was made acutely aware that the prevailing percep- tions of class and masculine behaviour excluded the possibility of his emotional and sexual fulfilment:

> Modern society provided no bond of comradeship whereby we may have been united. So my first love flowed to waste. I was unable to deal justly with him; the mortification of the anomalous position he and I were placed in did much to degrade my character.

It is significant that Symonds was made aware of the potential damage to Dyer's reputation by the liaison. Of course, concerns of class predominated – had Symonds decided to conduct a relationship with a girl of Dyer's class, social discomfiture would also have been acute. But the 'illicit passion' the two men shared transcended other socially unacceptable liaisons in its impropriety. The relationship was anathema throughout society. The connection with Symonds threatened to damage and stigmatise even Dyer's humble prospects and masculine status within his own social class and urban community. Symonds recalled the passing of this liaison with the deepest regret, 32 years after the break-up. The ending of the liaison 'exhausted [his] instinctive faculty for loving'. He never again 'felt the same unreason and unreasoning emotion for any other human being'.[51]

Symonds' recollections of the 1860s are dominated by his frustrated desires for other men. In his final year at Balliol, he fell in love with Alfred Brook, a fellow undergraduate. The men did not conduct, or attempt to conduct, a sexual affair. Symonds was deeply influenced by the ideal of pure love between men tolerated at Balliol in these years, fostered by an entirely chaste interpretation of Plato in the college curriculum. Symonds subsumed his sexual feelings for Brook in clandestine poetry, almost the only expression of his desires in these years. He described these years as a 'close unwholesome labyrinth of tyrannous desires and morbid thoughts in which [he] wandered'. He explained the principles governing his passions:

> A respectable regard for my father, an ideal of purity in conduct, a dread of the world's opinion forced upon me ... combined to make me shrink from action. Still I could not suppress my inborn unconquerable yearnings.[52]

Symonds' sexualised poetry from these years are revealing reminders of the isolation he felt. A stanza from one of his untitled poems encapsulates, with poignancy, his sense of disconnection from the men he desired:

> Four young men are bathing in the pond by the embankment. I pass; the engine screams and hurries me away. But the engine has no power to take my soul. That stays, and is the pond in which the bathers swim, the air in which they shout, the grass on which they run and dress themselves, the hand that touches them unfelt, the lips that kiss them and they know it not.[53]

Symonds' resolute maintenance of sexual chastity with the men he 'yearned' for, convinced him that he was able to continue his career in the homosocial environment of Oxford. After graduating from Balliol, Symonds was elected to a fellowship at Magdalene College, Oxford, in 1862. Unfortunately, the appointment was to have unfortunate consequences for him. In his last year at Balliol, he had befriended G. H. Shorting, an undergraduate who had come up from Rugby. Shorting was 'vain, possessive and strong willed'. He shared Symonds' 'Arcadian' tastes, or desires for other men, and, as Grosskurth states, Symonds strove to 'save Shorting from the ruinous eventuality towards which his desires were leading him'.[54] Unlike Symonds, Shorting refused to subsume his desires and 'pestered' a chorister at Magdalen. The authorities at Magdalen became aware of the potential scandal, predominantly because of the unbridled manner in which Shorting conducted his 'flirtations' with the chorister.[55] On his appointment to Magdalen, Symonds had naïvely agreed to coach Shorting privately in philosophy. Symonds insisted that the turorials were conducted in Shorting's rooms at Balliol, in order to frustrate Shortings' 'designs for easy access to the chorister' at Magdalen. Shorting was incensed at Symonds' actions and vowed to destroy him. Shorting made 'hysterical threats' that he was going to convince the Magdalen authorities that Symonds had encouraged him in his 'flirtations' with the chorister. Magdalen conducted an investigation, in which correspondence between Symonds and Shorting was examined. Symonds was completely exonerated, but the episode had shattered his nerve. Although exonerated, Linda Dowling argues that the scandal of an inquiry tainted Symonds' name with 'an unbearable suspicion of sexual guilt' amongst some at Oxford.[56] Shorting left Balliol 'in disgrace'[57] and Symonds resumed his teaching responsibilities at Magdalen. However, his health soon completely collapsed. Symonds had experienced, within three years of the Vaughan affair, another pointed reminder of the dangers of the desires that he and Shorting shared, and the impossibility of them being expressed without severe censure. Although Symonds' 'conscience was absolutely clear'[58] in the matter, the inquiry had provided an unequivocal example of the unacceptability of sexual relations between men in his society. He gave up his fellowship, on the grounds of ill health, and was sent by his father to Switzerland to recuperate.

Symonds regarded the suppression of his sexual desires and the emotionally shattering Magdalen incident as the cause of the chronic ill health he suffered as an adult.[59] He suffered from various chronic maladies of the lungs and eyes. He even described 'terrible disturbances of the reproductive organs'[60] and 'dangerous nervous erethism'[61], meaning that he experienced continuous and unrelieved erections. He consulted Dr William Acton, the famous genito-urinary physician who was a vehement condemner of masturbation. Acton was the author of the popular manuals *A Practical Treatise on Diseases of the Urinary and Generative Organs* (1841) and *The Functions and Disorders of the Reproductive Organs in Childhood, Youth, Adult Age and Advanced Life, Considered in their Physiological, Social and Moral Relations* (1859). The physician's treatment of Symonds involved cauterising his bladder and urethra in order to quell his 'dangerous nervous erethism'.[62] Symonds did 'everything in short, except what nature prompted ... nature bade me indulge my sexual instincts'.[63] Symonds argued that his desires 'drew [him] fatally to the male as a beast to be suppressed and curbed'. He regarded his sexual propensity as a problem 'to be down-trampled by the help of surgeons and their cautery of sexual organs'.[64] Symonds did not specify whether he revealed to Acton or any other surgeon the precise nature of his sexual desires. Symonds also consulted, on his father's advice, the famous surgeon, Sir Spencer Wells. Symonds told Spencer Wells about his 'constitution', for which the surgeon recommended marriage. Symonds was, unusually in the context of these memoirs, ambiguous about what was meant by his 'constitution', beyond 'nervous erethism', in relation to his consultations with surgeons. Wells impressed upon Symonds that

> marriage ought not to be regarded as a matter of idealised passion, but as the sober meeting together of man and woman for mutual needs of sex, for fellow service, and loyal devotion to the duties of social and domestic life in common.[65]

Wells was proffering to his patient the standard advice recommended by British doctors in this period for all 'aberrations in the sexual instinct', especially the urge to masturbate.[66] Symonds was tempted by this prospect as the solution to his inner problem:

> If instinct had to be followed, I must have found its satisfaction in male friendship. But this was what I had resolved to suppress and overcome. [Spencer Wells'] argument, therefore, made a strong appeal to my reason, when I considered the possibility of a suitable marriage. It seemed to be the one exit from my difficulties; and I found myself supported by my father.

Symonds strove, after this episode, to create a simulacrum of acceptable masculinity for himself that would have protected and guaranteed his social status as a man, at the expense of what he described in his memoirs as his 'real self'.[67] Taking a wife 'on calculation' ran against his instincts, but this was precisely what he did. In 1864, he married Catherine North, a woman from a family of social prominence and eminent connections.

In 1889, when writing his memoirs, Symonds regarded his marriage as 'the great mistake – perhaps the great crime of my life'. By 1889, Symonds had accepted his sexual desires as an integral part of his character. He had, since the late 1870s, been living permanently outside of Britain, in environments that were more convivial to and accepting of his propensities. However, whilst resident in Britain, Symonds' marriage had been an essential front to protect his masculine status and reputation. In this respect, Symonds regarded his marriage as 'not to be regretted' in the years before he emigrated with his family. He was 'urged to marry by [his] father, by [his]own earnest desire to overcome abnormal inclinations [and] by the belief that [he] should regain health'. By his own admission, marriage neither resolved his sexual inclinations or improved his health. But Symonds did regard the early years of his marriage as 'saving [his] life from wreckage and [prolonging his] power of moral resistance'.[68] He was able to abstain from sexual contacts with other men until he removed himself and his family permanently abroad. This preserved him and his family from the crippling social and professional disgrace of exposure and him personally from the severe penal and social consequences of successful prosecution.[69]

Symonds described his unsatisfactory sex life with his wife in considerable detail in his memoirs. Symonds was able to perform the sex act with her but it gave him no pleasure or fulfilment: 'there was something in it nauseous, and cohabitation in my case meant only the mechanical relief of nature'.[70] By these means, he was able to father four daughters and present himself to the world as a model of masculine aspiration. But what did his wife, Catherine, think of Symonds' sexual 'relief of nature' with her and a life devoid of 'any really passionate moments together'?[71] Symonds described Catherine North as a woman who 'married late ... and carried into matrimony the instincts of a virgin, for whom there is something ignoble in physical appetite and nauseous in childbirth'.[72] Symonds confirmed that Catherine's outlook on marriage was not at all unusual:

> We civilized people of the nineteenth century are more backward than the African savages in all that concerns this most important fact of human life. We allow young men and young women to contract permanent relations involving sex ... without instructing them. ... We

do all that lies in us to keep them chaste, to develop and refine their sense of shame, while we leave them to imagine what they like about the nuptial connection ... trusting that they will blunder upon the truth by instinct.[73]

Nonetheless, Symonds and his wife formed a bond of trust and friendship. Catherine was made aware by Symonds in 1869 of his own propensities. This was the year that Symonds fell passionately in love with 'Norman', or Edward Norman Moor[74], an ex-Harrovian who shared his sexual desires for men and a love of Ancient Greek literature. Norman was a constant visitor to Symonds' home, to an extent that aroused the concern of his wife. Symonds decided to be frank with Catherine. Following their discussion, the couple agreed to be celibate in marriage. Symonds described Catherine as having little problem with this arrangement. For Catherine, marriage with Symonds became companionship 'in the highest sense, when she is relieved of these necessities. ... After shillyshallying with an ill-participated nuptial bed, we have found it best to live as male and female quite apart'. Symonds claimed, on his wife's insistence, that she was quite happy with a celibate marriage: 'having realised by a life in common ... how much better it is to be married than to remain single, having found satisfaction in ... a sphere of activity in her domestic cares, she is satisfied'.[75] Catherine also engaged actively in elevated social circles in London and Bristol, for which a secure and respectable married status was prerequisite. Symonds used extracts from Catherine's own diaries, written in the early years of their marriage, to substantiate his assertions of her personal dissatisfaction with sex and childbirth. Catherine stated that

if girls knew all that marriage means, there would be less 'marrying in the abstract' less of that foolish longing for the temporary glitter and variety of the thing, possibly for the romance also, which has so often disgusted me in my contemporaries.[76]

Symonds, for his part of the compact between them, promised Catherine to keep his passions firmly 'within the limits of good sense and taste'.[77] In many respects, the couple had achieved the same mutually beneficial compact within marriage that Charles Vaughan and his wife had clearly maintained, until the threat of exposure by Dr Symonds imperilled the arrangement. Like Mrs Vaughan, Catherine was personally devoted to her husband. In addition, Catherine could maintain, through this private arrangement with Symonds, an appearance of highly respectable domesticity that was essential for a couple of their social status.[78] Symonds' arguments to Catherine for continuing to see his 'lover' were the 'increase in health since [he] knew Norman [and] the uncontrollable bias of [his] nature in this direction'. Symonds and Norman did not have a sexual liaison, fulfilling Symonds' promise to Catherine. In fact, Symonds had not experienced, at this stage in his life, the sexual experience he craved, with any man. Cook highlights that Symonds had had a brief encounter with a 'young grenadier' in the vicinity of Lecester Square in 1865. Although the encounter certainly captured Symonds' imagination, no sexual liaison took place and he declined the grenadier's proposition of sex with 'a passionate mixture of fascination and revulsion'.[79] Symonds and Norman kissed twice and he saw Norman naked once. It is clear from a letter from Norman to Symonds, written years later in 1886, that the two men did not have sex. Norman was quite sexually experienced with men before he met Symonds, but the relationship with Symonds 'did something to cure [him] of this'.[80] Symonds confirmed that, after their liaison ended, Norman became a schoolmaster and married. At the time of his relationship with Norman, Symonds was striving to achieve an understanding of his desires, through attempting to live the chaste and 'idealised passion' between men inherent in the Balliol interpretation of Plato's *Symposium*. Norman was considerably younger than Symonds, being 19 years old when they met. Symonds interpreted his feelings for Norman by the same light that Plato conceived of ardent passion between an older and a younger man. He claimed vehemently that he preserved a physically chaste relationship with Norman and, influenced by the ideals of Plato, did much to further the youth's education. 'I was content with contemplation, contact, kissing', he wrote, continuing,

> The candour with which I have set down everything about myself, and the admission which I here make of having at a later period indulged in such acts with other men, ought to be sufficient guarantee of my truthfulness.[81]

Symonds' new understanding with his wife and the 'platonic' love he maintained with Norman are of significant importance in the development of his ideas on sexuality between men. Symonds had, by the early 1870s, established himself as an independent scholar of classical Greek poetry of considerable promise. His passion for Norman inspired him to write, in 1873, his first private scholarly essay of the status accorded to sexuality between men in Ancient Greek society. Furthermore, Symonds conducted in this scholarship a comparative analysis between the Ancient and the Modern and formed a critique of the abhorrence with which 'Greek love' was regarded in contemporary British culture and society.

In his 1873 essay, 'A Problem in Greek Ethics', Symonds described, for the first time in English, sexuality between Ancient Greek men in its idealised form and its 'baser' forms. The essay was an important scholastic and personal milestone for Symonds. Elements of the piece informed his contributions to Hellenistic scholarship that established his literary reputation and the essay appeared posthumously, in emendated form, in Ellis' *Sexual Inversion*. In the essay, Symonds established that the Greeks, because they saw God in every manifestation of the human spirit, accepted sexuality between men. The Greeks accepted 'paiderastia' in all its physical and emotional forms and the philosophers, or the 'Greats', idealised the desire of an older man for a younger man into an enthusiasm and imbued the passion with piety.[82]

Symonds' approach to Greek paiderastia in the essay was fundamentally influenced by his experience of the curriculum as an undergraduate at Balliol and his continued scholarly contact with the college. Symonds' education at Balliol coincided with far-reaching reforms in the curriculum. Study of Greek classics had been part of an undergraduate's learning throughout the early modern and modern periods at Oxford and Cambridge universities. However, the texts in the curriculum were limited and students were confined to 'the dead weight of ... narrowly grammatical and rhetorical training'.[83]

Benjamin Jowett, the great pedagogue and reformer at Balliol and mentor to Symonds, sought in the late 1850s and the 1860s to expose undergraduates to 'the full range of philosophical and historical implication within the Greats texts, and allowing the best Continental thought and scholarship to play upon them'.[84] Linda Dowling argues, in her study *Hellenism and Homosexuality in Victorian Oxford* (1994), that Jowett's reforms had significant implications. Jowett approached the study of the Greats with 'an ethically relativising historicism'. This approach had unforseen consequences. Symonds, Walter Pater and Oscar Wilde found that 'Greek paiderastia was, through the agency of the Greats curriculum, brought vividly and compellingly to life'.[85] Jowett's historical relativism, deeply influenced by Rankeian historicism, minimised the relevance of 'English moral categories' in appreciating the culture and society of the Greeks.

Symonds' exposure to the Greats and his continued scholarship in this field, not only influenced his physical conduct with Norman in the early 1870s; it also informed Symonds' ideas on the difficulties in changing contemporary attitudes to Greek paiderastia. The late Victorians held an almost fetishistic obsession in the 1860s and 1870s with Greek culture, particularly with Homer, the Homeric ideal and its 'sway over the Victorian imagination'.[86] However, the Victorian admiration for the Greeks was largely silent on the matter of Greek cultural attitudes towards sexuality between men. Despite his insistence on minimising 'English moral categories' in examination of Greek history, even Jowett described paiderastia as 'the most degrading passion' and 'the greatest evil of Greek life'. Jowett provided 'obligatory phrases of English moral condemnation' to distance his work from more neutral German assessments of the phenomenon.[87] The new interpretation of Plato at Oxford translated into chaste, idealised relations between tutors and students for a specific time period at the university.[88] Reforms in 1854 opened competition for college fellowships and expanded non-clerical fellowships, meaning that graduates could teach at Oxford without taking Anglican orders. This established a period of 'particularly intense male homosociality' at Balliol, which based its outlook on Greek notions of masculine comradeship. Platonic masculinity was adopted almost as an alternative to the Anglican Christian homosociality that had traditionally predominated in an environment with an absence of women.

This 'unique moment of Oxford masculine comradeship' ended in 1877, when the Oxford commission abolished the celibacy requirement for fellows and ended the 'ethos of a wholly male residential society'.[89] Therefore the eminent Victorian *literateurs*, Pater and Symonds and the literary genius of Wilde, were educated at a particular period in Oxford when an idealised, though decidedly non-sexual notion of masculine platonic comradeship was being promulgated. 'Socratic' tutors at Oxford, including Pater and Connington, were at pains to subsume or ignore any suggestion of sexuality in teaching and interpreting the Greats.[90] Symonds himself had learned from Connington that the chaste ideal was the only acceptable form of 'Hellenistic' masculine comradeship in modern society. Connington's reaction over the Vaughan affair inculcated in Symonds the sense of absolute impossibility of paiderastia being expressed in physical form in modern Britain. Symonds' experience of the Magdalen inquiry into the Shorting incident compounded this conviction. Dowling argues that the 'Socratic' tutors at Balliol, including Connington, Jowett and Pater, lived constantly in fear of sexualised interpretations of paiderastia 'utterly' discrediting the legitimacy of the 'transcendental authority of philosophical thought, especially the thought of Plato' in modern, imperial Britain. Greek philosophy was an integral influence in Liberalism in these years and, in particular, in the thinking of the great Liberal Prime Minister, William Gladstone. It would have been highly unlikely, in this context, that a frank and genuinely historicist interpretation of Greek love between men could have been tolerated.[91]

The severe moral strictures in conduct and thought imposed by Symonds' colleagues at Balliol explains some of the reasons why he went to such lengths in his own life to emulate a chaste interpretation of paiderastia. Balliol's influence and his father's non-conformist and essentially plebeian moral rectitude, had combined to form a powerful amalgam that dominated Symonds' sexual conduct. Nonetheless, his sexual abstinence with men in these years, particularly in the 'platonic' relationship with Norman, and his highly respectable marriage, had their uses. Symonds' personal conduct gave him the prerequisite moral platform and intellectual 'objectivity' necessary for his broader studies of the Greeks to be taken at all seriously by his 'Socratic' peers at Balliol.

As an independent scholar, free from the celibacy requirements of senior academics at Oxford, Symonds had to present to 'the world' an unimpeachable display of respectable conduct, particularly after the Magdalen inquiry during his fellowship. His admirable family life protected him, to some extent, from close questioning of the nature of his friendships with men as an adult. Also, Symonds went to great lengths to avoid physical sexuality in his passionate attachments with men. The slightest hint that he might be conducting sexual relationships with men would have attracted the accusation of being a 'compositor', or, in other words, an active sodomite who used the Greek paradigm to justify his vices.[92]

Symonds, however, rejected these moral strictures when it came to his personal thoughts on the subject of Greek paiderastia. The essay 'A Problem in Greek Ethics' was a historicist and forthright account of sexuality between men, in all its forms, in Greek culture. Of course, Symonds' 1873 essay was, like his sexualised poetry, a work of unpublished private scholarship. However, unbeknown to his Oxford colleagues, elements of Symonds' research for 'A Problem in Greek Ethics' informed his published work on Greek morality. Symonds' analysis of the broad spectrum of Greek morality, appeared as a chapter in his highly successful *Studies of the Greek Poets*, published in 1873, 1875, 1876 and 1893.[93]

In *Studies of the Greek Poets*, Symonds made only very general references to Greek attitudes towards sensuality *per se*, with no specific references to paiderastia. The work received critical acclaim and established him as one of the pre-eminent Hellenist scholars of the day. Nonetheless, Symonds convinced himself that even though highly expurgated, his analysis of Greek morality in the work, cost him the Chair of Poetry at Oxford in 1877.[94] The Reverend Richard St John Tyrwhitt, rector of St Mary's, Oxford, attacked Jowett, Symonds and 'the pretentions of Balliol Hellenism' in an article in the *Contemporary Review* in March 1877. Tyrwhitt conducted a campaign to promote a 'forthright, fox-hunting [and] aristocratic' manliness at Oxford in an attempt to 'pierce the idealist glamour of Jowett's Platonising pedagogy'.[95] He stated in his article of 1877 that the 'emotions of Socrates at sight of the beauty of young Charmides … are not natural'.[96] Symonds withdrew his candidature for the elections to the Chair following publication of this article.[97]

Symonds was undoubtedly wise to withdraw his candidature for the Chair. Had he continued, the background research for his published comments on Greek morality might have come to light under scrutiny. Tyrwhitt continued to confront Jowett, who was in Anglican holy orders, with the cultural consequences of his 'abandonment of theological authority in favour of the merely intellectual mastery represented by Anglo-Hellenism'.[98] In other words, Tyrwhitt was accusing the Reverend Jowett and his movement, of atheism. Jowett survived these attacks, but it is doubtful whether Symonds would have, particularly if his uses of Greek paiderastia to criticise modern society, had been revealed. The analysis of Greek paiderastia had been used by Symonds in 1873 to critique modern British society in 'A Problem in Greek Ethics'. Symonds was not alone in realising the potential of studies of Ancient Greek society to appraise modern society, but was the first of his generation to use, albeit clandestinely, the Greek paradigm to criticise modern attitudes to sexuality between men. Symonds' sexual chastity with the men he loved also provided him with the 'dispassionate' approach he deemed necessary to use the Greek paradigm to criticise the modern.

In the essay, Symonds used Greek paiderastia to question the indiscriminate abhorrence of all forms of sexuality between men in modern British society:

> The reasons for evading the investigation of a custom so repugnant to modern taste are obvious … . [But] … the fact remains that the literature of the Greeks, upon which the best part of humanistic education rests, abounds in references to the paiderastic passion. The anomaly involved in these facts demands dispassionate interpretation. I do not, therefore, see why the inquiry should not be attempted.[99]

Symonds traced the idealisation of paiderastia amongst the Greeks to the traditions of the Dorian tribesmen. In that martial and homosocial milieu, passions between men were tolerated to such an extent that unions were cemented 'between man and man no less firm than that of marriage'.[100] Symonds argued that these unions were essential for the strength of the Dorian battalions and added that 'morality, according to modern conceptions, certainly did not enter into the account'.[101] This section, which eschews a moralising assessment of the Dorians, was, significantly, omitted from the posthumous essay incorporated by Ellis in the first edition of *Sexual Inversion* in 1897.[102] Symonds stressed the manliness and emphatic masculinity of Greek paiderastia and its expression in the arts: 'no prurient effeminacy degraded, deformed, or unduly confounded the types of sex idealised'.[103] Symonds went on to argue that the 'first reflection which must occur to even prejudiced observers is that paiderastia did not corrupt the Greek imagination to any serious extent'. However, Symonds regarded the ideals of paiderastia as unattainable in modern society. In a section that was also omitted from *Sexual Inversion*, he asserted that 'it is scarcely possible that the moral sense should resume paiderastia after resolutely through so many generations rejecting it'. Symonds argued that in modern society 'only in a camp, a prison, a convent, or a public school, some sequestered cyst within the social organism can the circumstances needful for its reappearance now be found'. In other words, modern marriage and its concomitant domesticity predominated, and excluded the conditions for 'noble' paiderastia to thrive. Nonetheless, Symonds regarded the contexts in which paiderastia occurred in the modern age as important:

> The manners of camps, prisons, convents, public schools, together with recurrences of vice in cities, prove that there is something persistent in human nature making for this habit.[104]

Symonds' memoirs articulated the repugnance he felt for the squalor of 'this habit' of human nature that prevailed in the 'sequestered cyst' of the English public school. Modern society had rendered paiderastia so shameful and secret, that its physical expression could be found only in depraved circumstances in esoteric single-sex institutions, or the anomic underworlds of modern cities. The timing of Symonds' reference to the 'recurrences of vice in cities' is significant. Symonds' essay was written only three years after the 'Stella and Fanny' arraignment at Bow Street in 1870, which received scandalised and garrulous coverage in the newspapers.[105] During the Bow Street proceedings, the *Pall Mall Gazette* published an article lambasting explicit details of the arraignment being published in the working-class Sunday newspapers. The *Pall Mall Gazette* also warned its classically educated readership in the article that men in 'drag' in the Burlington arcade, bore no relation whatsoever to passions between men, in Ancient and Pagan literature. The *Pall Mall Gazette* was clearly concerned that an apology for the defendants might be tolerated amongst some of its learned readership:

> There is a wide difference between objectionable and revolting deeds done and recorded by people who have for centuries been dust and ashes – deeds done in a wholly different state of society or under a different code of laws and morals – and the same deeds done in the London of the present day.[106]

In this unique style of newspaper commentary on a case of 'unnatural crime' in the period, the *Pall Mall Gazette* acknowledged what the 'Socratic' pedagogues at Balliol had been at pains to deny, in their interpretations of the Greats. It is significant that newspaper commentary on unnatural crime was subsumed in the case trial the following year; also that national newspaper coverage of unnatural crime all but ceased between 1872 and 1885.[107] No one, it appeared, could publicly tolerate the idea of physical sexuality existing between men in modern society. In this culture, 'Socratic' scholarship could only provide philosophical guidance for modern living when interpreted in a purified form, divorced from the morals of its Pagan originators. The *Pall Mall Gazette* added that the 'great sea of impurity in which the pre-Christian mind was wont to revel' resulted from 'an element wholly wanting in many men a hundred generations ago ... [in their] ... devotion to the female sex'. Modern, Christian marriage and concepts of uxorious masculinity excluded the possibility of a latter day 'Antinous in "drag" ' being tolerated in Britain. When such a 'creature' did surface, he was 'a thing abominable'. In addition, he was a 'lamentable anachronism' who did 'not know his epoch'.[108]

The commentary in the *Pall Mall Gazette* of 1870 mirrors Symonds' lament of the impossibility of paiderastia being tolerated in modern society. For Symonds, the difference between the Greeks and the Modern was that 'the Greek race made one brilliant, if finally unsuccessful, effort to regulate that gross persistent instinct'. Modern society, on the other hand, was obsessed with 'regulating and controlling intersexual relatinos [sic]'. In such a society, argued Symonds,

> it is rational to predict that what may still remain of an instinctive tendency towards paiderastia in the social organism will continue to

be treated much in the same manner as we treat the inconvenient survival of a superfluous member in the corporeal organism.

Symonds predicted that modern, Christian society would develop methods to eradicate paiderastia:

> Even if further researches into the history of primitive mankind do not confirm the Christian opinion that this habit, instead of being a normal instinct, is truly a disease ... which must be remorselessly stamped out like syphilis or madness.[109]

Symonds' comments were prophetic. Elements of Continental inversion theories were incorporated, in the twentieth century, into eugenic and fascist arguments for racial purity. However, in Britain, published scientific discourse could not even countenance the analysis of the phenomenon that would be necessary for such developments. Even pejorative and hostile commentary would have given legitimacy to the existence of 'this habit' in British society.[110] It is therefore understandable that Symonds' essay could not possibly have been successfully published in Britain, without risking prosecution for obscene libel. Also, publication would have jeopardised the merit of his established scholarship in the field.

In later life, Symonds railed against the hypocrisy underpinning the chaste homosociality that had been encouraged at Oxford. He criticised the notion that the chaste ideal of masculine love and comradeship promoted by Jowett's reforms bore any relation to the realities of this form of comradeship amongst the Greeks. In a letter to Jowett, written in 1889 in self-imposed exile from Britain, Symonds condemned his mentor and friend's interpretation of Greek love in the 'reveries of Plato'. Jowett regarded Greek love, or paiderastia, as being 'mainly a figure of speech' used by the Greeks. Symonds expressed surprise that Jowett, with his 'knowledge of Greek history', could be ignorant of the 'present poignant reality' of physical 'paiderastic love' amongst the Greeks. Symonds argued that this sexuality was so manifest in the texts of the Greats, that Jowett would be best advised to avoid the subject altogether, rather than interpreting paiderastia as a mere figure of speech. Symonds went as far to recommend that the study of the Greats be abandoned in Britain, on the grounds that it would be an 'anomaly' to make Plato 'a text-book for students, and a household book for readers, in a nation that repudiates Greek love'.[111]

Failure to achieve preferment at Oxford in 1877 and his continuing ill health, persuaded him to remove himself and his family permanently to

Switzerland. Symonds' emigration was to have a significant impact on his personal conduct. His 'new life' abroad profoundly influenced his ideas on sexuality between men and its concomitant difficulties in Britain. The Symondses were already regular visitors to Switzerland in the 1870s, mainly for the benefit of Symonds' health. Symonds had a house built in Davos and rarely made visits to England after 1880. Symonds undoubtedly suffered from debilitating bouts of lung disease and the climate in Switzerland proved beneficial to his health. But the permanent move to Davos was also a wilful and self-imposed exile from the torments that his sexual desires created for him in Britain. Tyrwhitt's criticisms and the attacks on Balliol 'Socratism' in 1877, was more than his constitution could bear. However, emigration created other personal problems for him. In a letter to Henry Dakyns, informing him of the completion of his new house *Am Hof*, Symonds revealed that 'Catherine hates Davos'.[112] Grosskurth argues that Catherine 'stoically' resigned herself to her life in Switzerland, though she never overcame her dismay at 'the prospect of being isolated for the rest of her life in a bleak valley whose less obvious attractions she never learned to appreciate'.[113]

Catherine's continuing loyalty to Symonds is indeed remarkable. She endured her sexless and emotionally bewildering marriage with Symonds, even in their exile. In the early days at *Am Hof*, Symonds sought the advice of Jowett, who continued to be his mentor and friend, as to whether he should send Catherine back to England for the sake of her happiness. Jowett, who was a regular visitor to *Am Hof*, pointedly underlined the social difficulties and possible scandal from such a move:

> I am certain that there is nothing about which your wife cares more than about your health and happiness, and that there is no sacrifice which she would not gladly make for it. It would be a fatal mistake for her to come and live in England: neither of you would know any happiness afterwards.[114]

Grosskurth regards Jowett's advice as 'comforting' to Symonds.[115] Jowett's advice also reveals the overarching presumption in this period, that a wife's place was beside her husband, come what may. Symonds, through publication and voluminous correspondence, continued to be a figure of prominence and importance in the English literary world. The Symondses may have lived in a self-imposed exile away from the gaze of their countrymen, but, as Jowett emphasised, Symonds' status demanded that the couple appear devotedly married. It is little wonder that Symonds regarded his marriage in these years as the 'great mistake' of his life. Catherine's removal to Switzerland cut her off from their considerable social circle, which included the reforming campaigner, Josephine Butler and the poet, Edward Lear. However, the Symondses were early settlers in a place that, within ten years of their arrival there, was to become one of the most fashionable resorts in Europe. As the years went by, the Symonds' played host at Davos to their many friends. Nonetheless, Catherine had to endure Symonds' new habit of 'moving between Davos and Italy as mood and weather dictated'.[116]

In Switzerland, Symonds was allowed intimate friendships with all classes of men, without censure from the local community. He insisted that manly love there did 'not interfere with marriage, when that is sought as a domestic institution, as it always is among men who want children for helpers in their work and women to keep their households'.[117] It is little wonder that Catherine hated Davos so much, as the culture of masculinity there relegated women to a domestic sphere even more completely than in England, with evidently little expectation of an affective parity in marriage. Catherine, educated, socially connected and sophisticated, could have had little in common with the women she encountered in the region.

Symonds, on the other hand, found the masculine culture of the canton in which he lived in Switzerland accepted the passions he felt for other men, to a degree that would 'astonish an Englishman who knows nothing of the Swiss'. Inspired by this structure of masculinity, he felt emboldened to neglect his wife and follow his sexual passions. Much time during the years of residence in Switzerland was spent in solitary visits to Venice. There, Symonds indulged his sexual desires to a considerable degree of promiscuity with gondoliers, 'soldiers on the streets, sailors ... professional male prostitutes and casual acquaintances'.[118] He described the ease with which a man could procure sex with a gondolier, without risking public censure: 'the gondoliers of Venice are so accustomed to these demands that they think little of gratifying the caprice of ephemeral lovers – within certain limits, accurately fixed according to a conventional but rigid code in such matters'. Symonds did not specify the 'certain limits' involved in the same-sex code of the gondoliers. However, in his love affair with the gondolier Angelo Fusato, which lasted eight years, Symonds hints that their sex life would have been considered in Britain a criminal 'misdemeanour', which indicates their sexual liaison did not involve anal sex.[119] Symonds' liaison with Fusato was important in the context of Symonds' own marriage. Fusato became a frequent visitor to Symonds' house in Davos, and the two men continued as lovers, until Symonds' death. When not in Symonds' company, Fusato lived with 'a girl by whom he had two boys'.[120] Symonds expressed some initial shock at this arrangement, indicating that a man of Fusato's class in England would be expected to be married in similar circumstances. Symonds revealed that he was not 'at that time fully aware how frequent and how binding such connections are in Venice'. By exiling himself from Britain, Symonds discovered cultures in which a man might live in an unmarried state with a woman – and conduct a sexual love affair with a man – without any threat to his masculine status.

Symonds would leave Catherine at Davos for up to a month at a time to indulge his sexual appetites in Venice and, after 1888, he kept a small flat in the city. In these years, Symonds was influenced by Horatio Brown, a regular '*Inglese Venezianato*'[121] and fellow admirer of male beauty and sexuality. Catherine had to endure the presence of her husband's Venetian lover at Davos and her husband's new coterie of likeminded friends, who also lived in semi-permanent exile away from the social hostility towards their propensities in Britain. Nonetheless, Symonds' new life abroad had emboldened him. In 1883, he had ten copies of 'A Problem in Greek Ethics' privately printed, and clandestinely circulated copies of the work amongst sympathetic friends at home and abroad.[122] He urged his small body of readers not to publicise the existence of the essay. He gave his reasons for circumspection and why he

> did not wish to give this study publicity. … The English public is almost totally devoid of scientific curiosity. … They go on putting the Greek classics in the hands of their sons … but they exact total silence upon the most significant anomaly in the life of … the race which has inaugurated nearly all our intellectual methods.[123]

Symonds' emigration also liberated his approach to his published work. His contacts with Italy encouraged him to write popular travelogues and his famous study: *Renaissance in Italy*. In the competition for the Chair at Oxford, Symonds expressed intense anxiety that the *Manchester Guardian* had described him merely as 'a writer for magazines'.[124] However, Symonds' professional ambition had all but evaporated on moving to the Continent. He studied what interested him, freed from the constraints of academic preferment in Britain. Symonds' overriding interest in these years, was his desires for men and the difficulties these desires created in society, particularly in Britain. This abiding interest motivated him to write his memoirs. He realised that the memoir was

> a very singular book – perhaps unique, in the disclosure of a type of man who has not yet been classified. I am anxious therefore that this

document should not perish. I want to save it from destruction after my death, and yet reserve its publication for a period when it will not be injurious to my family.[125]

Symonds' concerns about the piece were perceptive. The work was certainly not publishable at the time and would not be published for nearly a century. Nonetheless, the process of honest exploration of his inner self through the writing of the memoirs stimulated Symonds to examine the scientific writings on the subject that were available on the Continent.

It is remarkable that Symonds had not engaged with scientific discourse on the phenomenon of sexuality between men until 1890. Works of this kind were very difficult to obtain in Britain. Even after he emigrated, nearly all of Symonds' literary contacts, publications and book supplies were connected with Britain.[126] Scientific analysis of sexuality between men was freely available in published form on the Continent. Symonds found the encounter with this discourse a salutary experience. He added an alarmed postscript to his memoirs, stating that he had written them before he had

> studied the works of Moreau, Tarnowski, Krafft-Ebing, who attempt to refer all cases of sexual inversion to a neurotic disorder inherited or acquired. I had not then read the extraordinary writings of Ulrichs, who maintains that the persons he calls Urnings form a sex apart. ... It appears to me that the abnormality in question is not to be explained either by Ulrich's theory, or by the presumptions of the pathological psychologists.[127]

Continental theorists were, in Symonds' view, fulfilling his predictions in 'A Problem in Greek Ethics' that sexual desire between men would be considered by modern, Christian society as 'truly a disease' instead of 'being a normal instinct'. These developments prompted Symonds to write his critique of inversion theories: 'A Problem in Modern Ethics'. This essay is interpreted by Weeks and others as evidence of a medico-legal discourse on 'homosexuality' and the construction of 'the homo-sexual' in late Victorian Britain.[128] However, Symonds' work, although written in English, is best understood in the context of Continental discourse on the subject. Symonds was in self-imposed exile from Britain, in spite of his many contacts there, and his ideas on inversion theory were fostered by free access to literature that was proscribed in Britain. Also, Symonds used the perspective of Continental scientific freedom and relative legal liberality towards sex between men to criticise the indiscriminate social and legal hostility towards the phenomenon in Britain.

'A Problem in Modern Ethics' is the only contemporary humanist critique of Continental inversion theorisation. Examination of the critique is important, as the analysis informed Symonds' approach to the project of writing *Sexual Inversion*, a work he persuaded Ellis to co-author. Symonds' reading for the essay was extensive and included works by Karl Ulrichs, Paul Moreau, Benjamin Tarnowski and Richard von Krafft-Ebing, who were the leading luminaries in the discourse. Symonds recognised that 'medical writers upon this subject are comparatively numerous in French and German literature and they have been multi-plying rapidly of late years'.[129] He also recognised that there was an absence of this discourse in Britain, where 'no one dares speak of it; or if they do, they bate their breath, and preface their remarks with maledic-tions'.[130] He acknowledged that in England, Taylor's *Principles and Practices of Medical Jurisprudence* provided some comments on the mat-ter, but added that 'Taylor is so reticent upon the subject of unnatural crime that his handbook ... does not demand minute examination'.[131] During the study, Symonds engaged in correspondence with Ulrichs. Symonds did not 'incline to [Ulrich's] peculiar mode of explaining the want of harmony between sexual organs and sexual appetite in Urnings'.[132] However, he regarded Ulrich's theories of origin and argu-ments for decriminalisation of sex between men in states where penal statutes existed, as a sympathetic companion in the critique of medical literature in the field.

Symonds argued, using the perspective he had developed in 'A Problem in Greek Ethics', that Continental scientists had unconsciously adopted the mantle of the Christian theologian, in their discourse on sexuality between men. Symonds argued that

> the phenomenon of sexual inversion is usually regarded (by the med-ical writers) from the point of view of psychopathic or neuropathic derangement, inherited from morbid ancestors, and developed in the patient by early habits of self abuse.

Symonds understood the term psychopathic to mean 'derangement in the mind emotions'. In his opinion, concentration on the psychopathic by theorists such as Krafft-Ebing, was as subjective an approach to the phenomenon as the theologian's. Symonds argued that examination of the neuropathic, or a physical anomaly in the nervous system, was more objective and truly scientific. However, Symonds took issue with the use of a combination of the psychopathic and neuropathic by Krafft-Ebing, in forming conclusions on inversion in men. Symonds argued that such an approach did not provide conclusive evidence of the cause of inversion. Instead, that the approach simply raised philosophical questions of 'what is the soul, what are the nerves' and what were the exact distinctions between them.

Krafft-Ebing's predecessors had approached the phenomenon of inversion with methodologies that Symonds had little difficulty in finding flawed. Moreau concluded that inverts formed an intermediate class of persons that constituted 'a real link between reason and madness' and that this was caused by a neuropathic hereditary trait. However, Symonds highlighted that Moreau had contradicted himself in his work. Moreau had included the incidence of inversion in history and in modern Turkey and Persia, where sexuality between men was customarily accepted. His theories of morbidity applied exclusively to Christian Europeans, who had 'nothing to do with the morals of other countries'.[133] Moreau had treated the nineteenth-century European Christian as a species distinct from the rest of humanity, and Symonds took issue with 'the inefficiency of this distinction in a treatise of analytical science'. Symonds argued that 'in other words, an Englishman or a Frenchman who loves the male sex must be diagnosed as tainted with disease' but the Ancient and the 'Sodatic' male was simply yielding to instinct, supported by the custom of his society.[134]

Symonds critiqued other contributions to the field, which, like Moreau's, saved 'its victims from the prison [and delivered] them over to the asylum'. Krafft-Ebing's work, which Symonds regarded as a synthesis of its scientific predecessors, particularly alarmed him. Krafft-Ebing created categories of inversion and argued that they were caused by congenital as well as acquired factors. Krafft-Ebing argued that acquired inversion was caused by masturbation, which stimulated latent 'inverted neuropathy'. Symonds argued that Krafft-Ebing's theory was

so constructed as to render controversy almost impossible. If we point out that a large percentage of males who practice onanism in their adolescence do not acquire sexual inversion, he will answer that these were not tainted with hereditary disease.[135]

Symonds challenged the hereditary theory upon which medical men insisted, asking at 'what point in human history was the morbid taste acquired?'. Symonds posited his own theory as to why notions of heredity could not possibly explain the causes of inversion:

> There is probably no individual in Europe who has not inherited some portion of a neuropathic strain. If that be granted, everybody is liable to sexual inversion, and the principle of heredity becomes purely theoretical.

Symonds' analysis of the Eurocentricity of the inversion theorists was remarkable and perceptive for its time. He added that a scientific and medical analysis of inversion was unlikely to provide any answers about inversion:

> The problem is too delicate, too complicated, also too natural and simple, to be solved by hereditary disease and self abuse. ... we shall hardly be able to resist the conclusion that theories of disease are incompetent to explain the phenomenon in modern Europe. Medical writers abandon the phenomenon in savage races, in classical antiquity, and in the Sodatic zone. They strive to isolate it as an abnormal and specifically morbid exception in our civilisation.

Symonds concluded that inversion was 'a recurring impulse of humanity ... compatible with an otherwise healthy temperament'.[136]

Symonds' attempts to collapse the theories of Continental inversion theorists are also remarkable in the context of relative toleration of inverts in Continental cities, such as Paris and Vienna. Krafft-Ebing's inverted correspondents, overwhelmingly from Continental cities, regarded *Psychopathia Sexualis* as a work of liberation for them.[137] If inversion was a sickness, then it could not possibly be criminal or sinful. Symonds felt that this was a highly dubious category for inverts to resort to. He acknowledged that inverts, when discovered as such, displayed more than their share of nervous problems. He described the 'socially impossible' situation for the invert and his desires in modern society and questioned, from this perspective, who could not be

> astonished if the nerves of an individual in this position are not equal to the horrid strain? In some cases the nerves give way altogether: mental alienation sets in; at last the wretch finds in a madhouse that repose which life could not afford him. Others terminate their unendurable situation by the desperate act of suicide. How many unexplained causes of suicide in young men ought to be ascribed to this cause![138]

Symonds feared for the future development of science in this field and for possible treatments of 'congenital depravity in the brain centres'.[139] His engagement with the scientific discourse stimulated him to gather his own case histories from inverts, similar to those of Krafft-Ebing. Symonds wished to demonstrate, using a historical and culturally relativistic approach, that inversion was a rare but normal instinct in men in modern society. However, he realised that a riposte of this kind would not be taken seriously if conducted by a literary figure. He was inspired to persuade Ellis to undertake the authorship and medical analysis for the work.

The men had a keen mutual admiration for each other's publications and Symonds was convinced after reading Ellis' *The New Spirit* in 1890 that Ellis would be the most sympathetic medical figure to collaborate with.[140] In many respects, Ellis' *Sexual Inversion* was Symonds' brain-child. Symonds' aims with the work were twofold. He wished to provide a counterpoise to the emphasis on morbidity promulgated by the Continental theorists. Also, he wished to attack the social and legal opprobrium of the phenomenon in Britain. If published, *Sexual Inversion* would not only be the first work of its kind in Britain, but would also be an analytical departure in Continental discourse. Although Symonds had reservations about the implications of inversion theory, he recognised that the discourse on the Continent had been fostered in states where sex between adult males was either completely legal, or discussion of the phenomenon had altered patterns of prosecution. Symonds argued in 'A Problem in Modern Ethics' that in those countries, society had not suffered 'where legal penalties have been removed from inverted sexuality, where this is placed on the same footing as the normal – in France, Bavaria, the Netherlands ... [and] ... Italy'.

Symonds used his analysis of the medical and legal tolerance of the phenomenon in much of the Continent to argue for a change in British law. He argued that the problem in Britain in regards to sexuality between men was that

> assuming that they are all abominable, society is content to punish them indiscriminately. The depraved debauchee who abuses boys receives the same treatment as the young man who loves a comrade. The male prostitute who earns his money by extortion is scarcely more condemned than a man of birth and breeding who has been seen walking with soldiers.[141]

Symonds' assessment of the British paradigm supports the analysis that Britain had an indiscriminate cascade of legislation criminalising all sex between all men, rather than a legislative construction of 'the homosexual' in the late nineteenth century. Symonds addressed what he perceived would be obstacles to changing the law in Britain. He anticipated that society would object to change, on the grounds that 'unnatural vices, if tolerated by the law, would increase until whole nations acquired them'.[142] It is clear that Symonds regarded this as a prevalent perception. Symonds argued that the 'danger' of this notion being realised:

> Does not seem to be formidable. The position of women in our civil-isation renders sexual relations amongst us occidentals different from those of any country ... where antiphysical [sic] habits have hitherto become endemic.[143]

In other words, Symonds was arguing that modern marriage and prevailing cultural expectations for men to be uxorious, excluded the possibility of the propensity being more than an occasional occurrence. In 'Sodatic' cultures, such as Turkey and Persia, society did not demand the same kind of domesticity and relationship to women from its men. These cultures had entirely different structures of masculinity, where sexuality between men, within certain limits, did not threaten a man's masculine status.

In making his case for legal toleration of sex between grown men in Britain, Symonds argued that in France, 'sexual inversion has been tolerated under the same restrictions as normal sexuality'. He argued that in France, legal toleration of the phenomenon had caused 'no extension of it through society'.[144] However, during the 'Stella and Fanny' trial in 1871, the Lord Chief Justice enshrined in English case law a prohibition on rectal examinations for physical signs of sodomy. The Lord Chief Justice lambasted French medico-legal literature on the subject and inferred that the presence of such literature, legally tolerated in France, meant that French society was riddled with the vice of sodomy:

> Fortunately, doctors in England know very little about this matter. ... that vice [sodomy] has not yet tainted the habits of the men of this country. ... therefore the medical men here cannot give you ... what perhaps medical practitioners in other and less happy countries in that respect could give.[145]

It was highly unlikely, that using the French situation in regard to this matter, would persuade the legal authorities in England to tolerate the debate necessary to change the laws. Nonetheless, Symonds highlighted the illogical position of indiscriminate criminality of sex between men in English law:

> The severity of the English statutes render them almost incapable of being put into force. In consequence of this the law is not infrequently evaded, and crimes are winked at.

Symonds concluded that the English laws needed to be repealed because 'our legislation has not suppressed the immorality in question ... the English penalties are rarely inflicted to their full extent. ... [and] ... that our higher education is in open contradiction to the spirit of our laws'.[146] In other words, the English appeared content to tolerate the hypocrisy of indiscriminate and unworkable legislation, for fear that the unnatural vices might be publicly acknowledged to exist amongst its men. In correspondence with his friend Edmund Gosse, acknowledging the difficulties involved in English law being changed in this respect, Symonds urged that the law be changed 'without discussion'. He had convinced himself that 'the majority of unprejudiced people would accept the change with perfect equanimity' but that 'everybody' dreaded the scandal of a public discussion of the issue.[147]

In the final years of his life, Symonds dedicated himself wholeheartedly to the collaborative project of *Sexual Inversion*. In spite of the enormous potential difficulties, Symonds had convinced himself that the project and his aims for it were worth undertaking. From the safety of his Continental retreat, Symonds cared less and less in these years who knew of his proclivities. Grosskurth states that by the time he died in 1893, 'a large group of people' were aware of his tendencies. This contrasted sharply with Symonds' behaviour in Britain where, 'as a young man ... he was extremely careful to conceal his proclivities from all but his closest friends'.[148] Symonds had abandoned the constraints he had considered necessary in Britain to preserve his masculine and social status. Nonetheless, 'A Problem in Modern Ethics' was privately printed and circulated only to people he trusted. Symonds' new-found hopes in his final years, to contribute to the field of inversion theorisation and create a change in English law and social attitudes, were, however, completely unrealistic. In Continental exile, removed from the constraints of expectations of masculine behaviour in Britain, Symonds had corresponded predominantly with maverick thinkers there, on the margins of the late Victorian intelligentsia. However, British society had not, as Symonds had hoped, changed in its hostility towards public acknowledgement of sexuality between its men since he had emigrated.

If anything, in the aftermath of the trials of Oscar Wilde in 1895, this tendency in British society intensified. After his death, his family and his literary executor ensured that none of his work or ideas on the problems of sexuality between men in modern society became broader public knowledge. Grosskurth confirms that a 'conspiracy of silence' pervaded in Symonds' posthumous reputation. In his obituaries and the biography, written by Brown in 1895, 'so many friendships had to be omitted, so many activities had to be suppressed, so many motives had to be accounted for in innocuous terms'.[149] Symonds' family ensured that all copies of the first edition of *Sexual Inversion*, with Symonds' authorship, were withdrawn from publication. Ellis' second edition of the work, with Symonds' name removed, was banned in 1898 as a work of obscene libel.[150]

Edward Carpenter

Edward Carpenter was one of the maverick thinkers that Symonds encountered through the project of *Sexual Inversion*. Carpenter was an intimate friend of Ellis' wife, Edith Lees, and it was this connection that involved Carpenter with Ellis and *Sexual Inversion* in 1892. However, Carpenter was also influenced by the life and ideas of Symonds. Indeed, Carpenter felt compelled to undertake his own examination of sexuality between men after Symonds' death. In many respects, Carpenter's own struggle with his desires and his attempts to achieve some kind of accommodation of them in a hostile culture, were parallel to Symonds'. The men were from similar educational backgrounds, though Symonds' life was undoubtedly the more socially elevated of the two. Carpenter did not attend public school, but was educated at Cambridge in the early 1860s, and took Anglican holy orders. In 1874, plagued by religious and social doubts, Carpenter sued for his own defrockment and left Cambridge. Similar to Symonds' 'exile', Carpenter isolated himself from 'society' in order to free himself from the crippling social and behavioural restrictions of his upbringing. Of course, Carpenter's 'isolation' was initially from the upper and upper-middle class social circles in which he moved. As he stated in his 1916 autobiography, *My Days and Dreams*, 'I even gave my dress clothes away'.[151] Carpenter joined the new University Extension Movement and worked as an itinerant lecturer in the North of England. His purposes and motives after 1874 were to live 'almost entirely with the working masses'.[152] By 1892, when he came into contact with Symonds, Carpenter was well established as a leading intellectual figure in the socialist movements of the day.

Carpenter's involvement with Ellis, Symonds and *Sexual Inversion* was an understandable development in his ideas and thinking. Symonds had admired Carpenter for some years. He knew Carpenter's *Towards Democracy*, a highly influential poem of nearly four hundred pages, that predicted a socialist millennium. On these grounds, Symonds welcomed Carpenter's assistance with *Sexual Inversion*, though Carpenter's involvement never developed into full collaboration on the piece.[153] Carpenter had been part of a group of early socialists, 'The Fellowship of the New Life', in the early 1880s, which had included radical thinkers such as Ellis, George Bernard Shaw, William Morris and Henry Salt.[154] In the early years of 'The Fellowship of the New Life', socialists believed that personal transformation, based on instincts, was necessary to eschew the restrictions and prescriptions of contemporary life. In *Towards Democracy*, Carpenter prophesied that the socialist millennium would be achieved through 'liberation of man's natural desires or instincts from the repression of civilisation'.[155] It is difficult to overestimate the influence of Carpenter's *Towards Democracy* in these years amongst socialists, feminists and radical thinkers. One feminist commentator regarded *Towards Democracy* as 'our Bible'; in an era when socialists 'no longer believed in dogmatic theology, Edward Carpenter gave us the spiritual food we still needed'.[156] By the 1890s, most of the early socialist intellectuals had split and factionalised. Shaw and others went on to form the Fabian movement, which involved itself with industrial working-class politics and the *realpolitik* of parliamentary representation through a party of labour. However, Carpenter adhered to his highly esoteric vision of socialism in *Towards Democracy*.

Carpenter's persistence with his own particular vision of socialism is best understood through examination of his sexual desires for men and the ideas he expressed about this phenomenon. Carpenter regarded the process of writing *Towards Democracy* as 'the starting-point and kernel of all my later work, the centre from which other books have radiated'.[157] In the poem, Carpenter made explicit his view that sexual liberation was fundamental to liberation of other aspects of life. Carpenter believed that 'sex still goes first, and hands mouth eyes brain follow [sic]; from the midst of belly and thighs radiate the knowledge of self, religion and immortality'.[158] It is little wonder that Carpenter inspired many of the new socialists, particularly women, with this hitherto unexpressed emphasis on the pleasure of non-procreative sex and the essential nature of this pleasure in a fulfilled life. Carpenter was unable, even in this milieu, to express an equivalent liberation for his own desires for men. In a self-referential sentence, buried in a single stanza in the poem, Carpenter made the plea:

> Lovers of all handicrafts and of Labour in the open air, confessed
> passionate lovers of your own sex, Arise![159]

Carpenter had been aware of his desires for men since his adolescence.
Like Symonds, he felt unable to express his desires in physical form for
many years. As he stated in his autobiography,

> the desire had no expression, no chance of expression .... I natur-
> ally concluded that there was no room for them in the scheme of
> creation.[160]

Carpenter regarded his desires for men as central to his sense of difference from others in his class. However, his 'isolation' from society and
his self-imposed exile to the 'working masses' of the north did not provide him with any new outlet for his desires. His modern biographer,
Chushichi Tsuzuki, examines the 'desperation' felt by Carpenter in these
years, born out of the loneliness created by his desires. On one occasion,
in 1876, Carpenter went to Paris 'to see if by any means I might make a
discovery there'. In Paris he encountered male prostitutes, 'but the commercial samples of the Boulevards, though some of them deeply interested me, were nothing for my need'. It is significant that Carpenter, like
Symonds, regarded only the Continent as having the potential to fulfil
his sexual needs in these years. Carpenter resigned himself to living and
working with 'good enough people', but lamented that, emotionally,
'they too were only afar from me'.[161]

In 1883, Carpenter established his home at Millthorpe, an isolated
farm near to Sheffield. He described his farm as a 'happy valley ...
[with] ... no resident squire of any kind, nor even a single villa'.[162]
Carpenter had managed to achieve the personal isolation he felt he
needed, away from the gaze of the gentry and the haute bourgeoisie he
detested. Millthorpe also gave him refuge from the gaze of the working
classes amongst whom he had been working since the early 1870s. He
admired what he perceived to be the more instinctive and natural way
of living amongst the northern working classes. But the effort of relating
to the people he encountered was a constant strain for him. Carpenter
may have hated his own class, but he found the attempts to eschew the
preconceptions of his upbringing, intensified his isolation. Although
he continued to be involved in Sheffield working-class politics in the
late 1880s, his isolation made him into 'a being apart, carrying some

guru-like qualities'.[163] In other words, Carpenter had removed himself from prevailing expectations of masculinity and class. He belonged neither to his own class, nor to the class to whom he had dedicated his life. Also, the expectations of masculinity within his own class and the industrial working classes isolated Carpenter from other men. During these years, Carpenter sought emotional solace in Continental and oriental travel and the examination of oriental belief systems.

Carpenter's exploration of cultures other than Britain's in the 1880s and the 1890s were of significant influence in his efforts to understand and come to terms with his desires. His notions of sexual liberation expressed in *Towards Democracy* were inspired predominantly by the Hindu scriptural text, the *Bhagavad Gita*. Carpenter had been aware of the existence of Hindu philosophy since his adolescence. His eldest brother was in the Indian Civil Service and wrote regularly of events and religion in the country. Like many of Carpenter's contemporaries, a passing acquaintance with the beliefs of subject peoples was considered prerequisite knowledge for an English gentleman. After the creation, in 1876, of the Crown Imperial of India, knowledge of Indian beliefs was considered essential if 'the Empire was to last in India'.[164] Carpenter's exposition of Hindu philosophy was quite different from that of his peers. He was given the *Bhagavad Gita* to read in 1881, at a particularly low point in his 'desperation'. Reading the texts themselves, rather than learned Western interpretations, was something of a revelation to him:

> All at once I found myself in touch with a mood of exaltation and inspiration – a kind of super-consciousness – which passed all that I had experienced before.[165]

Carpenter had also been deeply affected at this time by the notions of masculine comradeship inherent in Walt Whitman's poem, *Leaves of Grass*. Whitman had been influenced by the *Bhagavad Gita* in his poetry of masculine friendship in the southern United States. Whitman vehemently denied any sexualised inspiration in his concept of male comradeship. The combination of Whitmanesque comradeship and the 'tenets of love between all men' in the *Gita* inspired Carpenter's particular concept of socialism. Also, Parminder Bakshi argues that the 'individual as part of the cosmic whole, preached in the *Gita*, would clearly have had an immediate appeal for Carpenter in his loneliness'.[166]

Bakshi argues that Carpenter's affinity with Indian scripture and his journey to Ceylon in 1891, was a particular form of Orientalism. Bakshi uses Edward Said's analysis of Orientalism and the creation of the Other by Western thinkers, in her assessment of Carpenter's travels in the East and the impact of these upon his acceptance of his desires. Said articulated the 'exaggerated boundary drawn between Europe and the Orient in terms of the notions of home and place' which was 'integral to the Western sensibility'. Bakshi takes the 'homosexual predicament' in nineteenth-century Britain as one of the most compelling and extreme examples of the oppositions identified by Said. As Bakshi states,

> against the context of social and religious intolerance, homosexuals invariably turned to places and ideas outside English society that accommodated love between men. Thus they became inveterate travellers to remote and unknown regions, forever in search of a viable lifestyle.

Bakshi extends this conception of 'homosexual Other' to Continental Europe, where 'attitudes to homosexuality were more lenient ... than in Britain'.[167] For Carpenter and, later, E. M. Forster, Europe was the first stage in a journey of liberating discovery, that culminated in the East. During the 1880s, Carpenter had travelled frequently to Italy, where he and his friends had 'intimate relations with Italian youths'. Bakshi argues that Carpenter regarded his journey to Ceylon in 1891 as 'replicating earlier trips to the Continent ... away from the constraints of England'.[168] Carpenter's journey to the East was undoubtedly a spiritual quest. He visited the Gnani Ramaswamy, a guru with whom Carpenter was to maintain correspondence for many years. Carpenter also had a sexual affair with a Singhalese man, named Kaula. The combination of spiritual enlightenment and sexual fulfilment that was free from local censure, left a powerfully enduring impression on Carpenter.[169]

Carpenter's travels had a liberating impact, inspiring him to live more openly as a lover of men. By doing so, he achieved what Symonds felt he never could in Britain. On his return from Ceylon, Carpenter met George Merrill, a working-class man whom he described as 'bred in the slums quite below civilization'.[170] Defying convention and the concerns of his friends, the two men became lovers in 1891. Carpenter had been honest about his proclivities amongst his inner circle of friends for some years and he had conducted an intermittent sexual relationship with George Hukin, a working-class man from Sheffield. However, Carpenter had been at some pains to conceal his sexual preferences from his wider reading public. Also, Carpenter had never confronted his friends with a potential sexual scandal. His relationships with other men had been passionate, but entirely ethically centred on notions of masculine and socialist comradeship, freed from class constraints. As Tsuzuki states, Carpenter's sexuality had 'remained a private affair'. Even the true nature of his attachment to Hukin was concealed from all but the closest of confidantes. By 1891, Carpenter was a well-known literary figure in radical circles. He had had passionate relationships with men, but these tended to be working-class 'comrades' involved with his isolated farm in Derbyshire or the milieu of socialist politics in Sheffield.

Carpenter had first formed a passionate attachment with Hukin in the mid-1880s. It is clear from Carpenter's correspondence with Charles Oates, his friend, confidante and fellow traveller to Italy, that Carpenter and Hukin had conducted a sexual relationship at some point in their friendship. Hukin was 'uneasy and even embarrassed' by the attachment with Carpenter.[171] Hukin eventually married a local girl, Fannie, in 1887, much to Carpenter's chagrin. Hukin was employed in the Sheffield razor trade and, by the mid-1880s, had become prominent in the local Socialist Society. It is probable that Hukin felt that marriage would provide him with a respectable and necessary masculine image amongst his peers. Carpenter described his intense jealousy at what he felt was Hukin's betrayal:

> Certainly, it is better for me to be away from the pair [George and Fannie Hukin] for the most part – for though they are <u>both</u> very affectionate, it causes me most horrible spasms of jealousy to see them.

This encounter, at Millthorpe, was apparently no less painful for Hukin. Carpenter complained to Oates that:

> George's illness <u>was</u> owing to seeing me – grief on my account and sorrow at having hurt me. He was so lovely on Thursday morning and kissed me and looked in my eyes so lovingly.

Carpenter raged to Oates about the impossibility of finding a lover, without the expectations of contemporary society intervening. Even in the working-class north, which Carpenter had expected to provide an alternative to the constraints of his upbringing, the possibility of fulfilling his sexual desires seemed just as unrealistic as amongst his bourgeois contemporaries in the south. Complaining of Hukin's marriage, Carpenter stated that

> these things are … <u>overpowering</u>. … The fierce and frightful waging for a mate – and the mockery of <u>woman</u> always thrust in the way. … I fear

it will be a lifelong struggle – with defeat certain – yet one <u>must</u> go on.[172]

A few months later, Carpenter revealed to Oates that he had engineered an encounter with Hukin and had sex with him: 'I went for a walk with George last Thursday and slept with him at Baslow – just as affectionate and loving as ever'.[173] This notwithstanding, Carpenter's relationship with Hukin cooled considerably during 1888. He remained friends with the Hukins, but the relationship centred entirely on concerns of local socialist politics.[174]

Carpenter continued to form passionate attachments to the working-class men with whom he came into contact. All of Carpenter's male 'comrades' whom he felt desire for in these years were either married, or in the case of Hukin, married during the friendship with him. Also, Hukin was the only man of this milieu, with whom Carpenter privately admitted having a sexual relationship. Amongst the other men he admired, Carpenter had to be satisfied with the chaste comradeship provided by his ethical socialist experiment at Millthorpe. He gave work to a series of working-class families who lived with him at Millthorpe. His relationships with the men of these families were certainly passionate, but decidedly non-sexual. To his friends, Carpenter appeared to be attempting to live the 'new life', with an absence of class distinctions, advocated by their new socialist beliefs. Nonetheless, Carpenter was to interpret the 'new life' in an entirely more radical fashion, that alienated even his most sympathetic friends.

Carpenter's relationship with Merrill, whom he met on his return from Ceylon, fulfilled his longings for a relationship with a man that was both sexual and emotional. Although they met in 1891, it took the couple seven years before they felt bold enough to live together. When Merrill did finally move into Millthorpe in 1898, Carpenter's friends were appalled. As Carpenter stated,

> they drew sad pictures of the walls of my cottage hanging with cobwebs, and of the master unfed and neglected while his assistant amused himself elsewhere. They neither knew nor understood the facts of the case. Moreover they had sad misgivings about the moral situation.[175]

The lack of understanding expressed by his friends is significant. Carpenter's friends were not narrow minded. Quite the reverse, as his friends included some of the most radical and controversial figures in

Victorian society. Some of them, including Shaw, Ellis and Lees, were contributors to underground publications such as *The Adult* in the late 1890s. The milieu of *The Adult* believed in free love, legitimation of the rights of illigitimate children and alternative coupling to marriage. However, even this radical milieu had severe reservations about two men living together as lovers. There are some inherent assumptions in the reactions of Carpenter's friends' to Merrill which merit attention. Prevailing concepts of domesticity regarded care of the home and the paterfamilias firmly as the realm of women. Even amongst feminists, such as Olive Schreiner and Carpenter himself, it was believed that society had 'exaggerated sex differences beyond sense and necessity'. It was this stance that made these thinkers radical in their time. Nonetheless, these radicals still firmly adhered to notions of divisions of labour between the sexes and used biological and evolutionary theories to substantiate these beliefs. Ellis' study, *Man and Woman*, published in 1893, argued about the 'perfection' of gender division of labour and 'sanctified the social roles that men and women inhabited'.[176] Ellis stated that 'woman breeds and tends; man provides; it remains so even when the spheres tend to overlap'.[177] By recognising that the 'spheres' overlapped between men and women, Ellis was being radical and innovative in his own society. But even amongst the radicals, the idea of two men living in a domestic setting, with an absence of women, was against nature.[178]

The fears of Carpenter's friends about his domestic arrangements after 1898, were based entirely on the presumption that a man needed a woman to tend to his domestic needs. Even the eccentric and isolated Carpenter, had relied on the wives of the working-class men who had lived with him, to attend to his home. Carpenter's domestic arrangement with Merrill was extremely unusual in its time. It is probable that the pair avoided prosecution and censure in 1898 only through the isolation of their home at Millthorpe. Carpenter commented that one of the attractions of Millthorpe had been the lack of a squire or middle-class residents. Had there been a squire, or a resident of a 'villa', it is likely that the arrangement might have elicited some hostility. Also, all classes of urban dwellers in the nineteenth century demonstrated increasing willingness to report sex between men to the authorities.[179] If Carpenter and Merrill had tried to live together as lovers in a town or a city, it is probable that their arrangement would have attracted more attention and been the cause of scandal. This notwithstanding, Carpenter's relationship with Merrill and, after 1892, his connection with Symonds and the project of *Sexual Inversion*, inspired Carpenter to write about sexuality between men.

Symonds had died in April 1893 and Carpenter continued to assist Ellis with the project of *Sexual Inversion*. Ellis did not collaborate with Carpenter on the authorship of the piece. Instead, Carpenter replaced Symonds in translating proscribed Continental works on the subject for Ellis. Carpenter's connection with *Sexual Inversion* inspired him to write his own material on the subject. For some years, Carpenter had been trying to find a way out of the sense of loneliness his proclivities created for him and a better understanding of the nature of his desires. As he stated to his friend, Charles Oates, in 1887, his hope was that

> we are going to form by degrees a body of friends, who will be tied together by the strongest general bond, and also by personal attachments. … the knowledge that there are many others in the same position as oneself will remove that sense of loneliness which one feels so keenly.[180]

Carpenter's keen sense of comradeship, inspired by his socialist and oriental beliefs, allowed him to prophesy that men who desired other men might form common bonds. This esoteric form of comradeship would serve to resist the atomisation and loneliness incurred by British society on men who had sex with other men. Although Carpenter was undoubtedly inspired by Symonds' work in this field, Carpenter's vision of the solution for the problem was quite different. Symonds' lament about modern society was based on its exclusion of all sexuality between all men. Symonds' aspiration in 'A Problem in Modern Ethics' was that all British men would be liberated to engage in consensual sexual relations with other men, if they so wished. Carpenter, on the other hand, visualised a community of men, separate and separated from the rest of British masculinity. The common bond between these men would be their desires for each other. This stance was reflected in his work, *Homogenic Love and its Place in a Free Society*.

Homogenic Love was written by Carpenter in 1894, as part of a series of works on more general problems of sex, marriage and gender roles in British society, called *Love's Coming of Age*. Weeks states that *Homogenic Love* was published in 1894.[181] However, Carpenter did not publish this work until 1906. Instead, he had the work privately printed in 1894 and, like Symonds with his essays, passed it to like-minded friends:

> I placed 'printed for private circulation only' on the title-page, and had only a comparatively small number of copies struck off – which were not sold but sent round pretty freely to those who I thought

would be interested in the subject. ... Even in this quiet way the pamphlet created some alarm.[182]

Although Carpenter did not include *Homogenic Love* in *Love's Coming of Age* and, as he stated, 'nor had I any intention of including it', his publisher, Fisher Unwin, withdrew *Love's Coming of Age* from publication in 1895, in the furore surrounding the Wilde Trials. Nonetheless, it is clear from Carpenter's comments that *Homogenic Love* would have created severe problems for him, had he published it in 1894.

In *Homogenic Love*, Carpenter attempted to demonstrate the special nature of 'homogenic love' between men and between women. He used the work of Continental scientists to differentiate the male 'urning' from other men who had occasional sex with men out of curiosity or circumstances, such as a barracks:

> Too much emphasis cannot be laid on the distinction between those born lovers of their own sex, and that class of persons with whom they are so often confused, who out of mere carnal curiosity ... or from the dearth of opportunities for a more normal satisfaction ... adopt some homosexual practices.[183]

It is interesting that Carpenter used the term homosexual for the first time in English in this work. The term had been in existence on the Continent since 1869. Carpenter did not use the term as a category or species of male, but as a general descriptor for sex between men. Carpenter cited Krafft-Ebbing's analysis of the kind of 'homosexuals' that were '*mutatis mutandis*', or exclusively attracted to their own sex.[184] However, Carpenter referred to *mutatis mutandis* as 'urnings' in his own analysis, using Ulrichs' nomenclature. He rejected Krafft-Ebing's nomenclature, which incorporated urnings with the activities of the merely 'carnal'. For Carpenter, Ulrichs' term urning best described the special and separate category he was trying to create in his work. In the 1894 edition, Carpenter was content to argue that the homogenic love of the urning, was as normal an instinct as love between men and women. Carpenter expanded on this essay considerably and included it in his 1906 and 1908 editions of *Love's Coming of Age*. By 1908, Carpenter had renamed the piece *The Intermediate Sex*.

The Intermediate Sex is an extraordinary and rather eccentric apologia for sexuality between men and between women. It was also the first published work on the subject in Britain to discuss the existence of the phenomenon of sex between men. *Homogenic Love* at least showed signs of the restraining influence of Symonds and Ellis in its claims for the propensity. However, by 1908, Carpenter had developed his ideas on the subject in a direction that was a distinct departure from either Ellis' or Symonds'. In *The Intermediate Sex*, Carpenter attempted to demonstrate that the urning was superior to 'normal' men and women. He embraced wholeheartedly Ulrichs' theory that urnings were a biologically intermediate type of being and added that these beings were gifted with special qualities:

> Urning men in their own lives put love before money making, business, success, fame, and other motives which rule the normal man. I am sure that it is also true of them that they put love before lust. I do not feel sure that this can be said of the normal man, at any rate in the present stage of evolution.[185]

Carpenter attributed these special qualities to the urning male because 'all this flows naturally from the presence of the feminine element in them, and its blending with the rest of their nature'. Carpenter regarded the 'place of the uranian in society' and the uranian temperament as 'an immense educational force; while, as between equals, it may be turned to social and heroic uses, such can hardly be expected from the ordinary marriage'.[186] Carpenter condemned the urning, in his millennial vision, to performing only the 'most valuable social work' and achieving the highest standards in the arts.[187]

Carpenter's eccentric vision of the urning in *Homogenic Love* and *The Intermediate Sex* was indicative of his own sense of social isolation and the conviction of his own genius. Carpenter always regarded himself and was regarded by others as a being apart, quite different from other men. This sense of isolation from all classes and masculinities he encountered in Britain partly explains why he was so enamoured of Ulrichs' conception of biological intermediacy to explain his own predicament. Also, his efforts to achieve some sense of masculine comradeship had always been frustrated with 'normal' men. Most of the men he encountered through his socialist mission were, ultimately, more dedicated to their wives and families than they were to his vision of masculine socialist comradeship.[188] Carpenter's comments on marriage in *Love's Coming of Age* reveal the sense that modern, British marriage excluded the possibility of his vision of masculine comradeship being realised. He criticised the

> kind of 'ring fence', which social opinion (at any rate in this country) draws around the married pair with respect to their relations to outsiders. ... marriage, by a kind of absurd fiction, is represented as

an oasis situated in the midst of an arid desert – in which latter, it is pretended, neither of the two parties is so fortunate as to find any objects of real affectional interest. If they do they have to conceal the same from the other party.

Carpenter's critique of marriage and the monogamous, uxorious expectation of men in modern marriage was predominantly aimed at the middle classes. Carpenter commented that these expectations were also the case for the working-class marriage. He argued that at any 'seaside place', one could see

the respectable working-man with his wife trailing along by his side, or the highly respectable stock-jobber arm-in-arm with his better and larger half – their blank faces, utter want of any common topic of conversation which has not been exhausted a thousand times already, and their obvious relief when the hour comes which will take them back to their several and divided occupations.[189]

Carpenter's only hope for his vision of masculine comradeship rested with the uranians. British legislation and society excluded the recognition of any kind of 'special being' that was elevated from the morass of sex between men. In these years, all sex between all men was a subject of the severest censure and taboo. When the authorities were forced to prosecute in these circumstances, the men involved had to be presented as rare and aberrant beings amongst British men.[190] Carpenter attempted to demonstrate in his work that these beings were not only more numerous than supposed, but also had the potential to form a band of comrades that would do work to alter and enhance society.

Carpenter's vision of uranianism in *The Intermediate Sex* elicited considerable hostility, even from sympathetic friends like Shaw. It is significant that Carpenter managed to publish the work in 1906 and 1908 without prosecution for obscene libel. So how did Carpenter avoid prosecution, whereas *Sexual Inversion* was banned? Part of the reason was the entire sublimation of the presence of sex in the milieu of the urning. As Carpenter stated in the work,

it would be a great mistake to suppose that their attachments are necessarily sexual, or connected with sexual acts. On the contrary, they are often purely emotional in their character; and to confuse Uranians ... with libertines having no law but curiosity in self-indulgence is to do them a great wrong.[191]

Sexual Inversion, on the other hand, contained case histories which admitted to the existence of proscribed sex. Nonetheless, Carpenter's outlandish claims for the special temperament of the urning had made him reticent to publish in 1894. Also, his critique of gender and marriage in the first *Love's Coming of Age* caused the publication to be hastily withdrawn in the panic over the Wilde trials.

The furore surrounding the Wilde trials had subsided by the time of the publication of *The Intermediate Sex*. By 1906, Carpenter regarded himself as the 'prophet of homosexuality' in Britain, supported by his lover, George Merrill and a milieu of contacts gained through the project of *Sexual Inversion*. Carpenter had also found himself a new progressive publishing house, Swan Sonnenschein. In 1906, against a 'background of the militant women's movement and its increasing attacks on sexual taboos', Swann Sonnerschein felt able, for the first time, to include *Homogenic Love* in *Love's Coming of Age*.[192] In the event, the authorities did not act against the publication. Had Carpenter elucidated on the presence of sex in the milieu of the urning, the work would have undoubtedly been banned. As late as 1915, when the authorities banned D. H. Lawrence's *The Rainbow*, Carpenter's *The Intermediate Sex* was also considered in this clampdown as a possible work of obscenity.[193] *The Intermediate Sex* was lambasted by those publications which deigned to recognise its existence. The *BMJ* excoriated Carpenter's 'praise and laudation for creatures and customs which are generally regarded as odious'. M. D. O'Brien, author of the pamphlet *Socialism and Infamy*,[194] lambasted the existence of the work in a letter to *The Yorkshire Post*. O'Brien went as far as to claim that Carpenter belonged to 'an international Communistic Brotherhood ... linked together by one common bond of guilt and infamy, for overthrowing private property, private homes and private families throughout the world'.[195]

Carpenter's connection of socialism with uranianism elicited the criticism of even sympathetic socialists. In private correspondence, Shaw railed against Carpenter's association of the socialist movement with this 'sex nonsense'. He argued that 'no movement could survive association with such propaganda'. Shaw had been sympathetic in the obscene libel trial of *Sexual Inversion* in 1898. *The Intermediate Sex*, on the other hand, appeared to recommend uranianism as a higher and more desirable form of masculine consciousness than the normal:

> I can sympathise with E.C's efforts to make people understand that the curious reversal in question is a natural accident. ... But to attempt to induce it in normal people ... would be ruinous, and

could seem feasible only to abnormal people who are unable to conceive how frightfully disagreeable – how abominable, in fact – it is to the normal, even to the normal who are abnormally susceptible to natural impulses.[196]

In other words, even the socialists who believed in the 'new life' based on instincts, could not countenance Carpenter's eccentric vision of a special place for uranianism in the socialist millennium.

Carpenter persisted after 1910 with his particular views on sexuality between men in publications in France, Germany and the United States. His work in this direction built on *The Intermediate Sex* in an attempt to prove, using scientific and anthropological techniques, a connection between the uranian temperament and 'unusual psychic or divinatory powers'.[197] None of these works were published in Britain, but the articles gained him an international reputation and notoriety. Carpenter used this reputation to garner international support for the foundation of the British Society for the Study of Sex Psychology in 1913. The Society was a highly marginal organisation for the first few decades of its existence. But it survived, without incurring censure and prosecution. The foundation of the Society represented a new tolerance in Britain of sex psychological theorisation, including inversion theorisation. Work of this kind had been conducted on the Continent for well over half a century by 1913. This notwithstanding, British newspapers could comment, as late as 1919, that toleration of sexological texts caused the perversions they described:

practically all that is filthy and degrading can be directly traced to the pernicious teachings of the Teuton criminal. ... the horrible practices of the unsexed were introduced to this country from Berlin and Vienna, and it is time that the professors of unnatural practices were plainly told that England has no place for them.[198]

It would not be until the 1950s that the ideas of the Society would be taken at all seriously by the medical professions and the legal authorities.[199] In the intervening years, British law retained unaltered its indiscriminate criminalisation of sex between men and British doctors remained largely ignorant of the ideas of Ellis and Freud.

The lives of Symonds and Carpenter provide ample evidence of the crippling social difficulties facing men who desired other men. It was not that British society actively and purposively sought out, classified and punished men with their sexual propensities. The problems facing both Symonds and Carpenter were that society resisted acknowledging that same-sex desires existed among British men at all. When society was confronted with this sexuality and the authorities were forced to act, punishments were severe and often indiscriminate. Both Symonds and Carpenter attempted to analyse the problems affecting men who shared their desires, in British society.

Symonds' life and work, in particular, recognised the dominance of uxorious masculinity in Britain. He also recognised that in a society which increasingly insisted upon marriage and the appearance of marital fidelity as the attainment of full adult masculinity, sexual desires between men could have no place. Freed from the constraints of British society, Symonds pursued his scholarly investigations of sexuality between men. His memoirs provide a unique autobiographical account and analysis of the difficulties of 'the problem'. In addition, Symonds critiqued the scientific analyses of sexuality between men that were freely available on the Continent. In the last two years of his life, Symonds gave himself wholeheartedly to the cause of reforming British society and legislation.

In Continental exile, Symonds had attempted to eschew and criticise the expectations of masculinity in British society and its disavowal of the existence of sexuality between men. But British society could not tolerate or countenance the existence of this phenomenon. Symonds had died in 1893 and Ellis attempted to include, posthumously, his contributions to *Sexual Inversion*. His posthumous reputation and his masculine status were preserved by his family from the damaging impute of his desires for men. This notwithstanding, Symonds' work inspired Carpenter in his attempts to force British society to recognise the existence of sexuality between men.

In many respects, Carpenter's struggle to understand, and achieve an accommodation with his desires for men, were similar to Symonds'. His own esoteric vision of socialism, encapsulated in the poem *Towards Democracy*, differentiated him from other socialists. Carpenter clung to his interpretation of socialism, involving the discovery of the personal through instincts, when other socialists had moved on to political representation of the industrial working classes. He alienated and alarmed many of his socialist friends by living with his working-class lover, George Merrill, after 1898. Nonetheless, Carpenter retained his literary reputation in socialist circles for the remainder of his life.

In *The Intermediate Sex*, the first successfully published work in English on the subject of sexuality between men, Carpenter promoted his vision of the special qualities of the urning, or uranian. Carpenter's thinking was an analytical departure from the ideas of Symonds and Ellis, and the work appears highly eccentric to the modern reader. Carpenter attempted to argue that the urning was somehow superior to the normal male. Also, relationships between urnings were presented in the work as devoid of sex. He regarded the urnings as having the potential to form a band of male comrades, that would work to heroic ends to alter and enhance society.

The publication of *The Intermediate Sex* and the foundation of the BSSSP did represent a new tolerance in Britain of discussion of sexuality between men. But Carpenter's other writings on sexuality between men had to be published abroad, for fear of proscription, and the anaemic and sexless *The Intermediate Sex* was his only publication in this field to be tolerated in Britain. In comparison, a voluminous corpus of inversion theories had been tolerated on the Continent for well over half a century.

In the final analysis, Symonds and Carpenter's critiques of the incapacity of British society to contemplate the existence of sexuality between men achieved little or nothing of their aims in the period in question. Before 1906, no work of this kind was tolerated. Even after Carpenter's publication of *The Intermediate Sex*, it took until the eve of the First World War before British academics had a forum with the potential to discuss the phenomenon of sex between men. British society remained, throughout the lifetimes of both Symonds and Carpenter, stoutly resistant to recognition of the existence of sexuality between men. In a culture that regarded uxorious and independent masculinity as the bedrock of society, recognition of the existence of sex between men in public discourse was unconscionable and deeply threatening to social stability.

7
Conclusion

Historiographies of male homosexuality in Victorian Britain that adopt a medico-legal analysis of homosexual identity construction are, frequently, problematic and ahistorical. The medico-legal analysis of male homosexual identity formations has resulted in highly mechanical, theoretical concepts of how late Victorian institutions constructed the modern male homosexual. Historians in the Weeks/Foucault tradition argue that the profession of medicine, or, more nebulously 'science', and the institutions of law, combined to construct a pathological and criminal concept. Few alternative approaches, such as essentialist and queer theory, have successfully deconstructed this approach to the question of male homosexuality in Britain. More recent historiography influenced by post-Sedgwick queer theory, such as Cocks' work, has identified the ambivalent status of the law with respect to male homosexuality and recognised that the phenomenon was 'nameless', which fostered a cultural silence around the matter. Cocks argues that it was this namelessness that fostered an epistemology of the closet. Homosexual self-making was influenced by the nameless nature of the crime of sex between men, rather than by purposive attempts by the authorities to construct a category of the homosexual in law. Cocks' work has done much to undermine the rigid legal analysis of a pejorative homosexual category. His work does not, however, deconstruct or effectively collapse the medico-legal analysis of homosexual identity formations.

This book has sought to collapse the medico-legal approach, that has dominated since Weeks' and Foucault's analyses in this field. Foucault regards the development of scientific classifications of sexual aberrations by sexologists, as the result of various historical processes. The ineluctable mission of science to push back the boundaries of knowledge, against a cultural background of superstition and ignorance, motivated scientists in the late nineteenth century to examine everything that exists in nature. The 'will to knowledge' included the pursuit of sexologists in the taxonomy of sex between men. Aberrant males who indulged in sex with other men were classified by a series of scientifically based nomenclature. This had the effect of creating new 'species' of human beings, separated from the rest of humanity by their sexual desires.[1]

In addition, Foucault argues that, in the nineteenth century, the sexologist somehow replaced the priest as the repository for people's sexual confessions. He states that after the Counter Reformation, Roman Catholic confessional practices had conditioned people to rigorous self-examination and confession to a priest. This cultural practice translated readily into 'confession' to the sexologist. Instead of interpreting sexual aberration as sin, the new science of sexology interpreted such phenomena as pathology. Of course, the Counter Reformation only affected Roman Catholic countries. This left Britain an outsider in the historical processes cited by Foucault. In Britain, the responses to the matter of sex between men was, increasingly, silence rather than confession. Unlike Continental states, no home-grown discipline of inversion sexology was tolerated in the nineteenth century.

Foucault claims that homosexuals shaped their identities by a process of reverse discourse. For Foucault, reverse discourse meant a form of self-definition by the homosexual, who engaged with dominant scientific discourse, often in defiance of its implications. Undoubtedly, British homosexual men, such as Symonds and Carpenter, examined scientific discourse that pathologised homosexuality. Symonds, in particular, formed a critique of scientific discourse that defied and collapsed many of the scientific analyses he encountered. However, inversion theorisation was not, by any means, a dominant form of discourse in Britain. Symonds, for example, only engaged with inversion theories in exile on the Continent. Inversion theories, written predominantly by Continental sexologists, were not legally available in Britain. Scientific discourse of this nature was completely unacceptable because it articulated the existence of sex between men, albeit in pejorative terms. In effect, the discourse was as abhorrent as the phenomenon it described.

Similar to Foucault, Weeks' studies in this field assert that medicine purposely sought to classify and pathologise the male homosexual. Weeks argues that, in Britain, medicine and the law combined, in apparent harmony, to construct a pejorative category of the homosexual. For Weeks, 'all homosexuals as a class' were constructed in the public imagination as pathological and criminal beings. It is difficult to overestimate the influence of Weeks' arguments in historiography. In spite of recent studies that problematise the approaches adopted by Weeks and others in this field, his arguments persist in broader historiographical works for the period and his studies have recently been republished. Criticism of the medico-legal analysis has tended to centre on the lack of agency inherent in this approach. As we have seen, the arguments presented by Weeks and others are, in the British context, ahistorical. The law and its concomitant institutions, such as parliament and the Home Office, were highly ambivalent in regard to the matter of sex between men throughout the nineteenth and early twentieth centuries. Also, doctors, or more specifically alienists in Britain, were remarkable for their lack of interest in the phenomenon of inversion, in comparison to Continental and American counterparts.

Concepts of sex and sexuality between men are presented as barely formulated before the 1880s, by Weeks and others in this field. The 'Stella and Fanny' trial of 1871 is used by historians to demonstrate that ignorance of the phenomenon amongst medical men called to give evidence at the trial, meant that sex and sexuality between men were not understood by society. Legal developments, such as Clause 11 of the Criminal Law Amendment Act and developments in medical analysis of the phenomenon, are presented as crystallising a new and unprecedented knowledge amongst the general public from the mid-1880s. As Cocks' work and the evidence and arguments here demonstrate, sex and sexuality between men were tacitly, but well-understood phenomena, before and during the 'Stella and Fanny' trial. In the 1880s and 1890s, medicine and the legal authorities were no more willing to investigate, classify and control sexuality between men, than before the 1870s. Examination of the broader context of the 'Stella and Fanny' trial reveals a deliberate 'unknowing' about the particular vices associated with the defendants. The British public, or at least urban dwellers, had sophisticated perceptions of types of men that would indulge in sex with other men. But to admit to this knowledge in public discourse was tantamount to recognising the existence of this propensity amongst British men. British attitudes towards sexuality between men were paradoxical. On one hand, the public, particularly urban dwellers, were increasingly willing to report incidents of sex between men to the authorities. Expansion in urbanisation in the nineteenth century coincided with an absolute increase in indictments for unnatural crime between men. On the other hand, the authorities demonstrated extreme reluctance to prosecute or pursue unnatural crime, except when forced to by individual incidents being brought to their attention.

So why did British society appear to have conflicting, but parallel attitudes towards sex between men? This book has examined the place of masculinity as a social status in shaping attitudes towards, and perceptions of, sexuality between men. Also, the writings of individual British homosexual men have been examined to assess the extent to which concepts of masculinity shaped and fashioned their lives. From the late 1860s, masculinity as a social status became the dominant indicator of social inclusion. For men to be considered fully masculine, they had to be married. Men had to demonstrate their authority and rights over wives and children. In addition, men had to maintain their masculinity through their abilities to support their wives and families. Attainment of full adult masculinity was contingent upon the ability of men to move freely between the home, the workplace and all male associations.

Masculine social status became the benchmark of middle-class male independence and citizenship. It also became the benchmark of working-class respectability and citizenship in this period. Trades unions and working-class newspapers valorised the skills and independent character of the working man and his abilities to support his family. Increasingly, trades unions promoted the male breadwinner wage as essential to working-class dignity. By the end of the nineteenth century, married working-class men who could not support their spouses as housewives, became the subject of concern by social commentators.

During this period, bachelorhood became an increasingly problematic and ambivalent status for adult men. In addition, it was not enough for men simply to be married. From the 1870s, men's sexual power over women was being vigorously questioned by popular mass campaigns. Middle-class and respectable working-class men were expected to preserve their sexual expression for marriage only. Men were enjoined to exercise stringent self-control in their expression of sex. Popular social purity campaigns targeted not only working-class men's sexual profligacy with women, but also habits of masturbation. However, the social purity campaigns of the 1880s made no mention of sex between men. Vigorous campaigning had resulted in the Criminal Law Amendment Act of 1885, which raised the age of consent for girls to 16. Contrary to what many historians claim, this campaign did not clamour for the criminalisation and prosecution of sex between men. To suggest that sexuality existed between British men, of any class, was anathema. Significantly, the highly popular social purity literature did not equate masturbation in young men with causing sexual inversion. This literature relied heavily upon medical theories, but ignored Continental inversion theories, which specifically targeted masturbation in the aetiology of male homosexuality.

Masculinity as a social status required men to undertake onerous and often conflicting responsibilities. Public acknowledgement of the existence of sexuality between men, even in pejorative terms, would have recognised an alternative to acceptable masculinity. This would have threatened and undermined the basis of British society. British politicians and moralists reinforced notions that the success of British society and the unparalleled power and extent of the Empire was due, in part, to the moral fitness of its men. Comparisons were made between the ancient civilisations of Rome and Greece and the modern, Christian, British Empire. The immorality of the ancients, particularly their propensity to sexuality between men, caused the collapse of their civilisations. The British Empire would prevail, it was argued, because the immorality of the ancients was an anachronism in modern Britain. In a society that was conscious of its pre-eminence in the world, sexuality between men had no place. In comparison, Continental states, such as France, not only tolerated sexuality between men, but allowed its scientific men to analyse the phenomenon. The absence of such literature in Britain was presented by the authorities, when forced to recognise the existence of French medical treatises, as a sure sign that sexuality between men was common to French society, but extremely rare and unusual in British society.

Masculinity as a social status had become, arguably, one of the cornerstones of British society by the end of the nineteenth century. Sex and sexuality between men complicated the free association of independent male citizens. Admitting to its existence challenged the ability of fathers of families to maintain authority in their homes. In 1896, attempts were made to ban completely the publication of details of court cases involving unnatural crime. The government of the day was prepared to infringe the constitutional liberties of the press in order to remove the existence of this 'evil' from public consciousness. Halsbury's Publication of Indecent Evidence Bill never became law, because of arguments that the 'evil' it proposed to suppress was almost absent in Britain. It was better to ignore the phenomenon, than advertise its existence by controversial, and internationally embarrassing, constitutional change.

To the British, sex between men threatened the structure of the family and flouted the work ethic. If recognised and tolerated, the phenomenon had the potential to tempt some men away from their procreative duties to their wives. Sexuality between men and its communitarian overtones also threatened the ability of independent men to maintain work, trade, commerce and politics. Halsbury was undoubtedly prompted to gag the press on this matter, following the furore of the trials of Oscar Wilde in 1895. But examination of national newspaper reporting of unnatural crime in the late nineteenth century, reveals that the British press was as reluctant to report and discuss the crime as the authorities. It is little wonder that claims that the phenomenon was nearly absent in Britain prevailed in the House of Lords debate in 1896. Prominent scandals, such as the 'Stella and Fanny' trials, the Cleveland Street Affair and the trials of Oscar Wilde, did receive press attention. Nonetheless, when contextualised against the scale of indictments for unnatural crime not reported in the newspapers, these scandals appeared as highly unusual, isolated and rare incidents.

Patterns of reporting unnatural crime in the newspapers altered during this period. *The Times* had persisted in occasional reporting of sodomy trials from the late eighteenth century. This discourse became an increasingly muted form of journalism in the 1850s. Nonetheless, readers of *The Times* were left in little doubt as to the nature of the crime reported. *The Times* demonstrated no particular pattern in its choice of trials for unnatural crime between males that made it to its pages. It is clear though, examining the cases that were reported, that it was a matter of supreme difficulty to convict a man of unnatural crime. In comparison to *The Times*, the *Daily Telegraph* did not report this crime, except on occasions when the trial involved men of social importance. Similarly, working-class newspapers, such as *Lloyd's Weekly Newspaper* and *Reynolds' Newspaper*, ignored cases of this kind, with occasional exceptions. All this changed with the 'Stella and Fanny' arraignment of 1870, involving cross-dressed actors and a Liberal MP. Garrulous reporting of this case in the newspapers revealed widespread knowledge of the location and guises of the drag sodomite. The newspapers came under severe criticism, mainly from the *Pall Mall Gazette* and the Society for the Suppression of Vice, for reporting the details of this case. In the trial the following year, the newspapers had entirely changed their tenor of reporting. The knowledge demonstrated at the arraignment had been suppressed, apparently by the newspapers themselves. The 'Stella and Fanny' trial was regarded as an international embarrassment. It was essential for the defendants to be found not guilty. Any other outcome would be tantamount to admitting that a deceased Liberal MP had been guilty of sodomy. In addition, a guilty verdict would have advertised to the world that a drag sodomitical subculture existed in London.

Between 1872 and 1885, reports of unnatural crime involving British men disappeared from the pages of *The Times* and other newspapers examined here. The furore of the 'Stella and Fanny' trials clearly warned newspapers, not usually given to reporting these kinds of cases, to avoid this kind of journalism. As most of these cases involved men of no social importance, it was not in the interests of publications that catered to the working classes, or the Liberal *Daily Telegraph*, to suggest that unnatural crime was a common occurrence amongst ordinary men. These publications increasingly presented the working man as an inherently dignified character. *The Times* also ceased reporting cases of unnatural crime after 1872. Significantly, in 1872, all newspapers refrained from reporting the disgrace of Simeon Solomon, the prominent pre-Raphaelite artist, in their pages. The problems arising from reporting the 'Stella and Fanny' trials had clearly had their effects. But the retirement of Delane as editor, and the efforts of new men at *The Times* to reflect changes in popular journalism, were also significant factors in avoiding reports of this nature. It was not in the interests of masculinity, and therefore social stability, to present the existence and extent of this crime in the newspapers.

Reporting of unnatural crime did, however, recommence in these newspapers after 1885. But the focus of newspaper reporting was quite different from the patterns detectable from *The Times* before 1872. After 1885, the newspapers were, predominantly, interested in reporting cases that involved sex between men and boys, whereas before 1872, the majority of cases reported involved grown men. The occasion for this new kind of journalism was the inclusion of Clause 11 in the Criminal Law Amendment Act of 1885. Clause 11 did not differentiate between sex between men and boys or sex between consenting adult men. Nonetheless, the protection of childhood appears to have interested these publications far more than reporting potentially destabilising cases of sex between adult males.

Clause 11 of the Criminal Law Amendment Act was not, as historians often claim, a revolution in jurisprudence. Nor did it replace or supersede the Buggery laws as the basis of legislation. There was little in the legal framework to suggest that the legislature purposively constructed a homosexual category. Indeed, it is remarkable how little British legislation altered in this respect. Even the addition of Clause 11, without debate, to the Criminal Law Amendment Act in 1885 did not, as historians claim, create a legal definition of a homosexual type that then, in turn, constructed notions of this type amongst the public. In the late nineteenth century, the state had at its disposal, an indiscriminate cascade of sexual acts proscribed by legislation, that could be applied to any male of any age, who forced the authorities to conduct criminal proceedings.

The addition of Clause 11, which simply reiterated the criminality of sexual acts that were already potentially punishable by law, was created more by accident than design. The Clause acted as no more than an accelerator to the already high rates of indictments for crimes of sex between males. Unlike the broader aims of the Act, which offered sexual protection for underage girls, Clause 11 did not differentiate between boys and men. However, the new concern for protecting boys, detectable in the newspapers, is also evident in secret Home Office sentencing policies for the period. But the protection and delineation of boyhood in the matter of sex between males remained secret, highly ambivalent and imprecisely defined, until well into the twentieth century.

The entire matter of sex between males remained a phenomenon the state preferred to ignore. Policies to distinguish between crimes of bestiality, sodomising of boys and sodomy between men, were only conducted when the Home Office was forced to do so. Campaigns for reform of punishments of juvenile offenders and reform of the penal servitude system, did not articulate a need to reform laws pertaining to sex between males. However, these campaigns and concomitant reforms to penal servitude legislation, forced the Home Office to bring some cohesion to the chaos of sentencing policy for unnatural crime. These changes, kept secret until very recently, resulted in extraordinary powers being given to the judges and the Home Secretary in the matter. Men prosecuted for anal sex with each other were completely at the mercy of the judge. The judges and the Home Office were happier to accept unfair and uneven treatment, than risk the parliamentary debate necessary to clarify the law in this matter.

Similar ambivalence is detectable in the attitudes of Britain's scientific community towards the matter of sexuality between men. In many respects, British scientists had the potential to be at the forefront of the quest to understand the phenomenon in scientific terms. British philosophers and scientists fostered the intellectual conditions for a science of inversion theorisation. The ideas of Malthus and Darwin had a direct effect in stimulating and expanding an already extant scientific enquiry of same-sex sexuality on the Continent. Darwin's thinking, in particular, provided the analytical basis for the discipline of inversion theorisation. However, Continental inversion theorists worked in societies where the milieu of the homosexual was, more or less, acknowledged. The ideas of theorists, such as Ulrichs and Krafft-Ebing, were controversial, but tolerated and widely disseminated.

In Britain, on the other hand, the ideas of Malthus and Darwin did not stimulate a home-grown discipline of inversion theorisation. The medical profession, the judiciary, the police and the government went to considerable lengths to suppress and resist any form of learned discussion of the matter of sex between men. Continental works on the subject were regarded as obscene and pornographic. The suppression of Continental ideas and the avoidance of the analytical implications of thinkers, such as Malthus, amounted to a culture of resistance. The rulings of the inadmissibility of 'physical signs' of sodomy as evidence in the 'Stella and Fanny' trial of 1871, ended any potential for British surgeons to conduct a scientific enquiry of this nature. Also, the Lord Chief Justice permitted the physical assault of any doctor who attempted to conduct such a study. After this case, the body of the British male was considered inviolate. This ruling was especially poignant at a time when the Contagious Diseases Acts permitted the state and doctors to enforce vaginal examinations of women suspected of prostitution, in Garrison towns.

Continental science was, at this point, developing neurological, biological and psychological analyses, influenced by the ideas of Darwin, rather than conducting studies of the physical signs of sodomy. Following the ruling of the Lord Chief Justice in 1871, the examination of the mind remained the only recourse left for British doctors wishing to conduct a scientific study of the phenomenon. But analysis of this kind was not forthcoming from British alienists. The notable exception was Havelock Ellis and his book, *Sexual Inversion*. His attempts to publish met with a wall of resistance. In the matter of sex and sexuality between men, Britain was one of the most hostile and intolerant cultures in the Western world. Sexually radical ideas, such as free love, were deemed by the authorities to be subversive to society and in need of eradication. Nonetheless, it was the presence of *Sexual Inversion* in the midst of sexually radical organisations, that provided the authorities with the evidence needed to suppress them. The banned *Sexual Inversion* offered the inverted male an analytical tool to understand and accept his propensities.

Ellis' co-author of *Sexual Inversion*, John Addington Symonds, had hoped that his ideas would bring about radical changes in British attitudes to sexuality between men. Symonds had died in Rome in 1893, before the work was published. He was, however, the instigator of the project and had persuaded Ellis to lend scientific authority to the work. In 1897, the first edition of the work, with Symonds' authorship, had been withdrawn from publication by his literary executor and his family. Many of Symonds' ideas on the matter of sexuality between men were not seen by historians until the mid-1980s and much of his correspondence was destroyed after his death.

Symonds' life provides ample evidence of the crippling social difficulties facing men who desired other men. Highly educated and socially prominent, his work in this field recognised the dominance of uxorious masculinity in Britain. He also recognised that in a society which increasingly insisted upon marriage and the appearance of marital fidelity as the attainment of full adult masculinity, sexual desires between men could have no place. Until the late 1870s, he strove to suppress his desires and conform to an accepted masculine social status. The moral vision of his father inculcated in him a deep sense of inadequacy and aberrance. Symonds' involvement in the downfall of the headmaster of Harrow School made clear to him the impossibility of his desires being realised in any kind of fulfilling way.

Exposure to the philosophy of the Greats at Balliol, Oxford, appeared to offer Symonds some possibility of the expression of his desires for men. However, the reformed curriculum at Balliol vehemently denied any interpretation of the Greats that recognised sexuality between men amongst the Ancient Greeks. Only a chaste homosociality among academic celibates could be inspired by the Platonic ethos. Deeply influenced by his education, Symonds went to great lengths to supress his desires for men. He married, on the advice of his father, and had a family. His marriage allowed him to present himself as fully masculine. He undoubtedly had passionate attachments with men, which his wife knew about after five years of marriage. His wife, Catherine, tolerated their sexless marriage in order to preserve their elevated social status. His attachments to men he loved remained sexually chaste. Symonds attempted to live the idealised Platonic attachment promoted at Balliol. Had he done otherwise, and conducted sexual relationships with men, his reputation would have been utterly destroyed. In spite of this, Symonds conducted his own private study of Greek paiderastia, in all its forms. 'A Problem in Greek Ethics', written in 1873, but never published, is a forthright and historicist account of sex between men in Ancient Greece. Significantly, Symonds used this account to criticise modern British morality. Had this work come to light, his other studies would have lost their scholarly authority and he would have been condemned as a compositor, even if his conduct showed no evidence of sexual impropriety. Symonds was convinced that a highly expurgated account of Greek morality *per se* in his famous published work, *Studies of the Greek Poets*, lost him the chance of academic preferment in 1877.

In self-imposed exile, Symonds also pursued his scholarly investigations of sexuality between men. His memoirs provide a unique autobiographical account and analysis of the difficulties of 'the problem' in

Britain. In addition, he conducted the first humanist critique of Continental inversion theories. Symonds' literary contacts, even in exile, were British, and he did not encounter this literature until the early 1890s, even though it was freely available on the Continent. In his essay, 'A Problem in Modern Ethics', Symonds also criticised British law on the matter, comparing its harshness with more tolerant arrangements on the Continent. But, as the fate of *Sexual Inversion* indicated, British society could not permit the discussion required to change legislation.

In many respects, the efforts of Carpenter to understand, and achieve an accommodation with his desires for men, were similar to Symonds'. Following a youth and young adulthood of Anglican asceticism, Carpenter attempted to understand his desires through involvement with socialism and pursuit of oriental beliefs and travel. Carpenter's own esoteric vision of socialism differentiated him from other Socialists. Believing firmly in the politics of the personal, Carpenter alarmed many of his Socialist friends by living openly with his working-class lover, albeit in the relative obscurity of the Derbyshire countryside. Part of Carpenter's isolation from other Socialists, was his insistence on critiquing modern marriage and promoting 'uranianism' in his writings. In 1895, Carpenter criticised the monogamous, uxorious expectation of men in marriage in *Love's Coming of Age*. His work, *Homogenic Love*, had been written as a companion to this series, but was not published until 1906. Published as the chapter, *The Intermediate Sex*, the work promoted the notion of the superior qualities of the 'urning'. Significantly, the urnings in Carpenter's work were devoid of sex, and existed to work towards heroic ends to alter and enhance society. Much of Carpenter's vision for urnings appears tame and rather eccentric to the contemporary reader. This did not protect his work from severe censure, even by sympathetic friends. *The Intermediate Sex* is historically important because it was the first successfully published work in Britain to discuss sexuality between men in any detail. In comparison, a voluminous corpus of studies had been available on the Continent for well over a century before its publication.

Neither Symonds' nor Carpenter's critiques achieved their stated aims. Throughout the second half of the nineteenth century and well into the twentieth century, British law remained ambivalent and imprecise in regard to sex between men, or the types of men that would have sex with other men. Indictments and prosecutions were high and the urban populace demonstrated its willingness to report incidents of sex between men to the authorities. This did not translate into a coherent policy of legal classification or punishment. Patterns of reporting in the newspapers and the refusal of the Home Office to clarify sentencing policies served to perpetuate the perception that the crime was unusual and highly aberrant. British society, probably more than any other in the Western world, regarded independent, uxorious masculine social status as its bedrock and the benchmark of social inclusion. In such a society, that was regarded, not least by the British themselves, as the moral exemplar in a rapidly transforming world, the existence of sex between men had no place. To allow scientists to analyse, quantify and classify sex between British men would dispel this perception. British surgeons and alienists, unlike their Continental counterparts, resisted and ignored the phenomenon. It was this culture of resistance and silence on the question of male homosexuality that fostered the self-making of inverted men in Britain.

Notes

Reference Abbreviations

PRO – Public Records Office, Kew.
Crim – Calendar of Prisoners Files.
DPP – Director of Public Prosecution Files.
HO – Home Office Files.
TS – Treasury Solicitors.

Introduction

1. Tosh, J, 'What Should Historians do with Masculinity? Reflections on Nineteenth-Century Britain', in *History Workshop Journal*, 1994, 38, p. 192.

1 History

1. Weeks, J, 2000 *Making Sexual History*, Polity Press, Cambridge, p. 1.
2. Ibid., p. 1.
3. Ibid., p. 6.
4. *International Encyclopaedia of the Social Sciences*, 1968, Vol. 15, p. 408.
5. McIntosh, M, 'The Homosexual Role', in *Social Problems*, Vol. 16, No. 2, 1968, p. 182.
6. Kutchins, H, and Kirk, S, 1999, *Making Us Crazy: DSM – the Psychiatric Bible and the Creation of Mental Disorders*, Constable, London, p. 57.
7. Weeks, J, 2000, p. 71.
8. Weeks, J, 'The Construction of Homosexuality', in Seidman, S (ed.), 1996, *Queer Theory/Sociology*, Blackwell, London, p. 44.
9. Weeks, J, 2000, p. 9.
10. Foucault, M, 1978, *The History of Sexuality Volume I: The Will to Knowledge*, Penguin, London, p. 101.
11. Foucault, M, 1978, p. 9.
12. Weeks, J, 2000, p. 9.
13. Foucault, M, 1978, pp. 9–13.
14. Ibid., pp. 17–20.
15. Ibid., p. 23.
16. Foucault, M, 1976, *Histoire de la Sexualité: 1: la Volonté de Savoir*, l'Imprimerie Gallimard, France, pp. 9–22. In this chapter, which Foucault uses to argue the Counter Reformational basis of the willingness to talk about sex in the nineteenth century, the term *Victorien* is used throughout and the title of the chapter is *Nous Autres, Victoriens* [Our other, the Victorians]. The epithet *Victorien* is then used throughout the work.
17. Even Carolyn Dean's excellent and highly critical essay on Foucault, which adds to the body of criticism of Foucault his lack of a theory of power and the

absence of a concept of gender in his work, accepts without criticism Foucault's concept of the 'modern confessional', or the practice of talking to psychoanalysts, psychologists and other 'experts' about sex since the late nineteenth century. Dean, C, 'The Productive Hypothesis: Foucault, Gender, and the History of Sexuality', in *History and Theory*, Vol. 33, No. 3, 1994, pp. 271–96.

The practice of talking about sex to experts became established in the United States long before such 'experts' were widely tolerated and respected in Britain. The remarkable exception in Britain in the interwar years was the 'expert' advice offered by Marie Stopes, the birth control campaigner (who was a palaeobotanist and not a psychologist or physician). It is probable that Stopes' popularity in the field of contraceptive and sexual advice in these years was, in part, due to the relative lack of 'experts' in this field in Britain until after the Second World War.

18. Halperin, D, 'Sex before Sexuality: Pederasty, Politics and Power in Classical Athens', in Duberman, M, Vicinus, M and Chauncey, G (eds), 1989, *Hidden from History: Reclaiming the Gay and Lesbian Past*, Penguin, London, p. 39.

19. Rowe, D, Introduction to Kutchins, H and Kirk, S, 1999, p. x.

20. Halperin, D, 1989, p. 38.

21. Ibid.

22. Padgug, R, 'Sexual Matters: Rethinking Sexuality in History', in Duberman, M, Vicinus, M and Chauncey, G (eds), 1989, p. 59.

23. Halperin, D, 1989, p. 40.

24. Chauncey, G, 1995, *Gay New York: The Making of the Gay Male World, 1890–1940*, Flamingo, London, p. 12.

25. See Barber, S, and Clark, D, 2002, *Regarding Sedgwick: Essays on Queer Culture and Critical Theory*, Routledge, London.

26. See Cocks, H, 2003, *Nameless Offences: Homosexual Desire in the Nineteenth Century*, I. B. Taurus, London. See also Cook, M, *London and the Culture of Homosexuality*, CUP, Cambridge, for contemporary analysis, languages and locations of 'the closet' in late nineteenth-century London.

27. Cocks, H, 2003, pp. 199–200.

28. Nottingham, C, 1999, *The Pursuit of Serenity: Havelock Ellis and the New Politics*, Amsterdam University Press, Amsterdam, NL, pp. 243–60.

29. Weeks, J, 1981, *Sex, Politics and Society: the Regulation of Sexuality since 1800*, Longman, London, p. 107 and elsewhere. Also Weeks, J, 1995 and Weeks, J, 2000.

30. Oosterhuis, H, 2000, *Stepchildren of Nature: Krafft-Ebbing, Psychiatry, and the Making of Sexual Identity*, University of Chicago Press, London, Frontispiece.

31. Ibid., p. 8.

32. Ibid.

33. Ibid., p. 9.

34. Ibid., p. vii.

35. Ibid., p. 248.

36. Ibid., p. 212.

37. Ibid., p. 254.

38. Ibid.

39. Ibid., p. 243.

40. Ibid., p. 249.

41. Ibid., p. 10.

42. See Symonds, J, 1896, 'A Problem in Modern Ethics', Privately Printed and Grosskurth, P (ed.), 1986, *The Memoirs of John Addington Symonds*, Hutchinson, London.
43. Porter, R and Hall, L, 1995, *The Facts of Life: The Creation of Sexual Knowledge in Britain, 1650–1950*, Yale University Press, London, p. 163.
44. See Chapter 3.
45. See Chapter 5.
46. Davis, N, ' "Women's History" in Transition: the European Case', in *Feminist Studies*, No. 3, 1975, p. 90.
47. Tosh, J, 1994, 38, p. 179.
48. The first sociologist to propose the theory that gender categories are histori-cally constructed is Jeffrey Weeks in *Sex, Politics and Society* (1981). However, Weeks does not develop this theory in relation to homosexual identity formations.
49. Connell, R, 2000, *The Men and the Boys*, Polity Press, Cambridge, pp. 23–31.
50. Cocks, H, 1998, *The Sodomy Trial in English Culture, 1780–1889*, University of Manchester Unpublished Thesis, p. 251.
51. Ibid., p. 30.
52. See Cocks, H, 2003, pp. 161–69.
53. See Sedgwick, E, 1994, *Epistimology of the Closet*, Penguin, London; Seidman, S (ed.), 1996, *Queer Theory/Sociology*; and Sullivan, N, 2003, *A Critical Introduction to Queer Theory*, Edinburgh University Press, Edinburgh.
54. Clark, A, 1997, *The Struggle for the Breeches: Gender and the Making of the British Working Class*, University of California Press, London, p. 225.
55. An example of this is inscribed into the *Address and Rules of the Working Men's Association for benefiting Politically, Socially and Morally the Useful Classes*, 1837, University of London Library.
56. See Tosh, J, 2004, 'Hegemonic Masculinity and the History of Gender', in Dudink, S, Hagemann, K and Tosh, J (eds), 2004, *Masculinity in Politics and War*, Manchester University Press.
57. See Chapter 2.
58. Tosh, J, 1994, pp. 187–91.
59. Connell, R, 2000, pp. 46–53.
60. Sinah, M, 1995, *Colonial Masculinity: The Manly Englishman and the Effeminate Bengali in the Late Nineteenth Century*, Manchester University Press, Manchester.

2 Masculinity

1. Tosh, J, 1994, and Doolittle, M, University of Essex unpublished thesis 1996, *Missing Fathers: Assembling a History of Fatherhood in Mid Nineteenth-Century England*.
2. Hammerton, J, 'Forgotten People? Marriage and Masculine Identities in Britain', in *Journal of Family History*, Vol. 22, No. 1, 1997, p. 111.
3. See *Address and Rules of the Working Men's Association for benefiting Politically, Socially and Morally the Useful Classes*, 1837.
4. See Clark, A, 1997.
5. Tosh, J, 1994, p. 191.

6. Ibid., p. 187.
7. See Chapter 5.
8. Ibid.
9. See Chapters 3, 4 and 5.
10. See Chapter 3.
11. See Chapter 4.
12. See Chapter 5.
13. Greenberg, D, 1988, *The Construction of Homosexuality*, University of Chicago Press, London, p. 352.
14. Symonds, J, 1896, 'A Problem in Modern Ethics', Privately Printed, p. 134.
15. Greenberg, D, 1988, p. 353.
16. Parry, J, 1994, *The Rise and Fall of Liberal Government in Victorian Britain*, Yale University Press, London, p. 92.
17. See Chapter 4.
18. See Perkin, H, 1969, *Origins of Modern English Society*, Routledge & Kegan Paul, London; Stedman-Jones, G, 1983, *Languages of Class: Studies in English Working Class History, 1832–1982*, CUP, Cambridge; and McKibbin, R, 1990, *Ideologies of Class: Social Relations in Britain 1880–1950*, OUP, Oxford.
19. Tosh, J, 1994, p. 190.
20. See Tosh, J, 1999, *A Man's Place: Masculinity and the Middle-Class Home in Victorian England*, Yale University Press, London.
21. Tosh, J, 1994, p. 190.
22. Ibid., p. 188.
23. Ibid.
24. McKibbin, R, 'Why was there no Marxism in Great Britain?', in *The English Historical Review*, Vol. 99, No. 391, 1984, p. 298.
25. Ibid., p. 302.
26. Ibid., p. 303.
27. Ibid., p. 304.
28. Ibid., p. 304.
29. Doolittle, M, 1996, p. 88.
30. McKibbin, R, 1984, p. 304.
31. Tosh, J, 1994, p. 192.
32. Tandy, H, 'Marriage in East London', in Bosanquet, B (ed.), 1895, *Aspects of the Social Problem*, Macmillan and Co., London, p. 77.
33. See Doolittle, M, 1996. Doolittle argues that increasing pressure was imposed on working-class families by charities and government to conform to new standards of hygiene, child care and nutrition in the late nineteenth century.
34. Ibid., p. 78.
35. Ibid., p. 81.
36. Ibid., p. 81.
37. Ibid., p. 80.
38. Ibid., p. 77.
39. Ibid., p. 78.
40. McKibbin, 1984, p. 300.
41. Ibid., p. 305.
42. Ibid., p. 305, citing Jebb, E, 1908, *Cambridge: A Brief Study in Social Questions*, p. 139.

43. Bourke, J, 1994, *Working-Class Cultures in Britain 1890–1960: Gender, Class and Ethnicity*, Routledge, London, p. 64.
44. Ibid., p. 68.
45. Tosh, J, 1994, p. 185.
46. McKibbin, R, 1984, citing Loane, M, 1908, *From their Point of View*, p. 324.
47. Ibid., p. 322.
48. Ibid., p. 323.
49. Ibid., p. 322.
50. Bourke, J, 1994, p. 65.
51. Tosh, J, 1994, p. 192.
52. Tandy, H, 1895, p. 78.
53. See also Summerfield, P, 'Patriotism and Empire: Music-Hall Entertainment, 1870–1914', in Mackenzie, J (ed.), *Imperialism and Popular Culture*, Manchester University Press.
54. See Chapter 3 for detailed discussion of these publications. See also Walkowitz, J, 1992, *City of Dreadful Delight: Narratives of Sexual Danger in Late Victorian London*, Virago, London.
55. Hobsbawm, E, 1987, *The Age of Empire 1875–1914*, Weidenfeld and Nicholson, London.
56. Doolittle, M, 1996, p. 226.
57. Ibid., p. 226.
58. Ibid., p. 230.
59. Ibid., p. 227.
60. Ibid., pp. 77–80.
61. Ibid., p. 68.
62. Bourke, J, 1994, p. 31.
63. Walkowitz, J, 1992, p. 132.
64. Ibid., p. 93.
65. Ibid., p. 92.
66. Ibid., p. 92.
67. Ibid., p. 105.
68. Hall, L, 'Forbidden by God, Despised by Men: Masturbation, Medical Warnings, Moral Panic and Manhood in Great Britain, 1850–1950', in *Journal of the History of Sexuality*, Vol. 2, No. 3, 1992, p. 371.
69. Ibid., p. 375.
70. Ibid., p. 374.
71. See Chapter 5 for broader discussion of British medical attitudes towards sex between men.
72. Mosse, G, 'Nationalism and Respectability: Normal and Abnormal Sexuality in the Nineteenth Century', in *Journal of Contemporary History*, Vol. 17, No. 2, 1982, p. 228.
73. Weeks, J, 1981, p. 107.
74. See Smith, F B, 'Labouchere's Amendment to the Criminal Law Amendment Bill', in *Historical Studies (Australia)*, Vol. 17, No. 67, 1976, p. 165. See Chapter 3 for full discussion of Smith's study.
75. Hall, L, 1992, p. 371.
76. See Chapter 5.
77. See Chapter 3.
78. See Chapter 4.

79. PRO, HO 45/24514.
80. Ibid.
81. PRO, HO 45/24514/473671.
82. *The Parliamentary Debates, Authorised Edition, 1896*, 59 Vic., Vol. xxxvii, Waterlow & Sons, London, House of Lords 1896, Halsbury, col. 1434.
83. Ibid., Halsbury, col. 1449.
84. Ibid., Salisbury, col. 1445.
85. Ibid., Halsbury, col. 1436. See also Chapter 3 for examination of newspaper reporting of 'unnatural crime'.
86. Ibid., Salisbury, col. 1445.
87. Ibid., Rosebery, col. 1446.
88. Ibid., Rosebery, col. 1447.
89. Ibid., Rosebery, col. 1448.
90. Ibid., Rosebery, col. 1448.
91. See Chapter 3.
92. *Parliamentary Debates, House of Lords 1896*, Glensk, col. 1448.
93. Ibid., Rosebery, col. 1448.
94. See Chapter 5.
95. See Chapter 6.
96. O'Brien, M D, 'Free Libraries', in Mackay, T (ed.), 1891, *The English Poor: a Plea for Liberty*, Murray, London; O'Brien, M D, 1893, *The Natural Right to Freedom*, Williams & Norgate, London; and O'Brien, M D, 1892, *Socialism Tested by Facts: being an account of Certain Experimental attempts to Carry out Socialist Principles and Containing a Criticism of 'Looking Backward' and the 'Fabian Essays'*, Liberty and Property Defence League, London.
97. *The Yorkshire Post*, 16 Feb. 1909.
98. O'Brien, M D, 1909, *Socialism and Infamy: the Homogenic or Comrade Love Exposed: an Open Letter in Plain Words for a Socialist Prophet*, Privately Printed, p. 2.
99. Ibid., p. 2.
100. Ibid., p. 4.
101. Ibid., p. 4.
102. Ibid., p. 21.
103. Ibid., p. 21.
104. McLaren, A, 1997, *The Trials of Masculinity: Policing Sexual Boundaries 1870–1930*, University of Chicago Press, London, p. 55.
105. See Connell, R, 1995, *Masculinities*, Polity Press, Cambridge.

3 National Newspapers

1. Weeks, J, 1981, pp. 100–2, and Cohen, E, 1993, *Talk on the Wilde Side: Toward a Genealogy of a Discourse on Male Sexualities*, Routeledge, London, p. 102.
2. Montgomery-Hyde, H, 1970, *The Other Love: An Historical and Contemporary Survey of Homosexuality in Britain*, Heinemann, London, p. 92.
3. Cocks, H, 1998, Unpublished Thesis, University of Manchester, *The Sodomy Trial in English Culture, 1780–1889*, pp. 31–4; and Cocks, H, 2003.
4. Waller, P, 1983, *Town, City and Nation: England 1850–1914*, OUP, Oxford, p. 54. The population of domestic animals actually increased in towns to

serve the expanding populations. By 1890, London had a population of three and a half million horses. *op. cit.*

5. PRO, HO files index.
6. See Chapter 2.
7. Such as abominable, unnatural, vile, evil, unmentionable.
8. Douglas, M, 1966, *Purity and Danger: An Analysis of the Concepts of Pollution and Taboo*, Ark, London, p. 2.
9. Ibid.
10. There is a relative abundance of evidence for these years, particularly in comparison with the 1860s and earlier. To name but a few, the essays on homosexuality by John Addington Symonds, the poetry and paintings of Simeon Solomon and the pornographic literature which celebrated the male prostitution trope in London all date from this period.
11. See Chapter 2.
12. See Chapter 6.
13. *The Times*, 9 July 1881, p. 14, col. a.
14. Ibid.
15. See Lees, L, 1979, *Exiles of Erin: Irish Migrants in Victorian London*, Manchester University Press, Manchester.
16. *The Times*, 23 Sept. 1825, p. 3, col. d.
17. PRO, *Index of British Trials, 1660–1900*.
18. T.E. Baker to Robert Peel, Home Secretary, PRO, HO 44/20.
19. See Cocks, H, 2003, p. 137.
20. *The Times*, 17 Aug. 1866, p. 9, col. a.
21. *The Times*, 8 March 1871, p. 11, col. f.
22. PRO, Crim 10/60, Central Criminal Court, 4736710, *Regina v. George Brett*.
23. *The Times*, 6 Feb. 1863, p. 12, col. d.
24. PRO, Crim 10/62.
25. *Pall Mall Gazette*, 30 May 1870, p. 5.
26. PRO, HO file 144/29 71577. Petition to Home Office to quosh life sentence for buggery imposed on Martin Martinelli, incarcerated on the evidence of one eye witness in 1878.
27. Cocks, H, 1998, Unpublished Thesis, pp. 143–85.
28. *The Times*, 6 Feb. 1863, p. 12, col. d.
29. See *Sins of the Cities of the Plain, or The Recollections of a Mary-Ann*, Anon, Privately Printed, 1881 and *Teleny, or The Reverse of the Medal, a Physiological Romance of Today*, Anon, Privately Printed, 1893.
30. *Reynolds' Weekly Newspaper*, 29 Jan. 1865. In an article 'The Times and the Working Classes', *Reynolds'* promised to keep its readership informed of the 'marvellous consistency' of *The Times* in its 'boundless belief in the potency of a falsehood as an instrument of popular delusion ... though for hundreds of years capitalists ... have combined and legislated for their own interests. ... *The Times* declares that the "unions" of the working classes have forced the capitalists to combine in their own defence'. *op. cit.*
31. *The Times*, 27 Nov. 1862, p. 11 col. e.
32. *The Times*, 23 Jan. 1865, p. 11, col. d.
33. *The Times*, 28 March, 4 Apr., 11 Apr., 4 Aug., 6 Aug., 2 Sept., 19 Sept., 21 Sept., 23 Sept., 2 Nov., 2 Nov., 9 Nov. and 16 Nov. 1825.
34. *The Times*, 5 Aug. 1833.

35. See Chapter 5 for discussion of lack of forensic literature in this field.
36. Montgomery-Hyde, H, 1971, pp. 90–3.
37. Cohen, E, 1993, pp. 117–19.
38. Potter, H, 1993, *Religion and the Death Penalty in England from the Bloody Code to Abolition*, SLM Press Ltd., London, pp. 40–3.
39. *Regina v. John Harris, otherwise called William John Bankes*, PRO, TS 11/897/3060.
40. *The Times*, 10 March 1871, p. 11, col. e.
41. Ibid., 5 Dec. 1862, p. 11, col. c.
42. Ibid., 27 Nov. 1862, p. 11, col. e.
43. Ibid.
44. *Guardian Index*, MS published on microfilm by Manchester Central Libraries, held at British Library Newspaper Collections, Colindale. Search terms for *Palmer's Index* for references in *The Times* to sexuality between men included: buggery, sodomy, unnatural acts, unnatural crime, nameless crime, infamous crime, abominable crime. Nearly all articles in the nineteenth century referred to sex between men as 'unnatural crime'. By the 1860s, references to 'unnatural crime' meant, exclusively, sex between men (an earlier nineteenth-century report used 'unnatural crime' to refer to a case of maternal infanticide).
45. Cocks, H, 2003, p. 78.
46. Ibid. Manchester Central Libraries *Introduction* to the *Guardian Index*.
47. Upchurch, C, 'Forgetting the Unthinkable: Cross-Dressers and British Society in the Case of the *Queen v. Boulton and Others*', in *Gender and History*, Vol. 12, No. 1, April 2000, p. 154.
48. Ibid., citing the *Pall Mall Gazette*, 8 June 1870.
49. Cocks, H, 1998, Unpublished Thesis, p. 114.
50. *Daily Telegraph*, 10 Nov. 1862, p. 4, col. c.
51. In 1865 *The Times'* circulation was 63,000 per edition. For the same year, circulation of *Reynolds'* and *Lloyds'* was 900,000 per edition. Ellegard, A, 1957, *The Readership of the Periodical Press in Mid-Victorian Britain*, University of Gothenberg Press, Gothenberg, Sweden, pp. 14–21.
52. Jones, A, 1996, *Powers of the Press: Newspapers, Power and the Public in Nineteenth-Century England*, Scholar Press, Hants, pp. 122–3.
53. *Lloyd's Weekly Newspaper*, 22 Jan. 1865, p. 12, col. c.
54. *Illustrated London News*, 1861–80, ULL, Senate House and BL Colindale. *Times'* articles cross-referenced with the editions of *ILN* for two weeks following publication.
55. *Lloyd's* and *Reynolds'*, 29 Jan. 1865.
56. Humpherys, A, 'The Newspaper Press and the Divorce Court', in Brake, L, Bell, B and Finkelstein, D (eds), 2000, *Nineteenth-century Media and the Construction of Identities*, Macmillan, London, p. 225.
57. Ibid., pp. 224–6.
58. Ibid., quoting *The Times*, 19 Jan. 1860.
59. Ibid., p. 226.
60. Walkowitz, J, 1992, p. 84.
61. McCalman, I, 1988, *Radical Underworld: Prophets, Revolutionaries and Pornographers in London, 1795–1840*, CUP, Cambridge, pp. 235–7.
62. Walkowitz, J, 1992, pp. 83–93.
63. Upchurch, C, 2000, p. 153n.15.

64. Upchurch, C, 2000, p. 153n.15.
65. Ibid., p. 129.
66. Ibid., p. 151.
67. Ibid., p. 129.
68. *The Times*, 7 May 1870, p. 11, col. f.
69. Ibid., 14 May 1870, p. 10, col. c.
70. Horn, P, 1997, *The Victorian Town Child*, Sutton Publishing, Gloucestershire, p. 169.
71. *Lloyd's Weekly Newspaper*, 22 Jan. 1865, p. 12, col. c.
72. *The Times*, 7 May 1870, p. 11, col. f.
73. *Daily Telegraph*, 9 May 1870, p. 6, col. c.
74. Ibid.
75. *The Times*, 31 May 1870, p. 11, col. d.
76. *The Times*, 16 May 1870, p. 13, col. a.
77. The contents of the letters not read out were not enough to convict Boulton, but deemed sufficient to remand him without bail, indicating that 'Louis' described his own sex life, but did not implicate Boulton. *Reynolds's Weekly Newspaper*, 22 May 1870, p. 5, col. d.
78. *The Times*, 16 May 1870, p. 13, col. b.
79. *Daily Telegraph*, 9 May 1870, p. 6, col. c.
80. The *Daily Telegraph* attests to Boulton earning his living as a female impersonator since the age of 14. *Daily Telegraph*, 9 May 1870, p. 6, col. c.
81. Ibid.
82. *Reynolds's Weekly Newspaper*, 29 May 1870, p. 8, col. b.
83. Cocks, H, 2003, p. 139; *Reynolds' Newspaper* carried an article on 'The Woolwich Affair', in October 1850.
84. Upchurch, C, 2000, p. 147.
85. *Lloyd's Weekly Newspaper*, 22 May 1870, p. 7, col. b.
86. In 1870, *PMG* was regarded as an exclusive, gentlemen's publication. This reputation persisted until W T, Stead's appointment in 1883. Pierce-Jones, V, 1988, *Saint or Sensationalist? The Story of W.T. Stead*, Gooday, West Sussex, p. 13.
87. See Chapter 6.
88. *Pall Mall Gazette*, 30 May 1870, p. 5.
89. Upchurch, C, 2000, p. 145.
90. Stenton, M, 1976, *Who's Who of British Members of Parliament, Vol. 1, 1832–1885: A Biographical Dictionary of the House of Commons*, OUP, Oxford. See also Adelman, P, *Gladstone, Disraeli and Later Victorian Politics*, Longman, Essex, for the political context of Clinton's election as MP.
91. Aronson, T, 1994, *Prince Eddy and the Homosexual Underworld*, CUP, Cambridge, p. 14. Aronson suggests that Clinton's death was a hushed-up suicide. The timing of his death was, in Aronson's assessment, just too convenient for everyone with interests in suppressing this case.
92. Upchurch, C, 2000, p. 157n.87.
93. See Fry, G, 1969, *Statesmen in Disguise: The Changing Role of the Administrative Class of the British Home Civil Service 1853–1966*, Macmillan, London, chapter 1; and MacDonagh, O, 1977, *Early Victorian Government 1830–1870*, Weidenfeld and Nicholson, London, chapter 11.
94. Koss, S, 1981, *The Rise and Fall of the Political Press in Britain: Volume One: The Nineteenth Century*, Hamish Hamilton, London, p. 9.

95. Reeve, H, 1855, from *The Edinburgh Review*, cited by Koss, S, 1981. Henry Reeve was Delane's correspondent-in-chief for foreign affairs at *The Times*.
96. Times Newspapers, 1939, *The History of The Times: Volume Two; The Tradition Established 1841–1884*, p. 492.
97. Ibid., p. 517.
98. See Cocks, H, 2003.
99. Delane's successor, Thomas Chenery, adopted a policy of destroying all correspondence received by *The Times*. This indicates an increasing culture of secrecy, apparent in government administration from the early 1870s. However, an internal memorandum from Chenery to his Assistant Editor, William Stebbing, on the subject of 'wild Indians' in North America, gives insight to prevalent attitudes to sex between men: 'One of the things that makes the Western men abominate them thoroughly can hardly be even hinted at. It is their practice to sodomize their captors before torturing and murdering them. No wonder the pioneer keeps a charge in his revolver to put an end to himself.' MS letter, TT/DepED/STB/1/11, 19 May 1877, News International Archive.
100. *The Times*, 16 May 1871.
101. Oosterhuis, H, 2000, p. 141.
102. *Regina v. Boulton and Others, 1871*, PRO, DPP 4/6.
103. *The Times*, 16 May 1871.
104. Cocks, H, 2003, p. 200.
105. See Cook, M, 2003.
106. See Chapter 6.

4 Legislation

1. www.justis.com, Statute Law, Criminal Law Amendment Act, 1885, Clause 11, 48 and 49 Vict.
2. Cohen, E, 1993, pp. 118–19.
3. Ibid.
4. Weeks, J, 1981, p. 103. Author's italics.
5. Cocks, H, 2003, p. 6.
6. Ibid., p. 104.
7. Walkowitz, J, 1992, p. 82. Clause 11 is referenced in Walkowitz's study as: 'In addition, the act made indecent acts between consulting [sic] male audits [sic] illegal, thus forming the basis of legal proceedings against male homosexuals until 1967.' This serious error of editing, in what is otherwise an important and influential study, is indicative of the lack of significance of controlling sex between men in the history of the campaign for the Criminal Law Amendment Act. Errata aside, Walkowitz replicates the impression in Weeks' study and the explicit argument in Cohen's study that Clause 11 superseded other legislation for punishing sex between men in 1885. This chapter will demonstrate that Clause 11 did not supersede the Buggery Act, which remained the basis of legislation until 1967.
8. See Chapter 5.
9. See Cook, M, 2003, chapter 1.

10. See Cocks, H, Unpublished Thesis, 1998, Appendix A, pp. 253–5. Cocks has tabulated the incidence of sodomy indictments, attempted sodomy indictments and convictions 1800–1900 and gross indecency indictments and convictions, 1885–1900.
11. See Chapter 3.
12. PRO, HO 144/20/58480a, Copy of letter from A.K. Hepburn to Adolphus Liddell, 8 Feb. 1877. The letter is part of a petition file for the release of James Smith, active between 1877 and 1896 and then closed for a century. Liddell is quoted by Hepburn as insisting that there be no prosecution in Smith's case unless there was certainty of conviction at trial.

    The position held by the civil servants cited in this chapter have been established by cross referencing the glossary of nineteenth-century Home Office staff in Pellew, J, 1982, *The Home Office 1848–1914: from Clerks to Bureaucrats*, Heinemann, London.
13. PRO, HO 144/20/58480a.
14. Ibid., Hepburn's underlining.
15. Ibid.
16. See Chapter 3.
17. See Cocks, C, 2003.
18. See MacDonagh, O, 1977, pp. 197–213.
19. Vincent, D, 1998, *The Culture of Secrecy in Britain, 1832–1998*, OUP, Oxford, p. 89.
20. Ibid., pp. 78–131. Vincent argues that the 'honourable secrecy' of gentlemen civil servants in the early nineteenth century was a chimera in many instances, with much government business being leaked to the press. However, by the late nineteenth century, the Treasury could no longer 'buy off' political loyalty from newspaper houses at election times. Also, there was a world of difference, in contemporary concepts, between an aristocratic civil servant using his discernment in deciding to 'leak' information and a clerk of working-class origins giving secrets to the papers, in an era of working-class male suffrage, particularly after 1884.
21. Cock's most recent study concentrates predominantly upon the relationship between the Home Office and the police in the matter of policing sex between men. The policy documents covered by the one hundred year rule, examined in this chapter and used to deconstruct Cohen's and Weeks' analysis, do not feature in this study. See Cocks, H, 2003.
22. Smith, F B, 'Labouchere's Amendment to the Criminal Law Amendment Bill', in *Historical Studies [Australia]*, Vol. 17, No. 67, 1976, p. 165.
23. Ibid., p. 170.
24. Ibid., citing *Parliamentary Debates*, Vol. CCC, 31 July 1885.
25. *The Truth*, 6 Aug. 1885, cited in Smith, F B, 1976.
26. Montgomery-Hyde, H, 1970, p. 133. The circumstances of the 'Golden lane Scandal' are cited from this work by other historians. However, much of the historical detail supplied by Montgomery-Hyde is anecdotal evidence, picked up from acquaintances in his student days in Dublin in the late 1920s. As Montgomery-Hyde states, 'none of the evidence was published either in the Irish or the English newspapers, and as all the court records were destroyed in the Irish Civil war, it is impossible to state the allegations in any detail'. It is interesting, nonetheless, that the 'Golden Lane Scandal', perpetrated by

the *United Ireland*, remained for years in oral legend as 'knowledge', in spite of the lack of publicity afforded the issue at the time.

27. Cocks, H, 2003, pp. 135–44.
28. Ibid., p. 144.
29. Walkowitz, J, 1992, p. 115.
30. *The Times*, 29 Oct. 1885, p. 7, col. d.
31. Ibid., 19 June 1886, p. 6, col. d.
32. *The People*, 20 June 1886.
33. *Lloyds' Weekly Newspaper*, 27 June 1886.
34. Between 1885 and 1900, *The Times* reported on only six cases of unnatural crime, other than the Cleveland Street Scandal and the trials of Oscar Wilde. Between 1861 and 1871, the publication reported on 17 cases, not including the coverage of the 'Stella and Fanny' trials in 1870 and 1871.
35. *The Times*, 3 Oct. 1891, p. 13, col. d.
36. PRO, HO 144/243/a53622, letter from Henry Matthews, Home Secretary, to the Lord Chief Justice, 6 Apr. 1892.
37. www.justis.com, Statute Law, Offences Against the Person Act, 1861, Clause 62, 24 Vict.
38. Cohen, E, 1993, p. 93.
39. Montgomery-Hyde, H, 1970, p. 7.
40. Ibid. The 1967 Act decriminalised sex between men in private in England and Wales only. Northern Ireland and Scotland retained criminalisation until the 1970s and the Republic of Ireland, which had retained its Victorian British criminal codes after independence, did not decriminalise until 1993.
41. The archaic Buggery Act remains on the British statute. Anal penetration of women by men remained criminal under this law until 2000. The British public was reminded in 2002 that this legislation was still the basis for criminalising acts of bestiality. A man was witnessed by passengers on a train copulating with a goat in February 2002. The man was initially charged using the archaic Buggery Act, but was then assessed for treatment using contemporary mental health legislation. *The Guardian*, 23 Feb. 2002.
42. All statistics are taken from Cocks, H, 1998, Unpublished Thesis, Appendix A. I am much indebted to Cocks' meticulous statistical tabulation of judicial returns from Parliamentary Papers.
43. www.justis.com, Statute Law, Offences Against the Person Act, 1861, Clause 63, 24 Vict.
44. In the case against George Brett in Chapter 1, the charge of attempted sodomy/indecent assault was thrown out of court because 'there was no corroboration of the prosecutors evidence, which, if true, showed consent on his part'. PRO, Crim 10/60, 4736710, CCC, Sept. 1868.
45. See also Cocks, H, 2003, chapter 1.
46. Of course, in relation to other crimes, sex between men remained a minute proportion of the business of the courts. In the five year period 1876–80, convictions for common assault accounted for 371,067 of all committals. *Source*: Sindall, R, 1990, *Street Violence in the Nineteenth Century: Media Panic or Real Danger?*, Leicester University Press, Leicester, table 4.10, p. 65. This notwithstanding, the levels of indictments for sexual crimes between men are surprisingly high before and after 1885, particularly in the light of the arguments for the rarity of cases or awareness of sexuality between men

before 1885 in historiography and the actions in the late nineteenth century to achieve this impression.

47. Read, D, 1990, *The Age of Urban Democracy; England 1868–1914*, Longman, London, p. 244.
48. Cocks, H, 2003, chapters 1 and 2.
49. Harvey, A D, 'Bestiality in late Victorian England', in *Journal of Legal History [GB]*, Vol. 21, No. 3, 2000, pp. 85–8.
50. PRO, HO 144/243/a53622. I have counted five convictions of sodomy in these files which do not stipulate whether the 'buggery' or 'attempted buggery' was 'with mankind or beast'.
51. Ibid.
52. This was certainly the interpretation in the 1960s of acts of anal sex between men, as opposed to other acts 'not amounting to buggery', before decriminalisation in the Sexual Offences Act of 1967. Montgomery-Hyde, H, 1970, p. 7.
53. Weeks, J, 1981, p. 102.
54. Cocks, H, 2003, pp. 34–9.
55. Ibid., p. 51.
56. DPP 4/6, *Regina v. Boulton and Others*, 1871.
57. *Dictionary of National Biography, 1901–11, Supplement*, 1927, p. 355.
58. Aronson, T, 1994, pp. 8–9.
59. PRO, DPP 1/95/4, file 2.
60. PRO, HO 144/216/a49134.
61. Tobias, J, 1967, *Crime and Industrial Society in the 19th Century*, B. T. Batesford, London, p. 175.
62. Tobias, J, 1979, *Crime and Police in England 1700–1900*, Gill & Macmillan, Dublin, p. 213.
63. Forsythe, W, 1991, *Penal Discipline, Reformatory Projects and the English Prison Commission 1895–1939*, University of Exeter Press, Exeter, p. 21.
64. PRO, HO 144/243/a53622.
65. Forsythe, W, 1990, p. 26.
66. Ibid., pp. 45–7.
67. PRO, HO 144/216/a49134.
68. Ibid.
69. Forsythe, W, 1990, p. 22.
70. Ibid., p. 45.
71. Ibid., p. 46.
72. PRO, HO 144/20/58480a/2.
73. PRO, HO 144/20/58480a.
74. PRO, HO 144/243/a53622, review by Charles Murdoch, Assitant Under Secretary, compiled for Herbert Asquith, Home Secretary, 29 Oct. 1892.
75. PRO, HO 144/216/a49134.
76. PRO, HO 144/21/71577/6, 'Karolyc' to Le Marquis de Salisbury, 17 Oct. 1879. 'Quoique ne doutaut nullement que la cour criminelle ne soit arrivé à sa décision qu'apres avoir par un examin conscientiaux approfondi la grâve accusation contre ... il ne paraît apendant que la sentence à vie est d'une sévérité exceptionelle ... en Autriche, du moins, le tribunal n'accrait pas en le droit décréter une peine plus sévère.'
77. PRO, HO 144/243/a53622, Godfrey Lushington to Herbert Asquith, Home Secretary, 29 Oct. 1892.

78. Ibid., Henry Matthews to the lord Chief Justice, 6 April 1892.
79. Ibid., Herbert Asquith to Godfrey Lushington, 29 Nov. 1892.
80. Montgomery-Hyde, H, 1970, pp. 212–13. Montgomery-Hyde highlights that there were, in 1952, 670 convictions for sodomy and bestiality and that the defendants were all tried under the archaic buggery laws.
81. PRO, HO 144/243/a53622.
82. Weeks, J, 1995, p. 53.
83. Walkowitz, J, 1992, p. 83.
84. Ibid., p. 275n.74.
85. Ibid., p. 83.
86. See Bristow, E, 1977, *Vice and Vigilance: Purity Movements in Britain since 1700*, Gill & Macmillan, Dublin; and Mort, F, 1987, *Dangerous Sexualities: Medico-Moral Politics in England since 1830*, Routeledge & Kegan Paul, London.
87. Smith, F B, 1976, p. 170.
88. Walkowitz, J, 1992, p. 83.
89. HO 45/9784/B2917.
90. Ibid., p. 159.
91. PRO, HO 45/9784/B29 17, Feb. 1898.
92. Walkowitz, J, 1992, p. 159.
93. PRO, HO 45/9928, May 1897.
94. The officials in this series initialled rather than signed their correspondence. None of the initials match the lists of senior Home Office officials listed by Pellew for this date.
95. PRO, HO 45/9784/B2917.
96. PRO, HO 45/9928/B25396.
97. PRO, HO 45/9784/B2917.
98. Ibid.
99. Greenberg, D, 1988, pp. 352–3.
100. The intolerance in Britain towards medical studies of sex between men, including physical studies along the lines of Tardieu's, are examined in detail in Chapter 5.
101. HO 45/9928.
102. Weeks, J, 1995, p. 53. Weeks acknowledges that 'figures are difficult to come by' for male prostitution until the differentiation of categories in 1954.
103. See Chapter 1.

5 Resistance

1. I am very grateful to Dr Harry Oosterhuis for confirming, in the discussion at a conference at the Wellcome Institute, London, in December 2001, that the vast majority of Krafft-Ebing's correspondents came from German-speaking lands or France. Very little correspondence emanated from England.
2. See Cook, M, 2003, p. 76.
3. *BMJ*, 1909, Vol. i, p. 1547, cited in, Porter, R and Hall, L, 1995, p. 162.
4. Porter, R and Hall, L, 1995, p. 142.
5. Ibid.
6. See Chapter 3.
7. Shaw, G B, letter to *The Adult*, Vol. ii, No. viii, p. 230, Sep. 1898.

8. Shaw, G B, letter to *The Adult*, Vol. ii, No. viii, p. 230, Sep. 1898.
9. Grosskurth, E, 1980, *Havelock Ellis: A Biography*, Quartet, London, p. 184.
10. This chapter will examine the single work in English that made this connection, using Malthus' work as its basis.
11. Porter, R and Hall, L, 1995, pp. 127–9. Citing nineteenth-century edition of *Aristotle's Master-Piece*, Porter and Hall chart the changes in this highly popular sexual manual, from its inception in the late seventeenth century to the late nineteenth century. By the reign of Victoria, the manual had become a 'fundamentally different work'. In the nineteenth-century editions, 'the plain discussion of sex [had] disappeared. In the Victorian version ... a greater stress was placed on marriage as distinct from mere "unions" ... the aim of these later editions was to uphold and dignify ... restraint ... desire [had] been unveiled as danger, and sex [had] been replaced by the higher ideals of "family affection" '. Ibid.
12. Oosterhuis, H, 2000, pp. 66–7.
13. Ibid., and Weeks, J, 1995, p. 70.
14. Oosterhuis, H, 2000, pp. 66–7.
15. Ibid.
16. See Mosse, G, 'Nationalism and Respectability', 1982, pp. 221–46.
17. Clark, J, 1985, *English Society 1688–1832: Ideology, Social Structure and Political Practices during the Ancient Regime*, CUP, Cambridge, p. 59.
18. See Collini, S, *Public Moralists: Political Thought and Intellectual Life in Britain 1850–1930*, Clarendon, Oxford.
19. Mason, M, 1994, *The Making of Victorian Sexual Attitudes*, OUP, Oxford, pp. 189–213; Benn, J, 1992, *The Predicaments of Love*, Pluto, London. Benn's excellent study is dedicated to Drysdale, the publication of *Elements*, its rejection by the medical establishment and its influence on birth controllers in the late nineteenth century. However, Drysdale's opinions on sexuality between men are ignored by this and other studies.
20. The earliest surviving edition of *Elements* dates from 1861 and has been used in this chapter.
21. Drysdale, G, 1861, *Elements of Social Science, or Physical, Sexual and Natural Religion: an Exposition of the True Cause and the Only Cure of the Three Primary Social Evils: Poverty, Prostitution and Celibacy*, Truelove, London, p. 247. Author's italics.
22. Ibid., p. 247.
23. Ibid., pp. 247–9.
24. Ibid., p. 70.
25. Ibid., p. 248.
26. Ibid., p. 249.
27. Porter, R and Hall, L, 1995, p. 150.
28. Ibid., 1905.
29. Benn, J, 1992, pp. 13–14, 24–26.
30. The Wellcome Library, London, has a complete collection of the first *Index-Catalogue of the Library of the Surgeon General's Office, United States Army*, and this has been searched for references to sexuality between men. All cumulative medical literature on the subject is catalogued under 'sodomy', published in Volume XIII (sialalgogues-sutgin) in 1892.
31. Ibid., p. 305. See also 'Perversion of the Sexual Instinct', in *The Alienist and Neurologist*, 1888, Vol. 9, Periodical Publications, St. Louis, Missouri, USA, p. 565. This article was not included in the *Index-Catalogue*.

32. 'Aberrations in the Sexual Instinct', in *Medical Times and Gazette*, 9 Feb. 1867, pp. 141–6.
33. Moscucci, O, 1990, *The Science of Woman: Gynaecology and Gender in England, 1800–1929*, CUP, Cambridge, p. 102.
34. Ibid., p. 142.
35. See Hardy, A, 2001, *Health and Medicine in Britain since 1860*, Macmillan, Basingstoke; Lawrence, C, 1994, *Medicine in the Making of Modern Britain, 1700–1920*, Routledge, London; MacLeod, R and Lewis, M, 1988, *Disease, Medicine and Empire: Perspectives on Western Medicine and the Experience of European Expansion*, Routledge, London and others.
36. Ibid., p. 423. Definition, *Oxford English Dictionary*, 'One who treats mental disease'.
37. Grosskurth, P, 1980, p. 180.
38. Kennedy, H, 'Karl Heinrich Ulrichs: First Theorist of Homosexuality', in Rosario, V (ed.), 1997, *Science and Homosexualities*, Routledge, London, pp. 36–9.
39. *The Journal of Mental Science*, Vol. XVII, No. 79, October 1871, p. 422.
40. Rosario, V, 'Inversion's Histories / History's Inversions: Novelizing Fin-de-Siecle Homosexuality', in Rosario, V (ed.), 1997, p. 91.
41. Ibid., p. 420.
42. See Chapter 3.
43. Ibid., p. 68.
44. PRO, DPP 4/6, *Regina v. Boulton and Others*, p. 252.
45. Ibid., p. 253.
46. Crozier, I, 'The Medical Construction of Homosexuality and its Relation to the Law in Nineteenth-Century England', in *Medical History*, Vol. 45, 2001, p. 67, citing Taylor, A, 1910, *Principles and Practice of Medical Jurisprudence*.
47. Rosario, V (ed.), 1997, p. 31.
48. PRO, DPP 4/6, p. 276.
49. Ibid.
50. Ibid., p. 71.
51. Ibid., pp. 997–9.
52. The Lord Chief Justice presided over the Queen's Bench which was the 'superior' English court of common law. The Queen's Bench conducted trials at Westminster Hall until 1882, when it was relocated, along with the Court of Common Pleas, to the Strand. Holdsworth, W, 1936, *A History of English Law, Vol. I*, Methuen & Co., London, p. 639; and Cornish, W, and Clark, G, 1989, *Law and Society in England 1750–1950*, Sweet & Maxwell, London, p. 22.
    The 'Stella and Fanny' trial for sodomy was, as far as I can ascertain, the only trial for sodomy conducted in Westminster Hall in the nineteenth century. Cornish and Clark state that trials in Westminster Hall became much less commonplace after 1750, with much of the business of the Queen's Bench being conducted on circuit. It is clear that the 'Stella and Fanny' trail was most unusual in every respect. Conducted and controlled in Westminster Hall, with a 'special jury' and the Lord Chief Justice presiding, the trial served as a very public and intimidating demonstration of the reprehensibility of the crime of sodomy, if proven, and the rarity of this vice amongst Englishmen.
53. PRO, DPP 4/6, p. 44.
54. Ibid., p. 1000.

55. Taylor, A, 1910, *Principles and Practice of Medical Jurisprudence, Vol II*, Churchill, London, p. 291.
56. The lack of material on sodomy in British nineteenth-century forensic text-books is remarkable, particularly if compared to material on the physical signs of rape in women in this literature, and in comparison to Continental forensic studies. See Male, G, 1818, *An Epitome of Judicial or Forensic Medicine: for the use of Medical Men, Coroners, and Barristers*, London; Ryan, M, 1831, *A Manual of Medical Jurisprudence, being an Analysis of a Course of Lectures on Forensic Medicine*, London; Husband, Henry, 1874, *The Student's Handbook on Forensic Medicine and Medical Police*, Edinburgh; *The Standard Cyclopaedia* [sic] *of Political, Constitutional, Statistical, and Forensic Knowledge*, H. G. Bonn, London; Williams, S, 1885, *Forensic Facts and Fallacies: a Popular Consideration of some Legal Points and Principles*, Macmillan & Co., London; and Guy, W, and Ferrier, D, 1888, *Principles of Forensic Medicine*. Male's work of 1818 makes a brief reference to the necessity of proof of penetration and emission for a sodomy conviction, but makes no suggestion of how this may be ascertained. All later works, apart from Taylor's, make no reference to the crime at all.
57. This is argued by Crozier in his unpublished research project, in progress, on Havelock Ellis and the construction of homosexuality. I am indebted to Dr Ivan Crozier for our discussions on reviews of inversion theorists in *JMS* in the late nineteenth century.
58. Summers, A, 'The Correspondents of Havelock Ellis', in *History Workshop Journal*, No. 32, 1991, p. 169.
59. For example, see Paul Robinson's influential study *The Modernization of Sex: Havelock Ellis, Alfred Kinsey, William Masters and Virginia Johnson*, Elek, London (1989).
60. Grosskurth, P, 1980, p. 122.
61. Nottingham, C, 1999, p. 32.
62. Grosskurth, P, 1980, p. 122.
63. Ibid., p. 126.
64. Ellis, H, 1940, *My Life*, Heinemann, London, p. 295.
65. Ellis, H to Symonds, J, 21 Dec. 1892, cited by Grosskurth, P, p. 177.
66. Olive Schreiner to Havelock Ellis, 5 May 1914. MS 568 in Draznin, Y, 1992, *My Other Self: The Letters of Olive Schreiner and Havelock Ellis, 1884–1920*, Peter Lang, New York, USA. Schreiner was commenting on Ellis' review of the third edition of *Sexual Inversion*, published in the United States in 1914. The comment is revealing of the social pitfalls for Ellis, even in these years when his work was a well-established publication in the US and increasingly clandestinely available in Britain.
67. Grosskurth, P, 1980, footnote on p. 180.
68. Ibid., p. 180.
69. Dr Hack Tuke was a visitor to Symonds' Swiss retreat and Symonds commented upon the 'warm affectionate way' Tuke senior would talk of his father, in correspondence to Henry Scott Tuke. Tuke senior, however, persistently refused to discuss Symonds' ideas on inversion with Symonds. J A Symonds to Henry Scott Tuke, 15 Oct. 1890, MS 1838, in Schueller, H and Peters, R (eds), 1969, *The Letters of John Addington Symonds, Vol. III*, Wayne State University Press, Detroit, USA.

70. Grosskurth, P, 1980, p. 180.
71. Sheffield City Archives, Carpenter Collection, MSS 357/6(1), Ellis to Carpenter, October 1894.
72. The work is listed in Babington's 1925 *Bibliography of the Writings of J.A.Symonds* as *Das Kontrare Geschlechtsgefuhl von Havelock Ellis und J.A.Symonds 1896*. Babington, P, 1925, *Bibliography of the Writings of J.A.Symonds*, p. 122.
73. Grosskurth, P, 1980, p. 179.
74. Ibid., p. 181. Brown did not quite manage to destroy all copies of the first edition. Fortunately, a copy exists at The London Library. Some of Symonds' other papers and the manuscript of his memoirs were deposited at the London Library by Brown at his own death, so it is possible that Brown had retained a copy of the first edition of *Sexual Inversion* for posterity.
75. Summers, A, 1991, p. 174.
76. Sweeney, J, 1904, *At Scotland Yard*, Grant Richards, London, p. 185.
77. Ibid., p. 178.
78. Grosskurth, P, 1980, p. 192.
79. Sweeney, J, 1904, p. 177.
80. Ibid., p. 181.
81. Ibid., p. 185.
82. Ibid., p. 185.
83. For example, a pirated translation of Tarnowski's essay on 'Morbid Manifestations of the Sexual Instinct' was available for 10s 6d, an exorbitant price for a book or pamphlet in the 1890s. *University Press Ltd., Watford*, December 1899, B.L., CUP 364/948.
84. See Bristow, J, 'Symonds' History, Ellis' Heredity: *Sexual Inversion*', in Bland, L, and Doan, L (eds), 1998, *Sexology in Culture: Labelling Bodies and Desires*. Brisow's work refers to Ellis' involvement with the Legitimation League at this time, but Grosskurth's study remains the most detailed examination of this connection. Like Grosskurth, Ellis' reputation is presented as aloof from the activities of the League, rather than his work being the catalyst for its supression.
85. Grosskurth, P, 1980, p. 180.
86. *The Adult*, March 1897.
87. Sweeney, J, 1904, p. 186.
88. Ibid., p. 189.
89. *The Adult*, June 1897, p. 1.
90. In her short article on the existence of *The Adult*, Patricia Anderson comments upon the lack of attention given by historians to the publication, in spite of its intriguing title. Anderson, P, 'Free Love and Free thought: The Adult, 1897–1899', in *Studies in Newspaper and Periodical History*, 1993, pp. 179–81. Grosskurth's biography of Ellis gives the publication some attention. Bristow's article in Bland, L and Doan, L, 1998, mentions *The Adult*, but does use the publication to place *Sexual Inversion* in the context provided here.
91. *The Adult*, Vol. 2, No. 7, Aug. 1898, p. 192.
92. Anderson, P, 1993, p. 180.
93. *The Adult*, Vol. 2, No. 7, Aug. 1898, p. 192.
94. Ellis, H, 1936, *Studies in the Psychology of Sex*, Vol. 2, Heinemann, London, p. 38.
95. *The Adult*, Vol. 2, No. 7, Aug. 1898, p. 189.

96. *The Adult*, Vol. 2, No. 6, July 1898, p. 183.
97. Ibid., Vol. 2, No. 7, Aug. 1898, p. 193.
98. Ibid., Vol. 2, No. 8, Sept. 1898, p. 224.
99. Ibid., Vol. 2, No. 9, Oct. 1898, p. 337.
100. Ibid.
101. Grosskurth, P, 1980, p. 204.
102. Lord Salisbury, House of Lords Debates, 20 March 1896, p. 38, col. 1445.
103. Davenport-Hines, R, 1990, *Sex, Death and Punishment: Attitudes to Sex and Sexuality since the Renaissance*, Collins, London, p. 139.
104. See Chapter 2.
105. *The Adult*, Vol. 2, No. 11, Dec. 1898, pp. 329–30.
106. Ellis, H to unidentifiable correspondent, 27 June 1913. MS Correspondence of Havelock Ellis, Harry Ramsden Center, University of Texas, USA. I am indebted to Dr Ivan Crozier, University of Edinburgh, for this piece of evidence.
107. *University Press Ltd., Watford*, December 1899, B.L., CUP 364/948.
108. Ellis, H, 1925, *A Note on the Bedborough Trial*, p. 10, Privately Printed, New York, USA, Reprint of 1898 edition, also published in New York, destroyed in the Second World War bombing of British Library.
109. Ibid., p. 16.
110. See Richards, G, 'Edward Cox, the Psychological Society of Great Britain (1875–1879) and the meanings of an Institutional Failure', in Bunn, G, Lovie, A and Richards, G, 2001 (eds), *Psychology in Britain: Historical Essays and Personal Reflections*, British Psychological Society, Leicester, pp. 33–53.
111. Lovie, A, 'Three Steps to Heaven: How the British Psychological Society attained its Place in the Sun', in Bunn, G *et al.*, 2001, pp. 95–103.
112. Rowe, D, introduction to Kutchins, H and Firk, S, 1999, p. x.
113. See Tucker, A, 'Army and Society in England 1870–1900: a Reassessment of the Cardwell Reforms,' in *Journal of British Studies*, Vol. 2, No. 2, 1963, pp. 110–41.
114. See Showalter, D, 'The Retaining of Bellona: Prussia and the Institutionalization of the Napoleonic Legacy, 1815–1876', in *Military Affairs*, Vol. 44, No. 2, 1980, p. 59; Wright, G, 'Public Opinion and Conscription in France, 1866–1870', in *Journal of Modern History*, Vol. 14, No. 1, 1942, pp. 26–45; Showalter, R, 'Army and Society in Imperial Germany: The Pains of Modernization', in *Journal of Contemporary History*, Vol. 18, No. 4, Oct. 1983.
115. See Blackborne, D, 'The Politics and Demagogy of Imperial Germany', in *Past and Present*, No. 113, 1986.
116. Hall, I, 'The Bourgeoisie and its Discontents: Reflections on Nationalism and Respectability', in *Journal of Contemporary History*, Vol. 17, No. 2, 1982, p. 222.
117. See Mosse, G, 'Nationalism and Respectability', 1982.

6 Lives

1. See Kutchins, H and Kirk, S, 1999.
2. *Homogenic Love* was not published until 1906, though Carpenter had an edition privately printed by the Manchester Labour Press in 1894, 'which [was]not sold but sent around pretty freely to those I thought would be

interested'. Carpenter, E, 1916, *My Days and Dreams: Being Autobiographical Notes*, Allen & Unwin, p. 195.

3. Greig, N, 1984, *Introduction to Edward Carpenter: Selected Writings Volume 1: Sex*, Gay Men's Press, p. 15.

4. See Osment, P, 1989, *Gay Sweatshop: Four Plays and a Company*, Methuen Drama, London.

5. Cook, M, 2003, discusses Carpenter's ideas on homosexuality and sex-psychology, but does not concentrate upon his ideas of masculinity and masculine social status. See also Hall, L, 'Disinterested Enthusiasm for Sexual Misconduct: The British Society for the Study of Sex Psychology, 1913–47', in *Journal of Contemporary History*, Vol. 30, No. 4, pp. 665–86. Hall briefly addresses Carpenter's connection with and contributions to the BSSSP after 1913, which falls outside the remit of this book, but does not offer a gendered analysis of Carpenter's ideas.

6. See Cook, M, 2003 for the most recent evaluation of this.

7. See Chapter 5.

8. Judd, D, 2001, *Empire: the British Imperial Experience from 1765 to the Present*, Phoenix, London. Judd highlights the sexual opportunities and adventures provided by the Empire for British men. In particular, he examines the activities of Sir Hector MacDonald, Commander-in-Chief of British forces in Ceylon. MacDonald committed suicide following the discovery of his sexual activities with Ceylonese boys. Judd highlights that many British men led uninhibited sexual lives in the imperial territories. However, discussion or discovery was the disgrace that had to be avoided at all costs; 'it had become virtually impossible to discuss sexual matters in public, and almost as difficult to speak of them in private. Rather than face condemnation, disgrace and ridicule, the overwhelming majority of British people ... refrained from mentioning sexual matters', pp. 178–9.

9. Weeks, J, 1990, *Coming Out: Homosexual Politics in Britain since the Nineteenth Century*, Quartet, London, p. 187.

10. Grosskurth's biography, in spite of being 40 years old and suffused with the prejudices of its time, remains the only comprehensive biographical treatment of Symonds' life, work and 'problem'.

11. Grosskurth, P, 1964, *John Addington Symonds: a Biography*, Longmans, London, pp. 189–93.

12. There are significant differences between Symonds' MS of 'A Problem in Greek Ethics' and the second edition of *Sexual Inversion*, published and banned in 1898.

13. See Chapter 5.

14. Grosskurth, P (ed.), 1984, *The Memoirs of John Addington Symonds*, Hutchinson, London. These memoirs will be examined throughout this chapter.

15. See Chapter 2.

16. British Medical Journal, 1909, Vol. i, p. 1547, cited in Porter, R and Hall, L, 1995, p. 162.

17. Tsuzuki, C, 1980, *Edward Carpenter 1844–1929: Prophet of Human Fellowship*, CUP, Cambridge, p. 127.

18. Grosskurth's editorial of Symonds' memoirs has been cross-referenced here with Symonds' MS in the London Library. Grosskurth has included nearly all of Symonds' memoirs unabridged, including material that did not form

part of the author's main narrative and relevant emendations made by the author.

19. Schueller, H and Peters, R (eds), *The Letters of John Addington Symonds*. Vol. 1 (1967), Vol. 2 (1968) and Vol. 3 (1969), Wayne State University Press, Detroit, USA.
20. Symonds' 'homosexuality' has tended to attract the attention of historians, rather than the difficulties his desires created for his masculine social status in Britain. Symonds' scholarly contributions to the lexicon of Renaissance and Classical studies has attracted the recent attentions of literary critics and historians in these fields. However, in recent literary/historical studies, Symonds'ideas on sexuality between men and masculinity appear only in parenthesis or in notes for broader scholarship in this field. See Shuter, W, 'The "Outing" of Walter Pater', in *Nineteenth-Century Literature*, Vol. 48, No. 4, 1994, pp. 480–506; Bristow, J, 'Churlsgrace': Gerard Manley Hopkins and the Working-Class Male Body, *ELH*, Vol. 59, No. 3, 1992, pp. 693–711; Danson, L, 'Oscar Wilde, W.H., and the Unspoken Name of Love', in *ELH*, Vol. 58, No. 4, 1991, pp. 979–1000.
21. Grosskurth, P, 1964, p. 5.
22. Grosskurth, P (ed.), 1984, p. 82.
23. Ibid., p. 94.
24. Ibid., p. 221.
25. Ibid., p. 96.
26. Ibid., p. 112.
27. Ibid., p. 112.
28. Ibid., p. 112.
29. Ibid., p. 113.
30. Symonds' daughter, Dame Katherine Furse, was the only person allowed to see her father's closed literary bequest in the London Library before 1976. Furse confirmed in correspondence with Virginia Woolf in 1939 that many of Symonds' papers had been destroyed, probably by the family of Symonds' literary executor, Horatio Brown; 'it is practically impossible to get to the root of what happened to all father's papers'. MS no. 7, Furse to Woolf, 11 Aug. 1939, cited in Fowler, R, 'Archives: Virginia Woolf and Katherine Furse: An Unpublished Correspondence', in *Tulsa Studies in Women's Literature*, 1990, Vol. 2, p. 211.
31. Chandos, J, 1984, *Boys Together: English Public Schools 1800–1864*, Hutchinson, London, p. 35.
32. Chandos, J, 1984, p. 296.
33. See Chapter 4.
34. Ibid., p. 315.
35. Ibid., p. 318.
36. Pearce, M and Stewart, G, 1992, *British Political History 1867–1990: Democracy and Decline*, Routledge, London, p. 38.
37. *Dictionary of National Biography*.
38. Mackie, J, 1964, *A History of Scotland*, Penguin Books, London, pp. 298–307.
39. Weiner, M, 1981, *English Culture and the Decline of the Industrial Spirit, 1850–1980*, CUP, Cambridge, p. 21.
40. Schueller, H and Peters, R, Vol. 1, 1967, Symonds to Dakyns, 14 Aug. 1866, MS 492.

41. Ibid.
42. Grosskurth, P, 1964, p. 5.
43. Cocks, H, 2003, pp. 118–19.
44. Ibid., p. 122.
45. Grosskurth, P (ed.), 1984, p. 97.
46. See Chapter 3 for discussion of newspaper reporting of unnatural crime.
47. See Chapter 4 for details of the 1861 Offences Against the Person Act.
48. See Chapter 5.
49. Grosskurth, P (ed.), 1984, p. 116.
50. Ibid., pp. 116–17.
51. Ibid., p. 104.
52. Ibid., p. 127.
53. Ibid., p. 167, stanza from a longer poem, untitled.
54. Grosskurth, P, 1964, p. 58.
55. Grosskurth, P (ed.), 1984, p. 132.
56. Dowling, L, 1994, *Hellenism and Homosexuality in Victorian Oxford*, Cornell University Press, London, p. 91.
57. Grosskurth, P, (ed.), 1984 p. 133.
58. Ibid., p. 133.
59. Ibid., p. 151.
60. Ibid., p. 152.
61. Ibid., p. 166.
62. Ibid., p. 141. Unfortunately, no correspondence between Symonds and Acton survives. However, Acton's brutal remedy, particularly if Symonds confided his sexual desires, would have been in keeping with the physician's recommendations about sex and masturbation. Acton recommended 'total ignorance' of sex in the education of the young and warned against a man prying 'into his mental and moral character with despicable morbid minuteness'. Acton, W, 1859, *A Practical Treatise on the Diseases of the Urinary and Generative Organs, in Both Sexes*, John Churchill, London, p. 14. Also see Porter, R and Hall, L, 1995.
63. Grosskurth, P (ed.), 1984, p. 151.
64. Ibid., p. 154.
65. Ibid., p. 152.
66. See Chapter 5.
67. Grosskurth, P (ed.), 1984, p. 152.
68. Ibid., p. 184.
69. See Chapter 3.
70. Grosskurth, P (ed.), 1984, p. 157.
71. Ibid., p. 185.
72. Ibid., p. 186.
73. Ibid., p. 158.
74. Symonds attempted in the memoirs to preserve the identity of this man by calling him 'Norman, though that was not his real name'. However, Symonds' correspondence to his friend Henry Dakyns, who shared Symonds' propensities and confidence, frequently refer to the love he bore for Edward Norman Moor between 1869 and the early 1870s. Scheuller, H and Peters, R (eds), Vol. 2, 1968. It is interesting that Symonds wished to hide the identity of a man of his own class, but revealed the name of Willie Dyer, his working-class 'lover' of the early 1860s.

75. Scheuller, H and Peters, R, p. 186.
76. Ibid., p. 160, citing Catherine Symonds' diaries, 30 Jan. 1866.
77. Ibid., p. 202.
78. See Davidoff, L and Hall, C, 1992, *Family Fortunes: Men and Women of the English Middle Class 1780–1850*, Hutchinson, London. Davidoff and Hall's thesis of 'separate spheres' in the middle-class marriage in the nineteenth century appears to be borne out by the domestic arrangement that the Symonds' achieved. Symonds was able to conduct his activities with men friends, without raising concerns that he was neglecting Catherine. For her part, Catherine was able to present to the world her sphere of domestic virtues and the provision of respectable family life for her eminent and literary husband.
79. Cook, M, 2003, citing Symonds' *Memoirs*.
80. Ibid., p. 297.
81. Ibid., p. 212.
82. Symonds, J, 1883, 'A Problem in Greek Ethics', pp. 17–24. Symonds had his essay of 1873 privately printed in 1883. Ten copies were printed. Number ten survives in the British Library. BL, CUP.402.c.2.
83. Dowling, L, 1994, p. 73.
84. Ibid., p. 73.
85. Ibid.
86. Jenkyns, R, 1980, *The Victorians and Ancient Greece*, Blackwell, Oxford, p. 192.
87. Dowling, L, 1994, p. 75. Citing Jowett, B, 1881, trans. *Thucydides*.
88. Ibid.
89. Ibid., p. 85.
90. Ibid., p. 102.
91. Ibid. See also Jenkyns, R, 1980.
92. Grosskurth, P (ed.), 1984, p. 297.
93. In *Studies of the Greek Poets*, Symonds outlined the Ancient Greek attitudes towards sexual activity *per se*, with only an implication that this included sexuality between men; 'the sensual impulses, like the intellectual and moral, were then held void of crime and harmless. Health and good taste the physical appetites of man, just as the appetites of animals are regulated by unerring instinct'. Symonds, J, 1893, *Studies of the Greek Poets*, A & C Black, London, p. 382.
94. Grosskurth, P (ed.), 1984, p. 228.
95. Dowling, L, 1994, p. 91.
96. Ibid., citing Tyrwhitt.
97. Ibid., p. 91.
98. Ibid., p. 92.
99. Symonds, J, 1883, p. 3.
100. Ibid., p. 24.
101. Ibid., p. 24.
102. Ellis, H H and Symonds, J A, 1897, *Sexual Inversion*, Wilson & Macmillan, London. I am indebted to The London Library for permission to view one of the very few examples of Ellis' first edition of *Sexual Inversion*, which included Symonds' authorship. The copy in the London Library has survived because it was part of Horatio Brown's bequest in 1926. Brown, as Symonds' executor, recalled nearly all copies for destruction at Catherine Symonds' behest. See Chapter 5.

103. Symonds, J, 1883, p. 35.
104. Ibid., p. 96.
105. Unfortunately, Symonds' correspondence does not refer to the 'Stella and Fanny' trial in his correspondence. However, Symonds subscribed to and was published in the *Pall Mall Gazette*, which conducted a refutation of the classical idiom in apologias for unnatural crime in the modern era. It is fair to suppose that Symonds followed this alarming coverage, given his private ideas on paiderastia at this time.
106. *Pall Mall Gazette*, 30 May 1870, p. 5.
107. See Chapter 3.
108. *Pall Mall Gazette*, 30 May 1870, p. 5.
109. Symonds, J, 1883, p. 97.
110. See Chapter 5.
111. Schueller, H and Peters, R (eds), 1969, Vol. 3, MS 1694, Symonds to Jowett, 1 Feb. 1889.
112. Schueller, P and Peters, R (eds), 1968, Vol. 2, MS 1270, Symonds to Dakyns, 10 April 1882.
113. Grosskurth, P, 1964, p. 192.
114. Cited in Grosskurth, P, 1964, p. 197.
115. Ibid.
116. Ibid., p. 198.
117. Schueller, H and Peters, R, 1969, Vol. 3, MS 2079, Symonds to Carpenter, 21 Jan. 1893.
118. Grosskurth, P (ed.), 1984, p. 275.
119. See Chapter 4. After 1885, Britain had a cascade of legislation criminalising sex of all descriptions between men.
120. Grosskurth, P (ed.), 1984, p. 276.
121. Ibid., p. 241.
122. Symonds' like-minded companions included the literary figures Henry Dakyns, Algernon Swinbourne, Edmund Gosse, Horatio Brown and Robert Louis Stevenson.
123. Schueller, H and Peters, R (eds), 1968, Vol. 2, MS 1381, Symonds to T S Perry, 22 March 1884.
124. Ibid., MS 1039, Symonds to Charlotte Symonds Green, 28 Feb. 1877.
125. Ibid., 1969, Vol. 3, MS 1943, Symonds to Brown, 29 Dec. 1891.
126. See Chapter 5 for details of the suppression of Continental scientific literature on inversion in Britain.
127. Grosskurth, P (ed.), 1984, pp. 64–5.
128. Weeks, J, 1989, pp. 104–12.
129. Symonds, J, 1896, 'A Problem in Modern Ethics', p. 29. There are no extant copies of Symonds' 1891 privately printed edition of the essay in Britain. However, the pornographer, Leonard Smithers, privately published a pirated edition in London in 1896. Nelson, J, 2000, *Publisher to the Decadents: Leonard Smithers in the Careers of Beardsley, Wilde, Dowson*, The Pennsylvania State University Press, Pennsylvania, USA, p. 332. A number from this edition [82/100] survives in the British Library and is used in this book.
130. Ibid., p. 3.
131. Ibid., p. 22. See Chapter 5 for discussion of Taylor's work.
132. Ibid., p. 33.

133. Symonds, J, 1896, p. 34, citing Moreau, P, 1887, *Des Aberrations du Sens Genesique.*
134. Ibid., p. 34.
135. Ibid., p. 46.
136. Ibid., p. 51.
137. Oosterhuis, H, 2000, p. 10.
138. Symonds, J, 1896, p. 15.
139. Ibid., p. 15.
140. Grosskurth, P, 1964, p. 286. See also Chapter 5 for discussion of Ellis' political work.
141. Symonds, J, 1896, p. 15.
142. Ibid., p. 133.
143. Ibid., p. 133.
144. Ibid., p. 133.
145. PRO, DPP 4/6, *Regina v. Boulton and Others*, p. 1000.
146. Symonds, J, 1896, p. 134.
147. Schueller, H and Peters, R, 1969, Vol. 3, MS1868, Symonds to Gosse, 23 Feb. 1891.
148. Grosskurth, P, 1964, p. 270.
149. Ibid., p. 320.
150. See Chapter 5 for fuller discussion of the problems facing Ellis in attempting to publish *Sexual Inversion* in Britain.
151. Carpenter, E, 1916, p. 149.
152. Ibid., p. 1.
153. In 1892, Symonds informed Ellis that 'I had a letter … from Edward Carpenter, to whom I am glad to see that you have communicated our joint project. He ought to be able to give some useful information'. Schueller, H and Peters, R, 1969, Vol. 3, MS 2036, Symonds to Ellis, 29 Sept. 1892.
154. Rowbotham, S, 'Commanding the Heart – Edward Carpenter and Friends', in *History Today*, No. 37, Sept. 1987, p. 41.
155. Pierson, S, 'Edward Carpenter: Prophet of a Socialist Millennium', in *Victorian Studies*, Vol. 13, 1970, p. 306.
156. Brockway, Frances, 'A Memory of Edward Carpenter', in *New Leader*, 5 July 1929, cited in Pierson, S, 1970, p. 301.
157. Carpenter, E, 1916, p. 190.
158. Carpenter, E, 1985, *Towards Democracy*, Gay Men's Press, London, p. 25. The 1985 edition is an unabridged reprint of the poem, published in eighteen editions until 1931.
159. Carpenter, E, 1985, p. 33.
160. Carpenter, E, 1916, p. 28.
161. Ibid., p. 61.
162. Ibid., p. 148.
163. Rowbotham, S and Weeks, J, 1977, p. 77.
164. Bakshi, P, 'Homosexuality and Orientalism: Edward Carpenter's Journey to the East', in *Prose Studies*, Vol. 13, No. 1, July 1990, p. 157.
165. Carpenter, E, 1916, p. 106.
166. Bakshi, P, 1990, p. 159.
167. Ibid., pp. 152–3.
168. Ibid., p. 161.

169. Tsuzuki, C, 1980, p. 105.
170. Carpenter, E, 1916, p. 159.
171. Tsuzuki, C, 1980, p. 73.
172. Carpenter to Oates, 27 Aug. 1887, MS 351/42, *The Carpenter Collection, Sheffield City Archives.*
173. Carpenter to Oates, 4 Jan. 1888, MS 351/44, *The Carpenter Collection.*
174. Tsuzuki, C, 1980, p. 77.
175. Carpenter, E, 1916, p. 161.
176. Rowbotham, S and Weeks, J, 1977, *Socialism and the New Life: The Personal and Sexual Politics of Edward Carpenter and Havelock Ellis,* Pluto, London, p. 170.
177. Ibid., citing Ellis, H, 1894, *Man and Woman.*
178. See Chapter 5 for discussion of the milieu of *The Adult.*
179. See Chapter 3.
180. Carpenter to Oates, 19 Dec. 1887, MS 351/43.
181. Weeks, J, 1989, p. 172.
182. Carpenter, E, 1916, p. 195.
183. Carpenter, E, 1894, *Homogenic Love and its Place in a Free Society,* Privately Printed, Labour Press Society, Manchester, p. 11.
184. Ibid., p. 12.
185. Carpenter, E, 1984, *Selected Writings: Volume 1: Sex,* p. 244. *Love's Coming of Age* in this edition, published by The Gay Men's Press, London, is a reprint of Carpenter's 1908 edition.
186. Ibid., p. 221.
187. Ibid., pp. 225–7.
188. Tsuzuki, C, 1980.
189. Ibid., pp. 141–3.
190. See Chapter 3.
191. Ibid., p. 194.
192. Fernbach, D, notes to Carpenter, E, 1984, p. 301.
193. Tsuzuki, C, 1980, p. 150.
194. See Chapter 2.
195. *The Yorkshire Post,* 16 Feb. 1909.
196. Laurence, D (ed.), 1972, *Bernard Shaw, Collected Letters,* Shaw to Louis Wilkinson, 20 Dec. 1909, p. 890, cited in Tsuzuki, C, 1980, p. 143.
197. Tsuzuki, C, 1980, p. 146.
198. *Illustrated Police News,* 24 April 1919, cited in McLaren, A, 1999, *Twentieth-Century Sexuality: A History,* Blackwell, Oxford, p. 108.
199. McLaren, A, 1999, pp. 107–9.

7 Conclusion

1. Foucault, M, 1978, p. 101.

Bibliography

Primary sources

Printed and published sources

Acton, W, 1859, *A Practical Treatise on the Diseases of the Urinary and Generative Organs, in Both Sexes*, John Churchill, London.

Address and Rules of the Working Men's Association for Benefiting Politically, Socially and Morally the Useful Classes, 1837, University of London Library.

Babington, P, 1925, *Bibliography of the Writings of J. A. Symonds*, John Castle, London.

Bosanquet, B (ed.), 1895, *Aspects of the Social Problem*, Macmillan & Co., London.

Carpenter, E, 1894, *Homogenic Love and its Place in a Free Society*, Privately Printed, Labour Press Society, Manchester.

Carpenter, E, 1916, *My Days and Dreams: Being Autobiographical Notes*, Allen & Unwin, London.

Carpenter, E, 1984, *Selected Writings: Volume 1: Sex*, Gay Men's Press, London.

Carpenter, E, 1985, *Towards Democracy*, Gay Men's Press, London.

Draznin, Y, 1992, *My Other Self: The Letters of Olive Schreiner and Havelock Ellis, 1884–1920*, Peter Lang, New York, USA.

Drysdale, G, 1861, *Elements of Social Science, or Physical, Sexual and Natural Relgion: an Exposition of the True Cause and the Only Cure of the Three Primary Social Evils: Poverty, Prostitution and Celibacy*, Truelove, London.

Ellis, H H, 1925, *A Note on the Bedborough Trial*, Privately Printed, New York, USA, British Library.

Ellis, H H, 1936, *Studies in the Psychology of Sex, Volume II*, Heinemann, London.

Ellis, H H, 1940, *My Life*, Heinemann, London.

Ellis, H H and Symonds, J, 1897, *Sexual Inversion*, Wilson & Macmillan, London.

Grosskurth, P (ed.), 1984, *The Memoirs of John Addington Symonds*, Hutchinson, London.

Guy, W and Ferrier, D, 1888, *Principles of Forensic Medicine*, H. Renshaw, London.

Hemming, W, 1878, *Aids to Forensic Medicine and Toxicology*, Balliere, London.

Husband, H, 1874, *The Student's Handbook of Forensic Medicine and Medical Police*, E. and S. Livingstone, Edinburgh.

Index-Catalogue of the Library of the Surgeon General's Office, United States Army, 1892.

Mackay, T (ed.), 1891, *The English Poor: a Plea for Liberty*, Murray, London.

Male, G, 1818, *An Epitome of Judicial or Forensic Medicine: for the use of Medical Men, Coroners, and Barristers*, T. & G. Underwood, London.

Medical Times and Gazette.

O'Brien, M, 1892, *Socialism Tested by Facts: Being An Account of Certain Experimental attempts to Carry out Socialist Principles and Containing a Criticism of 'Looking Backward' and the Fabian Essays'*, Liberty and Property Defence League, London.

O'Brien, M, 1893, *The Natural Right to Freedom*, Williams & Norgate, London.

O'Brien, M, 1909, *Socialism and Infamy: the Homogenic or Comrade Love Exposed: an Open Letter in Plain Words for a Socialist Prophet*, Privately Printed, The Carpenter Collection, Sheffield City Archives.

'Perversion of the Sexual Instinct', in *The Alienist and Neurologist*, 1888, Vol. IX, Periodical Publications, St. Louis, Missouri, USA, pp. 565ff.

Ryan, M, 1831, *A Manual of Medical Jurisprudence: Being An Analysis of a Course of Lectures on Forensic Medicine*, Renshaw & Rush, London.

Schueller, H and Peters, R (eds), *The Letters of John Addington Symonds, Volume 1 (1967), Volume 2 (1968) & Volume 3 (1969)*, Wayne State University Press, Detroit, USA.

Sins of the Cities of the Plain, or The Recollections of a Mary-Ann: with Short Essays on Sodomy and Tribadism, 1881, Volumes I and II, 'Privately Printed', British Library.

Sweeney, J, 1904, *At Scotland Yard*, Grant Richards, London.

Symonds, J, 1883, 'A Problem in Greek Ethics', Privately Printed 10/10, British Library.

Symonds, J, 1893, *Studies of the Greek Poets*, A. & C. Black, London.

Symonds, J, 1896, '*A Problem in Modern Ethics*', Privately Printed 82/100, British Library.

Taylor, A, 1910, *Principles and Practice of Medical Jurisprudence, Volume II*, Churchill, London.

Teleny, or The Reverse of the Medal: A Physiological Romance of Today, 1893, Volumes I & II, 'Cosmopoli', British Library.

The Adult, Watford University Press, 1897–99, British Library.

The Journal of Mental Science.

The Parliamentary Debates, Authorised Edition, 59 Vic., 1896, Vol.XXXVII, Waterlow & Sons, London.

The Standard Cyclopaedia [sic] of Political, Constitutional, Statistical, and Forensic Knowledge, H. G. Bonn, London.

University Press Ltd., Watford, Catalogue, December 1899, British Library, CUP 364/948.

Williams, S, 1885, *Forensic Facts and Fallacies: a Popular Consideration of Some Legal Points and Principles*, Macmillan & Co., London.

Public Records Office, Kew (now The National Archives)

Calendar of Prisoners, Crim 10/60–85.

Director of Public Prosecutions, DPP 4/6, *Regina v. Boulton and Others*, 1/95/4 file 2.

Home Office, HO 44/20, 45/9784/b2917, 45/9928, 45/9928/b25396, 144/20/58480a, 144/20/58480a/2, 144/21/71577/6144/29/71577, 144/216/a49134, 144/243/a53622, 144/243/a53622, 144/20/58480a.

Index of British Trials, 1660–1900.

Treasury Solicitors, TS 11/897/3060.

British Library Newspaper Collection, Colindale

Daily Telegraph

Guardian Index, MS published on microfilm by Manchester Central Libraries

Lloyd's Weekly Newspaper

London Illustrated News

Manchester Guardian
Pall Mall Gazette
Reynolds's Weekly Newspaper
The People
The Times
The Yorkshire Post

News International Archive, Wapping, London

MS Letter TT/DepED/STB/1/11, Chenery to Stebbing, 19 May 1877.

The Carpenter Collection, Sheffield City Archives

MS 351/42, 351/44, 357/6(1).

The London Library

MS: The Memoirs of John Addington Symonds.

Electronic databases

www.justis.com, 2003, Statute Law for England and Wales, University of London Library.

Unpublished theses

Cocks, H, 1998, *The Sodomy Trial in English Culture 1780–1889*, University of Manchester.
Cook, M, 2000, *The Inverted City: London and the Constitution of Homosexuality*, University of London.
Doolittle, M, 1996, *Missing Fathers: Assembling a History of Fatherhood in Mid Nineteenth-Century England*, University of Essex.

Secondary sources

Adelman, P, 1983, *Gladstone, Disraeli and Later Victorian Politics*, Longman, Essex.
Allen, D, 1993, *Sexuality in Victorian Fiction*, University of Oklahoma Press, Norman, USA.
Altman, D, 1993, *Homosexual Oppression and Liberation*, New York University Press, New York, USA.
Anderson, P, 'Free Love and Free Thought: The Adult, 1897–1899', in *Studies in Newspaper and Periodical History*, 1993, Part 3, pp. 179–81.
Aronson, T, 1994, *Prince Eddy and the Homosexual Underworld*, CUP, Cambridge.
Bakshi, P, 'Homosexuality and Orientalism: Edward Carpenter's Journey to the East', in *Prose Studies*, 1990, Vol. 13, No. 1, pp. 155–77.
Bartlett, N, 1988, *Who was that Man? A Present for Mr Oscar Wilde*, Serpent's Tail, London.
Benn, M, 1992, *The Predicaments of Love*, Pluto, London.
Blackbourne, D, 'The Politics of Demagogy in Imperial Germany', in *Past and Present*, 1986, No. 113.

Bland, L and Doan, L (eds), 1998, *Sexology in Culture: Labelling Bodies and Desires*, Polity Press, Cambridge.

Boswell, J, 1980, *Christianity, Social Tolerance and Homosexuality: Gay People in Western Europe from the Beginning of the Christian Era to the Fourteenth-Century*, University of Chicago Press, London.

Bourke, J, 1994, *Working-Class Cultures in Britain 1890–1960: Gender, Class and Ethnicity*, Routledge, London.

Bradstock, A, Gill, S, Hogan, A and Morgan, S (eds), 2000, *Masculinity and Spirituality in Victorian Culture*, Macmillan, London.

Brake, L, Bell, B and Finkelstein, D (eds), 2000, *Nineteenth-Century Media and the Construction of Identities*, Palgrave, London.

Brake, L, Jones, A and Madden, L (eds), 1990, *Investigating Victorian Journalism*, Macmillan, London.

Bravmann, S, 1997, *Queer Fictions of the Past: History, Culture and Difference*, CUP, Cambridge.

Bristow, E, 1977, *Vice and Vigilance: Purity Movements in Britain since 1700*, Gill & Macmillan, Dublin.

Bristow, J, ' "Churlsgrace": Gerard Manley Hopkins and the Working-Class Male Body', in *ELH*, 1992, Vol. 59., No. 3, pp. 693–711.

Bunn, G, Lovie, A and Richards, G (eds), 2001, *Psychology in Britain: Historical Essays and Personal Reflections*, British Psychological Society, Leicester.

Campbell, G, 1965, *The Civil Service in Britain*, Gerald Duckworth & Co., London.

Chandos, J, 1984, *Boys Together: English Public Schools 1800–1864*, Hutchinson, London.

Chauncey, G, 1995, *Gay New York: The Making of the Gay World, 1890–1940*, Flamingo, London.

Clark, A, 1997, *The Struggle for the Breeches: Gender and the Making of the British Working Class*, University of California Press, London.

Clark, J, 1985, *English Society 1688–1832: Ideology, Social Structure and Political Practice during the Ancient Regime*, CUP, Cambridge.

Cocks, H, 2003, *Nameless Offences: Homosexual Desire in the Nineteenth Century*, I. B. Taurus, London.

Cohen, E, 1993, *Talk on the Wilde Side: Toward a Genealogy of a Discourse on Male Sexualities*, Routledge, London.

Collini, S, 1991, *Public Moralists: Political Thought and Intellectual Life in Britain 1850–1930*, Clarendon, Oxford.

Connell, R, 1995, *Masculinities*, Polity Press, Cambridge.

Connell, R, 2000, *The Men and the Boys*, Polity Press, Cambridge.

Cornish, W and Clark, G, 1989, *Law and Society in England 1750–1950*, Sweet & Maxwell, London.

Craft, C, 1994, *Another Kind of Love: Male Homosexual Desire in English Discourse 1850–1920*, University of California Press, London.

Crozier, I, 'The Medical Construction of Homosexuality and its Relation to the law in Nineteenth-Century England', in *Medical History*, 2001, Vol. 45, No. 1, pp. 61–82.

Danson, L, 'Oscar Wilde, W. H., and the Unspoken Name of Love', in *ELH*, 1991, Vol. 58, No. 4, pp. 979–1000.

Davenport-Hines, R, 1990, *Sex, Death and Punishment; Attitudes to Sex and Sexuality since the Renaissance*, Collins, London.

Davidoff, L and Hall, C, 1992, *Family Fortunes: Men and Women of the English Middle Class 1780–1850*, Hutchinson, London.

Davis, N, ' "Women's History" in Transition: The European Case', in *Feminist Studies*, 1975, No. 3, p. 90.

Dean, C, 'The Productive Hypothesis: Foucault, Gender and the History of Sexuality', in *History and Theory*, 1994, Vol. 33, No. 3, pp. 271–96.

Dean, C, 'Queer History', in *History and Theory*, 1999, Vol. 38, No. 1, pp. 121–36.

Delamora, R, 'Victorian Homosexuality in the Prism of Foucault', in *Victorian Studies*, 1995, Vol. 2, No. 38, pp. 265–72.

Dictionary of National Biography, Smith & Elder, London.

Dollimore, J, 1991, *Sexual Dissidence: Augustine to Wilde, Freud to Foucault*, Clarendon Press, Oxford.

Douglas, M, 1966, *Purity and Danger: An Analysis of the Concepts of Pollution and Taboo*, Ark, London.

Dowling, L, 1994, *Hellenism and Homosexuality in Victorian Oxford*, Cornell University Press, London.

Duberman, M, Vicinus, M and Chauncey, G (eds), 1989, *Hidden from History: Reclaiming the Gay and Lesbian Past*, Penguin, London.

Dudink, S, Hagemann, K and Tosh, J (eds), 2004, *Masculinity in Politics and War*, Manchester University Press.

Ellegard, A, 1957, *The Readership of the Periodical Press in Mid-Victorian Britain*, University of Gothenberg Press, Gothenberg, Sweden.

Forsythe, W, 1991, *Penal Discipline, Reformatory Projects and the English Prison Commission, 1895–1939*, University of Exeter Press, Exeter.

Foucault, M, 1976, *Histoire de la Sexualité: 1: la Volonté de Savoir*, l'Imprimerie Gallimard, France.

Foucault, M, 1978, *The History of Sexuality: Volume One: The Will To Knowledge, translated from the French by Robert Hurley*, Penguin, London.

Foucault, M, 1984, *The History of Sexuality: Volume Two: The Use Of Pleasure, Translated from the French by Robert Hurley*, Penguin, London.

Fowler, R, 'Archives: Virginia Woolf and Katherine Furse: an Unpublished Correspondence', in *Tulsa Studies in Women's Literature*, 1990, Vol. 2, pp. 201–30.

Fry, G, *Statesmen in Disguise: The Changing Role of the Administrative Class of the British Home Civil Service 1853–1966*, Macmillan, London.

Golby, J (ed.), 1986, *Culture and Society in Britain*, OUP, Oxford.

Greenberg, D, 1988, *The Construction of Homosexuality*, University of Chicago Press, London.

Grosskurth, P, 1964, *John Addington Symonds: a Biography*, Longmans, London.

Grosskurth, P, 1980, *Havelock Ellis: a Biography*, Quartet, London.

Hall, I, 'The Bourgeoisie and its Discontents: Reflections on Nationalism and Respectability', in *Journal of Contemporary History*, 1982, Vol. 17, No. 2.

Hall, L, 'Forbidden by God, Despised by Men: Masturbation, Medical Warnings, Moral Panic and Manhood in Great Britain, 1850–1950', in *Journal of the History of Sexuality*, 1992, Vol. 2, No. 3, pp. 365–87.

Hall, L, 2000, *Sex, Gender and Social Change in Britain since 1880*, Macmillan, London.

Hammerton, J, 'Forgotten People? Marriage and Masculine Identities in Britain', in *Journal of Family History*, 1997, Vol. 22, No. 1, pp. 110–17.

Hampton, M, 'Journalists and the "Professional Ideal" in Britain: The Institute of Journalists, 1884–1907', in *Historical Research*, 1999, Vol. 72, No. 178, pp. 183–201.

Hardy, A, 2001, *Health and Medicine in Britain since 1860*, Macmillan, Basingstoke.

Harvey, A D, 'Bestiality in Late Victorian England', in *Journal of Legal History (Great Britain)*, 2000, Vol. 21, No. 3, pp. 85–88.

Hekma, G, 'Sodomites, Platonic Lovers, Contrary Lovers: The Backgrounds of the Modern Homosexual', in *Journal of Homosexuality*, 1989, Vol. 16, No. 2, pp. 433–55.

Hobsbawm, E, 1987, *The Age of Empire 1875–1914*, Weidenfeld and Nicholson, London.

Holdsworth, W, 1936, *A History of English Law, Volume 1*, Methuen & Co., London.

Horn, P, 1997, *The Victorian Town Child*, Sutton Publishing, Gloucestershire.

International Encyclopaedia of the Social Sciences, 1968, USA, Vol. 16.

Jenkyns, R, 1980, *The Victorians and Ancient Greece*, Blackwell, Oxford.

Jones, A, 1996, *Powers of the Press: Newspapers, Power and the Public in Nineteenth-Century England*, Scholar Press, Hants.

Judd, D, 2001, *Empire: the British Imperial Experience from 1765 to the Present*, Phoenix, London.

Koss, S, 1981, *The Rise and Fall of the Political Press in Britain: Volume One: The Nineteenth Century*, Hamish Hamilton, London.

Kutchins, H and Kirk, S, 1999, *Making Us Crazy: DSM – the Psychiatric Bible and the Creation of Mental Disorders*, Constable, London.

Lawrence, C, 1994, *Medicine in the Making of Modern Britain 1700–1920*, Routledge, London.

Lees, L, 1979, *Exiles of Erin: Irish Migrants in Victorian London*, Manchester University Press, Manchester.

McCalman, I, 1988, *Radical Underworld: Prophets, Revolutionaries and Pornographers in London, 1795–1840*, CUP, Cambridge.

MacDonagh, O, 1977, *Early Victorian Government 1830–1870*, Weidenfeld & Nicolson, London.

McIntosh, M, 'The Homosexual Role' in *Social Problems*, 1968, Vol. 16, No. 2, pp. 182–92.

McKibbin, R, 'Why was there no Marxism in Great Britain?', in *The English Historical Review*, 1984, Vol. 99, No. 391, pp. 296–331.

McKibbin, R, 1990, *Ideologies of Class: Social Relations in Britain 1880–1950*, OUP, Oxford.

Mackie, J, 1964, *A History of Scotland*, Penguin Books, London.

McLaren, A, 1997, *The Trials of Masculinity: Policing Sexual Boundaries 1870–1930*, University of Chicago Press, London.

McLaren, A, 1999, *Twentieth-Century Sexuality*, Blackwell, Oxford.

MacLeod, R and Lewis, M, 1988, *Disease, Medicine and Empire: Perspectives on Western Medicine and the Experience of European Expansion*, Routledge, London.

Mason, M, 1994, *The Making of Victorian Sexual Attitudes*, OUP, Oxford.

Medhurst, A and Munt, S (eds), 1997, *Lesbian and Gay Studies: a Critical Introduction*, Cassell, London.

Miller, N, 1995, *Out of the Past: Gay and Lesbian History from 1869 to the Present*, Vintage, London.

Montgomery-Hyde, H, 1970, *The Other Love: An Historical and Contemporary Survey of Homosexuality in Britain*, Heinemann, London.

Morrow, R, 'Sexuality as Discourse: Beyond Foucault's Constructionism', in *Australia and New Zealand Journal of Sociology*, 1995, Vol. 31, No. 1, pp. 15–31.

Mort, F, 1987, *Dangerous Sexualities: Medico-Moral Politics in England since 1830*, Routledge & Kegan Paul, London.

Moscucci, O, 1990, *The Science of Woman: Gynaecology and Gender in England, 1800–1929*, CUP, Cambridge.

Mosse, G, 'Nationalism and Respectability: Normal and Abnormal Sexuality in the Nineteenth Century', in *Journal of Contemporary History*, 1982, Vol. 17, No. 2, pp. 221–46.

Nelson, J, 2000, *Publisher to the Decadents: Leonard Smithers in the Careers of Beardsley, Wilde, Dowson*, The Pennsylvania University Press, Pennsylvania, USA.

Norton, R, 1997, *The Myth of the Modern Homosexual: Queer History and the Search for Cultural Unity*, Cassell, London.

Nottingham, C, 1999, *The Pursuit of Serenity: Havelock Ellis and the New Politics*, Amsterdam University Press, Amsterdam.

Oosterhuis, H, 2000, *Stepchildren of Nature: Krafft-Ebbing, Psychiatry and the Making of Sexual Identity*, University of Chicago Press, London.

Osment, P, 1989, *Gay Sweatshop: Four Plays and a Company*, Methuen Drama, London.

Parry, J, 1994, *The Rise and Fall of Liberal Government in Victorian Britain*, Yale University Press, London.

Pearce, M and Stewart, G, 1992, *British Political History 1867–1990: Democracy and Decline*, Routledge, London.

Pellew, J, 1982, *The Home Office 1848–1914; from Clerks to Bureaucrats*, Heinemann, London.

Perkin, H, 1969, *Origins of Modern English Society*, Routledge & Kegan Paul, London.

Philips, D, 1977, *Crime and Authority in Victorian England: The Black Country 1835–1860*, Croom Helm, London.

Pierce-Jones, V, 1988, *Saint or Sensationalist? The Story of W.T.Stead*, Gooday Publishers, East Wittering, West Sussex.

Pierson, S, 'Edward Carpenter: Prophet of a Socialist Millennium', in *Victorian Studies*, 1970, Vol. 13, No. 3, pp. 301–19.

Plummer, K (ed.), 1981, *The Making of the Modern Homosexual*, Barnes & Noble, New Jersey, USA.

Porter, R and Hall, L, 1995, *The Facts of Life: the Creation of Sexual Knowledge in Britain 1650–1950*, Yale University Press, London.

Potter, H, 1993, *Hanging in Judgement: Religion and the Death Penalty in England from the Bloody Code to Abolition*, SLM Press Ltd., London.

Pugh, M, 1999, *State and Society: A Social and Political History of Britain, 1870–1997*, OUP, Oxford.

Read, D, 1990, *The Age of Urban Democracy: England 1868–1914*, Longman, London.

Robinson, P, 1989, *The Modernization of Sex: Havelock Ellis, Alfred Kinsey, William Masters and Virginia Johnson*, Elek, London.

Rosario, V (ed.), 1997, *Science and Homosexualities*, Routledge, London.

Rowbotham, S and Weeks, J, 1977, *Socialism and the New Life: The Personal and Sexual Politics of Edward Carpenter and Havelock Ellis*, Pluto, London.

Rowbotham, S, 'Commanding the Heart – Edward Carpenter and Friends', in *History Today*, Sept. 1987, Vol. 37, pp. 41–6.

Sedgwick, E, 1994, *Epistemology of the Closet*, Penguin, London.

Seidman, S (ed.), 1996, *Queer Theory/Sociology*, Blackwell, Oxford.

Showalter, D, 'The Retaining of Bellona: Prussia and the Institutionalization of the Napoleonic legacy, 1815–1876', in *Military Affairs*, 1980, Vol. 44, No. 2.

Showalter, E, 1990, *Sexual Anarchy: Gender and Culture at the Fin de Siècle*, Viking Penguin, New York, USA.

Showalter, R, 'Army and Society in Imperial Germany: The Pains of Modernization', in *Journal of Contemporary History*, Oct. 1983, Vol. 18, No. 4.

Shuter, W, 'The "Outing" of Walter Pater', in *Nineteenth-Century Literature*, 1994, Vol. 48, No. 4, pp. 480–506.

Sinah, M, 1995, *Colonial Masculinity: The 'Manly' Englishman and the 'Effeminate' Bengali in the late Nineteenth Century*, Manchester University Press, Manchester.

Sindall, R, 1990, *Street Violence in the Nineteenth Century: Media Panic or Real Danger?*, Leicester University Press, Leicester.

Sinfield, A, *The Wilde Century: Effeminacy, Oscar Wilde and the Queer Moment*, Cassell, London.

Smith, F B, 'Labouchere's Amendment to the Criminal Law Amendment Bill', in *Historical Studies (Australia)*, 1976, Vol. 17, No. 67, pp. 165–73.

Stedman-Jones, G, 1983, *Languages of Class: Studies in English Working-Class History 1832–1982*, CUP, Cambridge.

Stenton, M, 1976, *Who's Who of British Members of Parliament: Volume One: 1832–1885: A Biographical Dictionary of the House of Commons*, OUP, Oxford.

Sullivan, N, 2003, *A Critical Introduction to Queer Theory*, Edinburgh University Press, Edinburgh.

Summerfield, P, 'Patriotism and Empire: Music-Hall entertainment, 1870–1914', in MacKenzie, J (ed.), 1986, *Imperialism and Popular Culture*, Manchester University Press.

Summers, A, 'The Correspondents of Havelock Ellis', in *History Workshop Journal*, 1991, No. 32, pp. 167–83.

The History of The Times: Volume Two: The Tradition Established, 1939, The Office of The Times, Printing House Square, London.

Tobias, J, 1967, *Crime and Industrial Society in the 19th Century*, B. T. Batsford, London.

Tobias, J, 1979, *Crime and Police in England 1700–1900*, Gill & Macmillan, Dublin.

Tosh, J, 'What Should Historians do with Masculinity? Reflections on Nineteenth-Century Britain', in *History Workshop Journal*, 1994, No. 38, pp. 179–202.

Tosh, J, 1984, *The Pursuit of History*, Longman, London.

Tosh, J, 1999, *A Man's Place: Masculinity and the Middle-Class Home in Victorian England*, Yale University Press, London.

Trumbach, R, 'Sodomitical Subcultures, Sodomitical Roles and the Gender Revolution of the Eighteenth Century: The Recent Historiography', in Macubbin, R (ed.), 1987, *Tis Nature's Fault: Unauthorized Sexuality during the Enlightenment*, CUP, Cambridge.

Tsuzuki, C, 1980, *Edward Carpenter 1844–1929: Prophet of Human Fellowship*, CUP, Cambridge.

Tucker, A, 'Army and Society in England 1870–1900: a Reassessment of the Cardwell Reforms', in *Journal of British Studies*, 1963, Vol. 2, No. 2, pp. 110–41.

Upchurch, C, 'Forgetting the Unthinkable: Cross-Dressers and British Society in the Case of Queen vs. Boulton and Others', in *Gender and History*, 2000, Vol. 12, No. 1, pp. 127–57.

Vincent, D, 1998, *The Culture of Secrecy: Britain, 1832–1998*, OUP, Oxford.

Walkowitz, J, 1992, *City of Dreadful Delight: Narratives of Sexual Danger in Late-Victorian London*, Virago, London.

Waller, P, 1983, *Town, City and Nation: England 1850–1914*, OUP, Oxford.

Weeks, J, 1981, *Sex, Politics and Society: The Regulation of Sexuality since 1800*, Longman, London.

Weeks, J, 1990, *Coming Out: Homosexual Politics from the Nineteenth Century to the Present*, Quartet, London.

Weeks, J, 1995, *Against Nature: Essays on History, Sexuality and Identity*, Rivers Oram Press, London.

Weeks, J, 2000, *Making Sexual History*, Polity Press, Cambridge.

Weiner, M, 1981, *English Culture and the Decline of the Industrial Spirit, 1850–1980*, CUP, Cambridge.

Young, J, 1997, *Britain and the World in the Twentieth Century*, Arnold, London.

Index